AGAINST THE ODDS

Studies in Slave and Post-Slave
Societies and Cultures

CO-EDITORS:

GAD HEUMAN
JAMES WALVIN

AGAINST THE ODDS

Free Blacks in the
Slave Societies of the Americas

Edited by
Jane G. Landers

FRANK CASS
LONDON • PORTLAND, OR

First published in Great Britain by
FRANK CASS & CO LTD
Newbury House, 900 Eastern Avenue
London IG2 7HH, England

and in the United States by
FRANK CASS
c/o ISBS
5804 N.E. Hassalo Street, Portland, Oregon 97213-3644

Transferred to Digital Printing 2004

Copyright © 1996 Frank Cass & Co. Ltd.

Library of Congress Cataloging-in-Publication Data

A catalog record of this book is available from the
Library of Congress.

British Library Cataloguing in Publication Data

Against the odds : free blacks in the slave societies of
the Americas. - (Studies in slave and post-slave societies
and cultures)
1. Free Blacks - America 2. Free Afro-Americans 3. Slaves -
Emancipation - America - History
I. Landers, Jane
323.1'1'96073

ISBN 0-7146-4710-1 (hb)
ISBN 0-7146-4254-1

This group of studies first appeared in a Special Issue on 'Free Blacks in the Slave
Societies of the Americas' in *Slavery and Abolion*, Vol.17, No.1, published by Frank
Cass & Co. Ltd.

Contents

Introduction

Twenty-five years ago a group of distinguished scholars gathered at The Johns Hopkins University to consider 'The Role of the Free Black and Mulatto in Slave Societies of the New World'. From that symposium was generated the fine collection of essays to which all scholars of race relations in the Americas have sooner or later turned, *Neither Slave Nor Free: The Freedmen of African Descent in the Slave Societies of the New World*, edited by David W. Cohen and Jack P. Greene.[1] Following the general comparative theses laid out by Frank Tannenbaum in 1947, that collection sought to assess the comparative character of slavery through the experience of its freed persons and to examine the pivotal role that group played in slave societies.[2]

After a quarter of a century, it seems appropriate to revisit many of the important themes introduced in *Neither Slave Nor Free* and examine the developments in the historiography of the intervening decades.[3] The authors whose work makes up this volume share many of the same interests as their notable predecessors, but they attempt a somewhat different perspective – from within the free black communities they study.

Four of the essays in this collection, those of John Garrigus, Kimberly Hanger, Jane Landers and Paul Lachance, were first presented at the 26th annual conference of the Association of Caribbean Historians, in San Germán, Puerto Rico, in 1994. Lachance organized the session and did such a good job of co-ordinating the papers within the panel that Gad Heuman and James Walvin saw the potential for a book and invited me to solicit additional pieces and edit the volume. Many of the authors have shared a common research agenda, know each other's work, and have collaborated before, so it is not surprising that some strong common themes emerged even within this comparative framework. The authors examine free black communities in Senegal, South Carolina, Louisiana, Florida, Cuba, Saint Domingue, Haiti, the Dominican Republic and Suriname allowing a comparison of the genesis of a free black class within Senegalese, British, French, Spanish and Dutch slave systems.

These essays are based on intensive archival work in notarial records, parish registers, government and military records, and wherever possible, in documents generated by, or as a result of the initiative of free blacks. As most of the authors will no doubt testify, such work requires extensive searching through vast amounts of material to turn up small scraps of evidence which must then be patched together to try to form whole patterns. It is analogous in many ways to restoring a fractured artefact whose scattered shards must be painstakingly excavated, examined and manipulated repeatedly to determine how they fit together.

In some places, for example, Suriname, there are gaps in the documentary record which can never be replaced, and reconstructing the early colonial past, especially that of people of colour, is made more difficult. In South Carolina, records for such work are also thin. But in the other areas under study in this volume (and potentially elsewhere as well) rich deposits of black history still wait to be mined. It is certainly not true, as was once thought, that because many were enslaved and illiterate, they had no history. The evidence is there, but it requires determination, creativity and, eventually, intimate familiarity with the historical communities to unearth it – not to mention inordinate amounts of time. But by working within a wide range of ground-level records of daily life, slowly reconstituting families and networks, and analysing manumission, property, wealth and inheritance patterns, the authors are able to get a real sense of the creative strategies people of African descent employed to achieve freedom and then live freely in societies in which most people of their colour were enslaved.

The authors highlight several important and common ways in which enslaved persons of African descent became free – notably, through gratis manumission, through political rewards for military service or religious conversion, or more commonly, through the arduous self-purchase process. In all manumission efforts kinship linkages were critical. Family, in nuclear and extended forms, played a key role in moving people out of slavery and through (and around) the difficult obstacles of legal and social discrimination. As Rosemarijn Hoefte points out, some extended families in Suriname were virtual representations of the social order – including free and enslaved members whose somatic descriptions ranged from white to black and whose economic status ranged from propertyless slaves to planter elites. Daniel L. Schafer's detailed reconstruction of Anna Kingsley's family demonstrates similar diversity in Florida and Haiti. Mutual aid cut across class and colour lines within these extended families.

Miscegenation was common in most of the areas studied and indeed facilitated emancipation for a few – particularly for the women of colour allied to white men studied by Hanger and Lachance in New Orleans, Garrigus in Saint Domingue, and Schafer and Landers in Florida. But as Hanger, Hoefte, Landers and Olwell demonstrate, more important over the long term, was the support of other black or coloured family members, whose co-operative efforts freed many more than a few white elites ever did. The essays by Hoefte and Hanger, in particular, demonstrate the shift from white male manumittors to white females and to blacks and show that, over time, family members were more important than masters in creating a free black class.

Still, as the essays also demonstrate, whites assisted in that process. Schafer describes how the Florida planter, Zephaniah Kingsley, regularly freed his own children by multiple co-wives, allowed slaves to purchase themselves at half their evaluated price and encouraged fellow planters to follow his lead. He published treatises advocating the increase and more fair treatment of a free population of colour and worked in the territorial legislature of Florida to promote the same goals. Sensing the hardening racial atmosphere in the United States, Kingsley finally transplanted many of these principles and many of his freed slaves and their families to Haiti.

In addition to freeing favoured slaves, white masters allowed slaves with artisanal or other skills opportunities to make them pay. Masters permitted slaves to hire out their time and services, market crafts and agricultural products, and operate small businesses – and to keep at least a portion of the proceeds for their own purposes. Whites also served as guarantors or creditors for enslaved persons trying to pursue self-purchase. Olwell describes how enslaved persons in Charleston frequently used white brokers to hide their own financial agency in manumissions. Collaboration by masters and other whites in the community facilitated such legal fictions. Hoefte also finds white complicity in the illegal manumissions of the *piki njan* in Suriname. Whites also covertly and overtly subverted the legal and social systems designed to prohibit race mixing and a breakdown of the slave order. They cohabited with and married blacks, and raised, educated, and bequeathed property to their mixed-race children.

Achieving freedom was a major accomplishment, but one that could not be taken for granted. Even after leaving slavery some people had to struggle to claim their civil rights and retrieve them if they were abrogated for some reason. The geopolitical turmoil of the eighteenth century meant that enemies might raid across a border and ensnare freed persons along with slaves. Changes of government often worsened race relations and put additional legal and economic pressures on freed persons. And as Olwell and Hoefte discovered, freed women living in a slave society sometimes found it such a struggle to survive that they voluntarily returned to slavery. Many more slaves, however, seized any opportunity to escape bondage and a significant number won their freedom on the battlefield. Many of these case studies are situated in the volatile eighteenth century, an 'era of revolutions', slave revolts, maroon and Indian wars. The geopolitical instability in the circum-Caribbean led colonial powers to create and depend upon black military units such as the Black Rangers and Free Corps in Suriname and the free black militias in Florida, Louisiana and Saint Domingue. These units move thousands of men (and often their families) out of slavery and had important political, social, and economic consequences for the free black community. The privileges guaranteed by these military organizations created a new community status for their members – the men were commanded by officers of their own colour, received government pay and recognition, and in most cases were exempt from civil prosecutions. Combat veterans in Florida and Suriname received lands as payment for their services and thus entered the peasant ranks. Some parlayed these homesteads into larger holdings and became known in their respective communities as hard-working, and successful farmers or, as in Suriname, 'small sugar gentlemen'. Moreover, as Garrigus, Hanger and Landers find, the corporate nature of black military organizations reinforced family and kin networks in important ways. Militia members formed marital alliances and godparentage ties which bound them in intricate webs of obligation and reciprocity. Pooling their material and social resources helped make all stronger and increased their chances of material success.

Once freed, former bondsmen and women had to sustain themselves and their families, which was no mean feat. A lucky few came to freedom gifted by white fathers or consorts with prosperous rice, cotton, sugar, indigo, or tobacco plantations, town houses and considerable 'moveable' property, including slaves. Most freed blacks, however, started with almost nothing. They had to work hard to accumulate property and 'wealth' to help secure their rights and those of their children and kin in an era when property defined citizenship.

Upward mobility was easier where free blacks derived from old planter families or became established early, as in Saint Domingue and Louisiana. Descendants of these families were often accepted as white after several generations. In Saint Domingue Garrigus shows that white notaries and clerks lied about the obvious, or well-known African heritage of respected and influential people of colour by using honorifics such as Sieur after it was forbidden to do so, or by simply avoiding any racial labelling, even as the government tried to require them to fix racial boundaries. Hanger finds similar patterns of clerical obfuscation in New Orleans. The blurring of colour lines and communal approval of certain privileged freed persons sometimes led them to identify more closely with their white families and to distance themselves from the slave masses. They created new identities as *gens de couleur*, creoles of colour, or *colons américains*. Lachance demonstrates, however, the 'limits of privilege'. Even if the creoles of New Orleans were wealthier than most of their free contemporaries elsewhere, their wealth did not compare to that of whites. The assessed wealth of a few very rich persons of colour (mostly women) has skewed the picture of collective coloured prosperity in Louisiana.

Despite the virulent white racism in plantation Suriname, a few favoured blacks and coloureds, like the famed Elizabeth Samson and her siblings, also managed to rise to great wealth, but they were clearly exceptional cases. In Suriname, too, there were limits to privilege and not even wealth and family connections could produce social acceptance. Planters violently opposed freedom for slaves and objected to Dutch manumission plans, but imperial interests overrode local racism. Forced to accept the freedom of many black soldiers, and an ever-growing number of illegally manumitted persons, the planter class resorted to making them the object of derision and scorn. Manumitted blacks and coloureds represented a very small proportion of Suriname's colonial population, which was primarily composed of slaves. Nevertheless, the free black class grew to represent one fourth of the free population in Suriname by the eighteenth century and two-thirds of the free population by the 1830s.

Racial distinctions and animosity were less significant in remote or frontier areas, where plantation systems and social hierarchy were less developed, but so, too, was the wealth and privilege of the free black class. In St. Augustine, Florida, most free blacks were either peasant farmers or artisans, although in Florida some free people managed to rise above that status, mostly through inheritance. Thanks to Zephaniah Kingsley, Anna Kingsley and her children owned vast estates in Florida and the Dominican Republic, and circulated among them. Without such white patronage Hoefte finds that in Suriname many freed blacks lived just above subsistence levels.

A free black peasantry failed to materialize in eighteenth-century South Carolina because free blacks never developed a rural land base as their contemporaries did elsewhere in the circum-Caribbean. Olwell describes the free black community of Charleston as 'small, colour-segregated, artisanal, and urban'. While it is true that the other free black communities studied in this volume also concentrated in urban settings, they had more opportunities to acquire land and live apart from whites if they chose. In Florida free blacks petitioned for and received contiguous land grants and sometimes worked their lands co-operatively. The rural concentration of free black families gave a sense of community and offered some protection on a volatile frontier.

Land-holding not only contributed to self-sufficiency, it was an important marker of free status and citizenship. Another was engagement in the local political system. Free blacks learned to use their respective legal systems to petition for rights to land, to pay, to inheritance and to marriage, among other things. They pursued legal grievances against those who cheated or defamed them – black or white. They recorded property and debts, dowries and wills. They testified in civil and criminal proceedings. Free blacks also took active roles in the larger politics of the region.

As noted above, the times were troubled and highly politicized. Empires were at war, territories were being contested, slave insurrection was a constant possibility and revolutionary rhetoric swept through the circum-Caribbean. Free blacks paid particular attention for their positions might change as suddenly as a government. They followed the major debates of the day and had to choose sides in all these contests. Free blacks could either be loyal allies or foes of the standing government, and this potential gave them leverage. They made political statements as they enrolled for military service (or deserted), as they attended political ceremonies and rallies, or contributed to political causes. They addressed petitions and memorials to European monarchs, Colonial and National Assemblies, and to their countrymen. Wealthy free blacks from Suriname, Louisiana, Saint Domingue, and the Dominican Republic crossed the Atlantic to pursue personal and collective interests. In other words, free blacks were fully engaged in the politics of their times. This sometimes led to tragic results – as warfare consumed property and lives and political transitions sometimes led to loss, imprisonment and exile, as it did for whites. Nevertheless, the participation of free blacks at these critical political junctures indelibly confirmed their membership in free society, as many chose, to quote Saint Domingue's Boissrond Tonnerre, 'to be independent, or die'.

In conclusion, while free black ascent within slave societies was difficult and limited, it was possible, and slaves and free blacks manipulated the possibility for all it was worth. Rigged the deck may have been, but persons of African descent found ways to work every loophole and contradiction in their respective legal systems. They quickly read geopolitical developments and were able to take advantage of imperial systems in crisis, and they created social leverage through extended kinship and patronage networks. The same networks supported co-operative economic ventures, and diffused the risks and losses. Using all these strategies, free blacks living in the circum-Caribbean slave societies were able to slowly advance themselves and their families, against the odds.

ACKNOWLEDGEMENTS

The papers of John G. Garrigus, Kimberly S. Hanger, Jane G. Landers and Paul Lachance are revisions of work first presented at the 26th annual conference of the Association of Caribbean Historians, Interamerican University, San Germán, Puerto Rico, March 1994. The authors would like to thank the members of the Association for their helpful comments and Gad Heuman and James Walvin for initiating this special issue.

NOTES

1. David W. Cohen and Jack P. Greene (eds.), *Neither Slave Nor Free: The Freedmen of African Descent in the Slave Societies of the New World* (Baltimore, 1972). Authors Gwendolyn Midlo Hall and Jack P. Greene mentored several of the authors of the current volume, who are, therefore, more directly indebted for their fine work.
2. Frank Tannenbaum, *Slave and Citizen: The Negro in the Americas* (New York, 1947).
3. Important monographs on free blacks which have appeared since *Neither Slave Nor Free* include: Jerome S. Handler, *The Unappropriated People: Freedmen in the Slave Society of Barbados* (Baltimore, 1974); Gad Heuman, *Between Black and White: Race, Politics, and the Free Coloreds in Jamaica, 1792–1865* (Westport, CT, 1981); and Edward L. Cox, *Free Coloreds in the Slave Societies of St. Kitts and Grenada, 1763–1833* (Knoxville, 1984). A new study is that of Christine Hunefeldt, *Paying the Price of Freedom: Family and Labor Among Lima's Slaves, 1800–1854* (Berkeley, 1994).

Becoming Free: Manumission and the Genesis of a Free Black Community in South Carolina, 1740–90

ROBERT OLWELL

If antebellum South Carolina's free black community was 'a world in shadow', its eighteenth-century predecessor was cloaked almost entirely in darkness. The dearth of documentation for the colonial and revolutionary eras has led most students of the subject to date the beginning of South Carolina's free black community from the first federal census in 1790. At that time, according to the census takers, the state contained 1,801 free blacks living amid 107,094 slaves. More than half of these free blacks were concentrated in the city of Charleston and its immediate vicinity. The year 1790 also saw the establishment of the city's first freedmen's social organization, 'the Brown Fellowship Society'. With the arrival a few years later of several hundred refugee *gens de couleur* from the revolution in Saint Domingue, South Carolina's free black community attained most of the basic characteristics (small, colour-segregated, artisanal and urban) that it maintained for the next seventy years.[1]

Although South Carolina's free blacks had to wait until the end of the eighteenth century before they could stand up and be counted, they did not spring from the ground in 1790. Even when allowances are made for a late burst of revolution inspired manumissions, a large proportion of the free people of colour recorded in the first census were the children of, or were themselves, slaves who had gained their freedom in the preceding half-century. The experience of individual free blacks in the colonial and revolutionary eras played a significant and formative role in the development of South Carolina's subsequent free black community. In the long darkness before the 1790 dawn, the region's free people of colour first learned to make their way in the midst of a suspicious and hostile slave society.

In colonial South Carolina the words 'free' and 'black' were regarded as almost a contradiction in terms. Even the title of the 1740 slave code: 'An

Act for the Better Ordering and Governing of *Negroes and Other Slaves*',
assumed a conflation of race and caste. The code's more popular name, 'the
Negro Act', made the process complete. Although the makers of the Negro
Act grudgingly acknowledged the existence of 'negroes ... who are now
free', they appeared uncertain as to the status of such peculiar people. On
the four occasions that the twenty-page act even bothered to acknowledge
free blacks, it contradicted itself, twice combining their treatment with that
of slaves, and twice drawing a distinction on the basis of freedom (or at least
self-ownership).[2]

Rather than make allowances for an intermediate caste between white
and black, slave and free, colonial legislators and jurists endeavoured to
eliminate this ambiguous middle ground. To this end, the Negro Act
directed that it 'shall always be presumed that every negro ... is a slave',
until or unless otherwise proved. The law's strong presumption of servitude
could lead the court to render bizarre verdicts. For instance, in one 1767
case, a black woman suing for her freedom ended up as the property of the
presiding judge.[3]

The law's discomfort toward free blacks was paralleled in the almost
complete elision of such persons from other parts of the documentary record
during the colonial period. There is, for example, simply no reliable way to
determine the number of free blacks living in the colony at any one moment.
Because they were not considered part of the ruling white minority, free
blacks were not listed in the jury or militia rolls which are used as the basis
of white population estimates; nor were most free blacks counted in tax
records or in the censuses of adult male slaves produced by parish road
commissioners since they were not considered to be either property or
bound labour.[4]

On those few occasions when free blacks came to the attention of
colonial record keepers, it was seldom to their advantage. Free black men
were at the centre of two of the largest conspiracy scares in the eighteenth-
century low country. In 1759, two free blacks, Philip Jones and John
Pendarvis, along with 'Mr. Broadbill's Caesar', a slave, were charged with
'promoting and encouraging an insurrection of the Negroes against the
white people'. Of the three, Caesar was 'Headman', Jones was the plot's
promoter and recruiter, and Pendarvis, who was described as 'a person of
credit and property', was to provide the money to purchase arms and
ammunition. Perhaps because Jones had been the most active, he was put to
death while Caesar and Pendarvis were whipped and released.[5]

Sixteen years later during the outbreak of the revolution, Thomas
Jeremiah, a free black man well known in Charleston as a harbour pilot and
fisherman, also stood accused of attempting 'to encourage our Negroes to
Rebellion & joining the King's Troops if any ... [were] sent here'. Although

Jeremiah staunchly insisted upon his innocence, he was sentenced to 'be hanged and afterwards burned'. The following winter, another free black fisherman, Scipio Handley, was captured while carrying messages between Charleston loyalists and British warships in the harbour and was condemned to be executed as a spy.[6]

Other references to free blacks, more mundane although no less rare, are occasionally encountered elsewhere in the archives. The letters sent to the Society for the Propagation of the Gospel by the colony's Anglican missionaries, for example, include one written in September 1748 by William Orr, minister in St. Paul's parish west of Charleston, which noted that:

> ... I have baptised two free Negroe women after proper Instruction, both of them very sensible and sober; and each of them answered to full satisfaction when examined concerning their belief, and expressed their sincere desire to be admitted into the Christian Church by the Holy Sacrament of Baptism.

But not all free blacks were as satisfyingly pious. In 1753, for instance, the Charleston Grand Jury complained of '... Hugh Jones a mulatto Man – free or said to be free – as a vagabond and Idle person not following any business or livelihood, but a sham Doctor among the Negroes and slaves of Charlestown and has often been seen gaming among the Negroes on the Sabbath Day'.[7]

Olaudah Equiano offers further testimony of the precarious place free blacks occupied in the colonial low country. Arriving in Savannah, Georgia, soon after buying his freedom in 1766, Equiano narrowly escaped being 'being flogged all round the town' by the master of a slave whom he had struck. A few months later, on a subsequent visit, he was taken into custody by the town watch, threatened with whipping and forced to spend the night in the workhouse. Soon after his release he was accosted by two white men who claimed that he was a runaway slave. Had he not been armed with a 'revengeful stick', Equiano feared that he might well have been kidnapped and sold back into slavery.[8]

Beside these impressionistic fragments, one other, more substantive, source survives to shed a glimmer of light on the lives of South Carolina's free blacks before 1790. The collections of the South Carolina Department of Archives and History include several dozen folio-sized volumes which contain the 'miscellaneous records' of the colony/state from the early eighteenth until the early nineteenth century. As their name suggests, the miscellaneous records are a compilation of minutiae. For a small fee a government clerk copied the details of leases, contracts and other agreements, creating a public record of a private transaction for the security of

either or both of the parties involved. Most of the thousands of such
engagements are of little interest except to genealogists, but the deeds of
several hundred slave manumissions are also transcribed among the
miscellany.

A comprehensive search through the miscellaneous records complied
between 1737 and 1785 gleaned 379 separate deeds of manumission. The
consent of the slave owner was a prerequisite of manumission, and studies
of the practice have commonly focused upon the motives and attitudes of
the manumittor rather than the manumitted. But every manumission
involved two parties. Seen from another perspective, manumission was the
first act of a free person as much as it was the last act of a slave. This essay
will use these 379 recorded deeds of manumission as a source from which
to delineate the character of the free black experience in the colony/state of
South Carolina in the half-century before the first census.[9]

To draw a portrait of the pre-1790 free black community merely from a
roster of manumissions is something like crafting a biography from a single
diary entry. Although Olaudah Equiano described his own manumission as
the 'happiest day I had ever experienced', it was still but one day in his long
and varied life. Yet, despite their obvious limitations, manumission records,
like diary entries, can offer important insights into their subjects. While
slaves' desire for liberty can safely be taken for granted, the means or
method through which individual slaves bargained for, and obtained their
freedom can suggest something of the character of their life both before and
after becoming free.[10]

A few more words of caution are in order. The deeds of manumission
that survive in the miscellaneous records cannot provide a comprehensive
portrait of manumission in this era. While a newly freed person's interest in
creating such a public document may appear obvious, it is nonetheless clear
that not all manumissions were publicly recorded. In 1762, for example,
Jane Massey issued (and recorded) a duplicate deed of manumission for a
woman whom she had freed fifteen years earlier. The previous (and perhaps
sole) copy of the original deed had been 'burnt and destroyed' in a house
fire. If in the intervening fifteen years, Massey had died or left the city, it is
not inconceivable that her freed slave might also have ended up as the
possession of a judge.[11]

Before a free person could appear before the public registrar to enter
their deed into the record, he or she needed to have some familiarity with
legal procedure, access to Charleston, and a small monetary fee. Some
manumittors provided the first, as did the couple who after 'cheerfully'
freeing a slave woman via a letter, added soberly, 'if you can get this
registered, do it'. The latter two requirements would have not exceeded the
capabilities of any determined individual. Given what was at stake, it might

be assumed that the vast majority of freed people took the trouble to enter their deeds of manumission into the public record, but there is no way of knowing if this was the case.[12]

Nor can it simply be assumed that the recorded manumissions provide a representative cross-section of the total (albeit unknowable) global figure. The urgency with which a freed person undertook to register their deed of manumission might have been closely tied to the degree of apprehension they were under as to whether or not their freedom was likely to be challenged. Perhaps significant in this regard, is the fact that while three fourths of nineteenth-century South Carolina's free people of colour were described as 'mulatto', only a third of those whose manumissions were recorded before 1786 were similarly perceived. There are several ways to explain this discrepancy, but it may well be that freed people of white parentage felt less need to register their manumission deeds because they expected to be able to turn to their white father (or other kin) for assistance if their status was questioned.[13]

Nonetheless, while acknowledging that the 379 recorded manumissions cannot be taken as either a comprehensive or even a representative sample of all manumissions, it is worthwhile to consider them collectively before proceeding to examine particular cases. Analysed chronologically, the importance of the Revolution immediately becomes apparent. Of the entire sample, 199 or fifty-three per cent, were recorded in the ten years after 1775. In this final decade, the registrar transcribed an average of twenty deeds of manumission per year. In the peak year of 1784, thirty-five deeds were recorded. By contrast, in a typical year in the period from 1737 to 1774, only five deeds were entered into the miscellaneous record book, and there are years in which no manumissions were registered at all.[14]

Categorization of recorded manumissions on the basis of perceived skin colour, sex, and age, reveals that two-thirds of those freed were blacks, almost two out of three were women, and three out of five were adults. When these ratios are compared to their estimated proportions in the total slave population, it is apparent that perceived skin colour (i.e. mulatto before black) was enormously important, sex (i.e. women before men) held considerable weight, and age (children before adults) was of only small influence in determining who was most likely to become free (see Table 1).

Combining categories creates a composite portrait of which slaves were most and least likely to be freed (and to have their deeds of manumission recorded). The most favoured group were mulatto, female, children, and the least favoured were black adult men. Interestingly, while the American Revolution greatly increased the total number of manumissions, it had very little influence on these characteristics. The percentages of mulattoes, women, and children among those freed did not differ to any significant

TABLE 1

RECORDED MANUMISSIONS, 1737–85
CATEGORIZED BY PERCEIVED SKIN COLOUR, SEX, AND AGE

| | Among Rec. Manumissions | | Among Total Slave Pop., Est. | |
	No.	(%)	No.	(%)
Perceived Skin colour:				
Black	249	(66)	2596	(96)
Mulatto	130	(33)	113	(4)
Sex (adults only):				
Female	151	(65)	3736	(44)
Male	83	(35)	4766	(56)
Age:				
Adult	234	(62)	8502	(66)
Child	145	(38)	4359	(33)

Sources: MR\SCDAH, 1737–1785. The estimated percentage of mulattoes in the total slave
population is extrapolated from their percentage in a tally of runaway advertisements
compiled by Philip Morgan. While admittedly crude, this source seems the nearest one
can come to this important but illusive figure, Philip D. Morgan, 'Colonial South
Carolina Runaways: Their Significance for Slave Culture', *Slavery and Abolition*, Vol.6
(1985); I have also relied upon Morgan's pioneering work for my other figures
concerning sex and age ratios, Philip D. Morgan, 'The Development of Slave Culture
in Eighteenth-Century Plantation America' (Ph.D. dissertation, University of London,
1977), pp.289, 293. I am very grateful to my colleague, Gunther Peck, for his assistance
in designing the data base from which my tables are drawn.

degree on either side of the 1775 divide.

Only a few deeds openly acknowledged a blood tie between manumittor
and manumitted. When John Williams freed two of his slave children in
1754, he claimed to be moved by the 'natural love and affection' he felt
toward 'my own proper children & issue of my body'. Twenty years later,
in a change perhaps indicative of a growing social disquiet toward
miscegenation (and one reason for its absence in the manumission records),
such an admission had to wait until after the father's death. In 1774, the
executors of the estate of Benjamin Williamson reported that 'amongst the
slaves which he was possessed of and entitled to at his Decease there are ...
[two] Mullatto children, ... there being reason to believe they are his issue,
... [the executors] are therefore unwilling that the said children should
continue in a state of slavery'.[15]

However, given the high proportion of women among the freed, the
common presumption that eighteenth-century manumission was often
granted to women involved in relationships with their masters or other
whites cannot be entirely discounted. Three instances survive from the mid-
eighteenth century of slave women who married white men and later
became free. In 1753, a planter in Colleton County wrote that the 'negro

woman Peggy is and hath been the wife of me, John Bond, for many years past'. Bond also acknowledged Peggy's three children as his own before granting freedom to them all. In the other two cases, white servants were wed to slave women with the permission of their owners. Both women were later manumitted although one had to agree to remain 'subject to ... [her ex-master] and no other during his natural life, to mend, make, and serve him, as occasion required', which suggests something less than complete freedom.[16]

Slave women were also freed for motives that while familial, were neither sexual nor conjugal, suggesting the complex interracial dependencies and emotive ties that could develop within slaveholding households. Tilly, described as 'a thick short Negro wench about forty years of age', was manumitted in 1782 in return for 'having carefully attended ... [her master's] Children during their Infancy'. Two years later, the incumbent governor of South Carolina, Benjamin Guerard, granted freedom to an elderly slave woman named Bess. The Governor wrote that he was moved to act from 'the great respect & gratitude due from me most justly to her, she having carried me in her arms when a very infant as my dry nurse'.[17]

A slaveholder's willingness to free one or several slaves should not be taken as evidence of an unspoken (or perhaps even unconscious) anti-slavery sentiment. The manumission of a tiny minority of especially favoured slaves might just as accurately be taken as the ultimate bestowal of patriarchal benevolence. Like the modern lottery's Midas touch, the example of a fortunate few may have served to validate an inherently unequal system.

The easy co-existence of slavery and manumission is nowhere better illustrated than in those cases wherein people simultaneously were transformed from slaves into masters. In 1764, William Philips, a 'mulatto slave', was manumitted in the last will and testament of Elizabeth Jehne. In the same document Jehne bequeathed to Philips 'one negro girl named Lucey with her issue and increase and one negroe boy named Demboe to have & to hold forever'. Such arrangements remained possible even after the revolution. In the will of Frederick Brindley, who died in 1782, Chloe received her own freedom, as well as fifty guineas, the household furniture, and her 'pick' of any two of Brindley's other slaves.[18]

In a manner that resembled new world slavery itself, manumission could be made to fit a wide variety of circumstances and purposes. Nine per cent of the recorded manumissions were conditional upon the freed person either agreeing to undertake certain obligations, or consenting to accept limitations upon their freedom.

One way that a slaveholder could ensure that valuable and troublesome slaves applied themselves to their work was to hold out the offer of future freedom, conditional upon the slaves' provision of obedience and labour. This arrangement might be for a specified term of years, such as the bargain which William Stone struck with Tartar in 1740. Soon after purchasing Tartar, Stone promised to set him free in exchange for eight years of 'good and faithful service'. Or there is the case of Dandy, who in exchange for providing Joseph Allston with seven years of hard work, was promised his own and his family's freedom, as well as 'two Mulch Cowes'.[19]

Dangling the carrot of freedom as well as the whip provided slaveholders with a powerful incentive with which to extract slaves' labour. Moreover, masters were not legally bound to keep such pledges. A slave promised freedom in eight years upon good behaviour could be sold after seven. Because the agreements were not carried through, such betrayals would have left little trace in the records. Nevertheless, it is interesting to note, for example, that Tartar, who was promised that he would be freed in 1748, did not actually become a free man until twenty years later.[20]

In the colonial era, the hope of future emancipation usually rested not only upon the slave's good behaviour but also upon the master's death. Masters, like other patriarchs, could use the prospect of the rewards that would be dealt out after their death, in their last wills, as a tool to encourage their subordinates to toe the line while they lived. Such acts of post-mortem generosity offered a mode of control over slaves at no cost to the owner (although it did come at the expense of their heirs). That such agreements gave slaves a reason to wish for, if not hasten, their master's death, seems not to have prevented such promises from being made.

Commonly, such agreements took the form of suspended acts of manumission that were to take effect only upon the master's demise. In 1773, for example, Peter Manigault drew up a document freeing one of his slave women and her children but 'provided that this Deed of Manumission shall not have any force during ... [my] natural life'. Similarly, Daniel Roofs promised 'a negro wench slave named Phillis' her freedom 'immediately after my decease', but reserved 'all ... [claim] to the slave as long as I live'.[21]

As such slaves legally remained their master's property, their future freedom was precarious. Like any of the provisions of a will, while testators lived they were free to change their minds (and their wills) at any time. In the same deed in which Manigault promised his slave her freedom at his death, he also reserved the right 'at any time hereafter to revoke, disannul and make void' the act. An extreme example of such a change of heart occurred in the fall of 1750, when a master who had freed his slave from his death bed made an unexpected recovery, suffered manumittor's remorse, and rescinded the deed.[22]

When such promises of post-mortem manumission were only verbal, they were even more likely to miscarry. John Colleton had pledged a 'slave woman named Lissey' that if she served him faithfully 'to the hour of his death', she would be freed. But when Colleton was 'taken with a sudden illness' and died, 'he was prevented from carrying his said resolution fully into execution'. Fortunately for Lissey, Colleton's executors both knew of his promise and chose to honour it. Had they not done so, no record of the event would have survived.[23]

Executors could also take advantage of their position to act against the would-be free person's interest. Just as executors could attempt to defraud the estates in their charge of other forms of property, they could also rob slaves of their promised self-inheritance. In 1780, George Galprin, executor of the estate of Brian Kelly, overruled a provision of Kelly's will that freed Dick, his wife Juno, and their eight children. Instead, because Kelly died owing him 'a considerable debt', Galprin declared that the slaves' freedom must wait upon his own death, until which time they would belong to him.[24]

Some of the manumissions did not seek to set the conditions upon which the slave would become free, but rather sought to define or restrict the nature of the proffered freedom itself. In one case, freedom was defined according to situation. Isaac Barksdale manumitted his slave woman Nanny on condition 'that whenever I shall reside in Charles Town ... the said Negro woman shall ... then & there attend, be subject to, serve, and obey me as a good and faithful slave ought to do'. In other words, Nanny was only to be free when Barksdale was out of town.[25]

In other cases, the boundaries of freedom were geographic. In 1744, Yanaka, a slave woman, was freed only after agreeing that she not would leave her ex-master's plantation without his consent. Conversely, Judy, a 'mullatta wench', was manumitted by John Colleton 'upon this express condition and not otherwise, that she shall not at any time during my life ... come or stay in Charlestown or come or reside to or at any place within Ten miles of my Plantation'. Such bargains might be seen as the price slaves were willing to pay for their liberty. Better a freedom constrained than none.[26]

The strangest of all the engagements struck between masters and freed blacks defies such a ready explanation. Betty was manumitted in 1784 upon her mistress's death. Two years later, she reappeared before the registrar. In this second document, Betty agreed to

> ... put and bind herself [as] a Servant to ... James Lamar and to his heirs for and during the Term of Fourteen years with him to dwell & serve as a true orderly and faithfull Servant to obey all his lawful & reasonable commands by night or by day & never absent myself ... without leave... [In return] Lamar [was to provide] sufficient and

comfortable clothing diet and lodging suitable to one in her Station
and in Case of sickness to supply her with the usual & necessary helps
and comforts commonly afforded to servants in such cases and to pay
her annually two dollars.

The clerk, clearly taken aback by such an unequal exchange, added to the
bottom of the record: 'The above Negro Betty was particularly examined by
me and declared she had from her own desire and inclination made the
above Indenture ... without any force, compulsion, or persuasion.' While
most slaves would do anything and accept any terms in order to become
free, it seems that Betty was just as eager to trade her liberty away. Betty's
bargain may serve as a reminder of the dark and dangerous world in which
South Carolina's free blacks lived. Having been a free woman for two years,
Betty may have had reason to desire the protection and security which a
white patron could provide. Betty may have thought that she made the best
of a series of bad choices. In her mind, perhaps, taking another master did
not make her once again a slave.[27]

In 105 of the 379 manumissions that were copied into the miscellaneous
records between 1737 and 1785, the bargain struck between master and
slave was financial, as the slave became free through the act of self-
purchase. Self-purchase was a common, although never the most common,
avenue of manumission throughout the entire period. As with other modes
of manumission, the American Revolution lead to a dramatic increase in the
number of masters who were willing to sell their slaves their freedom. But
self-purchase did not overtake other non-economic motives. The proportion
of self-purchase cases among total recorded manumissions (twenty-eight
per cent) did not vary on either side of the revolutionary watershed of
1775.[28]

However, the average amount slaves paid for their freedom showed a
significant change over time. The same proportion of slaves may have
bought themselves in each era between 1740 and 1785, but the price they
paid for their freedom steadily increased. Over the course of the entire
period, the average cost of self-emancipation more than doubled, from less
than thirty pounds sterling in the era 1737–54, to nearly seventy pounds by
1775–85. This increase may have reflected the rising cost of slaves, more
than a rising rapacity on the part of manumittors, but the mere fact that the
price of freedom was linked to the price of slavery indicates the central
place of financial calculation in these transactions. If, as Ira Berlin asserts,
'egalitarian ideals motivated most manumittors in the years following the
Revolution', masters did not allow their love of liberty to impinge upon
their pocketbooks (see Table 2).[29]

Moreover, considering self-purchase according to perceived skin colour,

TABLE 2
RECORDED MANUMISSIONS BY SELF-PURCHASE
CATEGORIZED BY YEARS, 1737-85

| | | Average Amount Paid | |
	No.	S.C. Currency	(£)
1737–54	11	206.4	(29.5)
1755–64	20	246.9	(35.3)
1765–74	12	363.2	(51.9)
1775–85	62	483.3	(69.0)

Source: MR\SCDAH, 1737–85. A note on currency exchange rates: during the colonial period South Carolina currency held steady at approximately 7 to 1 against the pound sterling. I have undertaken to convert one to the other in my table for the sake of comparison. After 1775, the monetary situation becomes far more confused and comparison is difficult. In this era however, (and perhaps for this reason) a large proportion of self-purchases are described in pounds sterling or British guineas. Consequently, the right column (pounds sterling) may offer a more reliable basis for comparison over time.

sex, and age indicates that, among the group of people whose deeds of manumission were recorded, those who gained their freedom by means of self-purchase were disproportionately drawn from blacks, males and adults. Although mulattoes and women are still hugely over-represented among the self-manumittors when compared to their numbers in the total slave population, if cases of self-purchase are compared only to all other recorded manumissions these trends are reversed. Although children whose freedom was bought by their parents are included in the sample, the financial prerequisites of self-purchase probably explain the increased proportion of adults. The higher percentage of blacks and males among the self-purchased is far more significant. This may indicate that just as slaves with these characteristics were less likely to be freed at all, they were also less likely to be given their freedom without having to pay for it. That black adult men may have walked a steeper road to their freedom is also suggested by the fact that they paid a substantially higher price when bargaining for their liberty (see Table 3).

In several cases, the enormous efforts through which slaves raised the money needed to purchase themselves were explicitly acknowledged. In 1770, Jacob Willeman sold Leander his freedom for 900 pounds current money (approximately 130 pounds sterling). In the deed of manumission, Willeman wrote: 'I ... do hereby declare that the said sum ... was delivered to me by ... Leander from time to time as Monies which he had by his great care, dilligence, and industry in his business Trade or occupation of a Butcher for several years past got together and earned.' Similarly, seven years later, Diana was able to buy freedom for herself and her daughter out of 'the earnings and gains arising from her Labour and Industry [which she

TABLE 3

RECORDED MANUMISSIONS BY SELF-PURCHASE, 1737–85
BY PERCEIVED SKIN COLOUR, SEX, AGE, AND AVERAGE COST

Perceived Skin colour (adults only)				
Black	61	(80%)	465.0	(£66.4)
Mulatto	15	(20%)	406.0	(£58.0)
Sex (adults only)				
Female	45	(59%)	415.1	(£59.3)
Male	31	(41%)	509.3	(£72.8)
Age				
Adults	76	(72%)	453.5	(£64.7)
Children	29	(28%)	243.4	(£34.8)
Total	105	—	395.5	(£56.5)

Source: MR\SCDAH, 1737–85

was] from time to time, ... allowed to carry on and transact during the term of her servitude'.[30]

The terms under which slaves bought their own freedom, or the methods they employed to raise the necessary capital, varied enormously. One woman paid her master fifty pounds sterling and in return received only his pledge that she would be freed upon his death. Another black woman borrowed the money to purchase the freedom of her three children, in effect mortgaging her own and her children's freedom on her ability to repay the debt. James persuaded his owner, Ann Yarborough, to allow him to buy himself through an instalment plan. Perhaps, the strangest arrangement was the bargain struck between Daniel Legare and his slave woman Grace in 1784. Legare wrote that he agreed to manumit Grace 'in consideration of a Negro girl named Hagar which she purchased from John Young [and] to me in hand delivered'.[31]

As with masters' promises to free slaves in their wills, such financial understandings were always at risk of being rendered void by the sudden death of one or both of the principals. In 1763, for example, Daniel Crawford agreed with George, a 'free negro', to sell George his wife and son for £488 'current money'. As a down payment and mark of good faith, George gave Crawford £288. Before the transaction could be finished, however, both Crawford and George died. Ultimately, Abah, George's wife, was able to pay Crawford's heirs the balance due and gain freedom for herself and son. Only the completion of this bargain allowed it to survive in the record. Slaves in similar circumstances that ended less happily would never have had cause to appear before the registrar.[32]

A slave had no legal right to property, thus arrangements through which slaves bought themselves were of no legal force. By law, masters had the right to any and all money that their slaves might earn. Consequently, that slaves should buy their freedom with cash they earned themselves was in a legal sense impossible, as both slave and money already belonged to the master before any 'sale' was made. The fact that slaves and masters struck such bargains anyway was neither the first nor last time that the everyday practices of the slave society deviated from its laws and logic.[33]

This lack of a legally enforceable contract placed any slaves who sought to buy their freedom entirely at the mercy of their master. When slaves appeared before their master bearing their hard-earned cash in order to buy their freedom, there was nothing to prevent their master from reneging on the deal, or even claiming the money as their own. Equiano's master, for example, agreed to sell him his freedom for forty-seven pounds sterling. When Equiano actually presented him with the money, he changed his mind and only consented to honour the bargain when shamed into doing so by another white man.[34]

The fear (or expectation) of such a betrayal or back-sliding may have induced many slaves to purchase their freedom through the assistance of another white person who agreed to act as a screen or front hiding both the true nature of the transaction, and the actual source of the funds, from their master. In 1761, for example, Mary Underwood bought Binah and her child from the estate of Jacob Martin for 252 pounds 'currency'. Three years later, however, when Underwood manumitted the two, she admitted that the cash she used to make the purchase 'were the proper moneys of the said Negro woman named Binah and was by her delivered to the said Mary Underwood in order to free and discharge her the said Binah and her child Tub from the Bond of Slavery'.[35]

In some cases, the existence of such 'freedom brokers' can only be surmised from circumstantial evidence. For instance, Alexander Oliphant purchased three slaves Flora, Fatima, and Fatima's child, from Edward Rutledge for 155 guineas on 10 August 1783. Thirteen days later, Oliphant manumitted Flora in return for seventy-five guineas, and Fatima and child in exchange for eighty guineas. In other cases, the deeds are far more explicit. When John Speed purchased and immediately freed Betty for the enormous sum of two thousand pounds currency (£286) in 1778, he declared that this 'was her own money & my name was only made use of for her'. Similarly, on 6 June 1782, Robert Ballingall bought 'a mulatto girl named Jane' from Samuel Prioleau for thirty-two guineas. One month later, Ballingall appeared before the registrar to declare: 'I hereby acknowledge to have received from the above mentioned mullatto girl, Jane, the sum of thirty-four pounds sixteen shillings and ten pence sterling, being the sum I paid for her. In consideration whereof, I hereby manumit the said girl named Jane.'[36]

Of course, nothing prevented the slave's chosen freedom broker from absconding with the money, or from refusing to free a slave whom they had bought with the slave's own earnings. In the end, because slaves were themselves legal non-persons, any slave wishing to buy their liberty had first to place both their freedom and their cash in someone else's hands.

The manumission records offer testimony for the existence of a free black community in colonial and revolutionary South Carolina. One source can be found in those cases in which blacks who had already become free extended the blessings of liberty to other members of their family. The earliest example of such 'familial manumission' occurred in 1754 when 'Free Bing' appeared before the clerk in Charleston and proudly testified that 'by the fruit of my own industry I have been enabled to purchase and actually have purchased of Hugh Bryan deceased, my wife named Judy and her children Bing, Johnny, Judy, Bess and Jemmy'. Bing cited the 'love and affection' he felt toward his wife and children as his motive for granting them their freedom. Three years later, 'Matthew Daniel, free negro' paid John Edwards, a Charleston merchant, 700 pounds currency for 'Betty, my wife, together with her three children, named Matt, Quash, and Betty', all of whom he immediately freed.[37]

Several records survive in which free black or mulatto women bought and freed daughters who presumably had been born while the were still slaves and thus legally remained the property of their ex-masters. One of these cases is particularly noteworthy. Nanny Barksdale, who had been granted a conditional freedom by her master in 1754, apparently found sufficient time while her master was away to earn and save a large amount of money. In 1759, Nanny paid 300 pounds 'lawful money' for the freedom of her daughter Sarah, a slave to Sarah Wright.[38]

The three appearances in the record made by 'Carolina Lamboll, a freed Negro man', provide another family history. Lamboll first came before the registrar in January 1779 to record the manumission of 'Jane, my wife, lately purchased by me of Mrs. Rachel Caw'. Five years later, Lamboll was back. First as a master, selling freedom to his slave Pompey in exchange for 122 pounds sterling, then later in the same year, as a father, buying his son Quash for the same amount and then setting him free. The near sequence of these two records (and the exact coincidence in price accepted and price offered) suggests that Lamboll may have acquired the money to buy his own son's freedom by selling freedom to another slave.[39]

Lamboll's strategy draws attention to the ways in which blacks who were already free could serve as a conduit to freedom for others besides the members of their own family. In such cases, the black master often was not averse to making the freedom of their slave conditional upon a cash payment. It may be significant, however, that in cases where blacks bought their freedom from other blacks, the prices are far lower than in the majority of cases where the manumittor was white. In 1782, for example, John Lamputt, a free black wheelwright, sold a 'mestizo boy (slave) named George' his liberty for only ten pounds sterling. Leander Fairchild, the free black butcher who had paid 130 pounds sterling for his own freedom in 1770, asked only one third as much from his own slave, Robin, before he manumitted him in 1786.[40]

Perhaps the best evidence for the emergence of a free black 'community' lies in the cases in which Charleston free blacks took on the role of freedom brokers, agreeing to act as the agent for slaves who sought to purchase their liberty from untrustworthy masters. On 10 August 1786, for example, Scipio Guignard, who described himself as 'a free black man of the city of Charleston, cooper', bought Cato, a slave, from William Kelery for thirty-seven guineas. Later the same day, Guignard manumitted his new property, declaring to the registrar that he acted from 'consideration of the Sum of thirty-seven guineas to me in hand paid ... by my Negroe man named Cato'. Perhaps slaves who were forced to place their liberty and money into another's hands, felt safer if the proffered hand was the same colour as their own.[41]

The deeds of manumission recorded in South Carolina's miscellaneous record books offer a window into the lives of South Carolina's free blacks before the first federal census, but manumission, in the last half of the eighteenth-century, was also a door between slavery and freedom. Manumission records illuminate the process through which individual slaves became free and South Carolina's free black community was born. On 1 January 1791, the free blacks of South Carolina, who in the previous year had been 'discovered' by the census and who had collectively 'found' themselves in the formation of the Brown Fellowship Society, found something else: their voice. On this day, the General Assembly of the State of South Carolina received the 'memorial of Thomas Cole, Bricklayer, P.B. Matthews, and Matthew Webb, Butchers, on behalf of themselves & others free-men of Colour'. The petitioners declared that

> ... in the enumeration of free Citizens by the Constitution of the United States for the Purpose of Representation of the Southern States in Congress your memorialists have been considered under that description as part of the Citizens of this State. Although by the 14th and 29th clauses in an act of Assembly made in the year 1740 ... commonly called the Negroe Act ... [they] are deprived of the rights and privileges of Citizens by not having it in their power to give testimony on oath in prosecutions on behalf of the state from which cause many culprits have escaped the punishment due to their

atrocious crimes, nor can they give testimony in recovering debts due
to them ... whereby they are subject to great losses and repeated
injuries without any means of redress ... [they] have at all times since
the independence of the United States contributed and do now
contribute to the support of government by chearfully paying their
taxes ... they are ready and willing to take and subscribe to such oaths
of allegiance to the state as shall be prescribed ... Your memorialists
do not presume to hope that they shall be put upon an equal footing
with the free white Citizens of the state in general they only humbly
solicit such indulgence as the wisdom and humanity of this House
shall dictate in their favour by repealing the clauses of the Act before
mentioned.

Taking the constitution at its word, and accepting the limitations of the
world that they lived in, the free blacks of Charleston apparently felt that
'three-fifths' citizenship was better than none.[42]

For two of the three signers of this petition, the tone of hard-headed
pragmatism, as well perhaps of careful calculation, contained in their
memorial had been learned years earlier. In 1755, John Webb, a Charleston
merchant, in exchange for sixty-six pounds sterling, 'confirm[ed] and
deliver[ed] in plain and open market ... freedom & liberty' to his slave
Matthew, who thereby became Matthew Webb. Eight years later, Benjamin
Smith, in return for eighty-six pounds that he was paid by 'Thomas Cole, a
free Mulatto man, and bricklayer', drew up deeds of manumission for 'one
woman named Ruth and her two children named Tom & Barbary, being also
the children of the said Thomas Cole'. The lessons of diligence,
determination, and industry, and of caution and conservatism that served
slaves well as they bargained for their own and their family's freedom in the
colonial and revolutionary eras continued to shape Charleston's free black
community from 1790 until the outbreak of the Civil War.[43]

NOTES

1. Marina Wikramanayake, *A World in Shadow: The Free Black in Antebellum South Carolina* (Columbia, 1973), pp.22, 81, 18; Ira Berlin, *Slave Without Masters: The Free Negro in the Antebellum South* (Oxford, 1974), pp.221–3; for a vivid portrayal of one Charleston free black family in the mid-nineteenth century, see Michael P. Johnson and James L. Roark (eds.), *No Chariot Let Down: Charleston's Free People of Colour On the Eve of the Civil War* (Chapel Hill, 1984). An article on this subject which I was unable to locate but which may be of interest is John D. Duncan, 'Slave Emancipation in Colonial South Carolina', *American Chronicle, A Magazine of History*, I (1972).
2. Thomas Cooper and David J. McCord (eds.), *The Statutes at Large of South Carolina* (10 vols.; Columbia, SC, 1836–41), VII, p.397. Beside the exception made for 'negroes, mulattoes, and mustizoes, who are now free' in the first paragraph of the Act (which otherwise defines all members of these groups as *ipso facto* slaves), the category of 'free

negroe' appears three times in the slave code. In paragraph XIV, the law first directs that slave testimony would be admissible in the trial of 'free negroes' (as it was in the trial of slaves but not whites) but then immediately afterward decreed that free negroes accused of crimes would be tried in the same manner as slaves, which rendered the preceding point moot. In paragraph XVI, free blacks are also to suffer death if convicted of any of the 'peculiar' crimes (i.e. arson, poison, conspiracy, etc.) directed at slaves. This conflation of slave and free blacks is contrasted however by section XXIX which subjected 'free negroes' convicted of harbouring runaways to a fine while slaves convicted of the same offence were to be whipped. Ibid., VII, pp.397, 402 and 407.

3. Ibid.., VII, p.398; In this case, Clarinda, a black woman, was brought before the Charleston court after having escaped from Spanish territory. Although Clarinda claimed to free she had no evidence to support her case. A white man came forward claiming to be her master but he also could provide neither witnesses nor written proof. In rendering his verdict, the presiding justice, Charles Skinner, faced a dilemma: while Clarinda was, by law, a slave, she also had no known master. With a deft hand, the judge solved his problem by dismissing Clarinda's suit, paying the court costs himself, and claiming the woman as his own property; Memorial of Charles Skinner to Governor Montague, 2 May 1767, in 'Garth Correspondence', *South Carolina Historical Magazine*, XXX (1929), pp.36–7.

4. See for example, Robert M. Weir, 'Muster Rolls of the South Carolina Granville and Colleton County Regiments of Militia, 1756', in *South Carolina Historical Magazine*, LXX (Oct. 1969), pp.26–39; Records of the Commissioner of the High Roads of St. John's Parish, Berkeley County, 1760–1853, South Carolina Department of Archives and History, Columbia, South Carolina; and 'A 1786 Tax Account', in H. Roy Merrens (ed.), *The Colonial South Carolina Scene: Contemporary Views, 1697–1774* (Columbia, 1977), pp.250–1, (the tax account lists only 77 'free negroes' in the colony (amid 79,817 slaves) and is almost certainly a gross under count of the true figure. The lack of evidence with which to apprise the number of free blacks in colonial South Carolina has not deterred scholars from positing their own guesses. Both Robert Weir and Peter Wood estimate the number of free blacks in the colony as being about one per cent of the slave population, or about 800 in 1768. See Robert M. Weir, *Colonial South Carolina: A History* (Millwood, NY, 1983), pp.199–200; Peter H. Wood, *Black Majority: Negroes in Colonial South Carolina from 1670 to the Stono Rebellion* (New York, 1974), p.103.

5. Details of this affair are drawn from two sources: the Journal of the Council, 20 June and 9 July 1759, originals at the South Carolina Department of Archives and History (SCDAH), Columbia, South Carolina, and the British Public Record Office (BPRO), London, microfilm at the Library of Congress, Washington, DC, pp.105–6, 110–11; and Governor Henry Lyttleton to the Board of Trade, 1 Sept. 1759, original at the BPRO, microfilm SCDAH, C05/376, D438, pp.107–8.

6. Both of these incidents are described at greater length in Robert Olwell, '"Domestick Enemies": Slavery and Political Independence in South Carolina, May 1775–March 1776', *Journal of Southern History*, LV (1989), pp.33–4, 38, 43.

7. Quoted in Frank J. Klingberg, *An Appraisal of the Negro in Colonial South Carolina: A Study in Americanization* (Washington, DC, 1941), p.81; Journal of the Council, 4 April 1753, p.360.

8. Olaudah Equiano, *The Interesting Narrative of the Life of Olaudah Equiano, or Gustavus Vasa, The African, Written by Himself*, reprinted in Henry Louis Gates (ed.), *The Classic Slave Narratives* (New York, 1987), pp.103–4, 117–18.

9. Hereafter the Miscellaneous Record Books at the South Carolina Department of Archives and History, Columbia, South Carolina, will be cited: MR\SCDAH, followed by the date and volume reference. My sample stops in 1785 rather than 1790 because at the time the research was conducted, I was in the midst of an earlier and larger project. Had the search continued to 1790, more samples would certainly have been found, although I do not believe that they would have differed significantly in character. I thank my wife, Julie Hardwick, for collecting this data.

10. Equiano, *The Interesting Narrative*, p.101.

11. MR\SCDAH, 18 Feb. 1762, LL454; A similar incident occurred three years later when a

duplicate deed of manumission was drawn up to replace an earlier one which 'by some accident … is lost or mislaid'; MR\SCDAH, 18 May 1765, MM276.

12. I assume the registrar's fee was five shillings because of the common inclusion of this paltry sum, 'to me in hand paid', in many manumission accounts; see for example MR\SCDAH, 12 July 1757. Equiano reported that he paid the registrar in Montserrat one guinea when he was freed in 1766, a sum he described as 'half-price'; Equiano, *The Interesting Narrative*, p.101; MR\SCDAH, 6 March 1777, RR433.

13. See, Johnson and Roark, *No Chariot Let Down*, pp.6; 130 (or thirty-four per cent) of the 379 recorded deeds describe their subjects as 'mullato'.

14. Despite this increase in the incidence of manumission, only one manumittor (from 1779) was willing to admit to being moved by anti-slavery sympathies:

> I, John Peronneau of Charlestown in the state aforesaid gentleman, in consequence of my aversion to and abhorrence of slavery which natural religion and common sense do equally condemn and in consideration of the sum of five shillings currency do hereby manumit infranchise and make set free from the state of slavery & bondage forever the within named slave Romeo.

MR/SCDAH, 16 Oct. 1779, TT36.

15. MR\SCDAH, 6 June 1754, KK148; 18 June 1774, WW77.

16. MR\SCDAH, 14 Feb. 1753, II381; 19 Oct. 1754, KK290; 19 Nov. 1746, KK270.

17. MR\SCDAH, 27 March 1782, TT127; 22 April 1784, UU95.

18. MR\SCDAH, 10 May 1784, UU115; 12 Feb. 1782, TT103.

19. MR\SCDAH, 21 April 1740, FF434; 2 June 1784, WW256.

20. MR\SCDAH, 22 May 1768, FF436.

21. MR\SCDAH, 12 May 1773, ZZ354; 3 May 1765, MM265.

22. The case reads as follows:

> … [last fall while] the deponent was afflicted with sickness & so very ill that he kept his bed … he is informed that by a Certain Instrument of Writing said to be executed by the Deponent he had manumised or set free his negro man slave Kingston … if he did execute such instrument of Writing he the deponent was not then of sound mind … the deponent further saith that the manumission or freedom of his … slave would be [a] manifest & trying loss [to him] … if he did execute the original of the written copy he was greatly imposed on and if he … the deponent had been in his right senses [he] would not have done [it] & therefore the deponent doth declare that he doth make null and void & of none effect the said deed of manumission.

MR\SCDAH, 20 Jan. 1750, HH382.

23. MR\SCDAH, 20 May 1752, NN79

24. MR\SCDAH, 24 Nov. 1780, CCC96. In a similar case, an executor delayed a slave's post-mortem manumission until the slave (who was a skilled carpenter) built the executor a storehouse in Charleston; 10 Aug. 1763, MM245.

25. MR\SCDAH, 30 April 1754, KK204.

26. MR\SCDAH, 3 April 1744, GG330; 6 July 1775, RR201.

27. MR\SCDAH, 19 Nov. 1784 and 7 Aug. 1786, WW315.

28. Just as the 379 deeds of manumission that survive in the miscellaneous records must be regarded as a sub-set of the unknowable global figure of all manumissions, the 105 of these 379 that explicitly describe a self-purchase transaction must be regarded as a lowest possible figure (or per centage) for this phenomenon. Deeds did not have to accurately describe the bargains that led to their creation. For example, 78 (or twenty one per cent) of the manumittors explained their action via an ambiguous piece of boiler-plate that may have been supplied by the registrar. It is certainly conceivable that among the unnamed 'diverse good causes and considerations' that these manumittors claimed had motivated them to act, was a large cash payment received from the slave now become free.

29. Berlin, *Slaves Without Masters*, p.30.

30. MR\SCDAH, 11 Oct. 1770, OO385; 16 April 1777, SS49.
31. MR\SCDAH, 21 Nov. 1782; 3 July 1784, UU142; 23 Aug. 1782, TT173; 10 May 1784, UU115.
32. MR\SCDAH, 5 May 1763, LL611.
33. Cooper and McCord (eds.), *The Statutes at Large of South Carolina*, VII, pp.407–9. The complex interplay between ideology and practice in the colonial lowcountry is treated at length in my forthcoming book, *Slaves & Kings: The Culture of Power in a Colonial Slave Society, The South Carolina Lowcountry, 1740–1783*.
34. Equiano, *The Interesting Narrative*, pp.100–1.
35. It is unclear whether three year's labour was Underwood's fee for acting as Binah's agent, or whether the delay was merely in getting the manumission officially registered; MR\SCDAH, 23 June 1761, MM158.
36. MR\SCDAH, 10 Aug. 1783, TT355; 23 Aug. 1783, TT353, 23 Aug. 1783, TT354; 29 Sept. 1778, RR572; 13 July 1782, TT165. Six months before he sold Binah her freedom for 2,000 pounds currency, John Speed sold 'Judy and her son Billy' their freedom for the similarly inflated sum of 1,500 pounds, which raises the question as to whether some white men may have endeavoured to make a living by acting as 'freedom brokers'; 25 March 1778, SS228.
37. MR\SCDAH, 4 June 1754, KK98; 7 July 1757, LL255; 12 July 1757, LL254.
38. MR\SCDAH, 5 Feb. 1759, MM502. For other mother-daughter manumissions see UU187, SS322, and SS340.
39. MR\SCDAH, 19 Jan. 1779, RR586; 9 Oct. 1784, VV195; UU 427.
40. MR\SCDAH, 9 April 1782, TT128; 16 Dec. 1786, WW34. Between 1775–85, the average amount paid for the freedom of a mulatto boy was 52 pounds, and for a black, adult, male 74 pounds.
41. MR\SCDAH, 10 Aug. 1786, WW251; 10 Aug. 1786, WW252.
42. General Assembly Petitions, SCDAH, 1791-00181.
43. MR\SCDAH, 7 Sept. 1755, KK223; 5 May 1763, LL603.

Colour, Class and Identity on the Eve of the Haitian Revolution: Saint-Domingue's Free Coloured Elite as *Colons américains*

JOHN D. GARRIGUS

Although wealthy free coloured planters played a central role in transforming the French Revolution into the Haitian Revolution, the origins of this class are still poorly understood.[1] To date only the colony's most conspicuous pre-revolutionary free coloured elite has been studied in any detail. That group, the indigo planters of Aquin parish, was descended from early French settlers and African slaves and built its prosperity on family connections and smuggling. These families saw themselves, with good reason, as island-born French planters, *colons américains*, not *gens de couleur*.[2]

This self-identification as both creole and French was the basis of the political stance Saint-Domingue's free people of colour adopted in the French Revolution. From 1789 their leaders argued that they should participate in the 'regeneration' of the French nation. In various colonial parishes free people of colour drafted petitions for reform, formed National Guard units and tried to participate in colonial elections. In Paris Julien Raimond, a wealthy man of colour from Aquin parish, made free coloured civil rights the central colonial issue facing the Revolutionary National Assembly.[3]

But was Aquin, whose affluent, Franco-centric planters played an important role in the Revolution, unusual? Although its fertile valleys attracted early settlers, mountains separated Aquin from Saint-Domingue's major cities and sugar planting regions. This parish's free coloured elite has been described as more an example of white misalliance than representative of Saint-Domingue's free population of colour.[4] Certainly most free people of colour were not as wealthy, well travelled or self-confident as Julien Raimond.

Nevertheless, men like Raimond could be found throughout Saint-Domingue. This paper examines the origins and activities of three families in Torbec parish. This area was far closer to Saint-Domingue's great sugar plantations than Aquin (see Map 1). Torbec had been the seat of the rich Cayes du Fond region from the beginning of organized French settlement in 1698. A town named Torbec was already in place in the western corner of that plain in the early 1700s when the royally chartered Saint-Domingue Company established its officers there. In 1720 the Company dissolved and Versailles joined the peninsula to the rest of the colony. In 1726 royal officers founded the parish of Torbec, distinct from Cayes du Fond.[5]

For the next decade Torbec was the more important of the two parishes. By the 1750s, however, it was overshadowed by Cayes, to the east. The city of Les Cayes became Saint-Domingue's third largest port and, in 1779, was named the administrative capital of the southern peninsula. In the 1780s the town of Torbec had only about 20 occupied houses, two-thirds less than it had once had. Nevertheless, the district's rural population continued to grow. In 1784 a new parish was carved out of Torbec's boundaries.[6]

Although Torbec lost its commercial and official importance to Cayes, the parish maintained a distinctive political identity from 1769 into the Haitian Revolution. Free coloured resistance to militia reforms in 1769, support for Julien Raimond's civil rights proposals in 1784, an armed uprising for free coloured citizenship in 1790 and racial warfare in 1792 have been described as occurring at Cayes, but all took place in the Torbec plain and hills.[7]

Torbec's planters, like those of Aquin, had a past that supported their Revolutionary claim to be *colons américains* – legitimate citizens of Saint-Domingue. By the 1780s new racial laws prevented many people of mixed European and African descent from identifying themselves as 'white'. Yet these families were neither African slaves nor newly manumitted freedmen. Like Aquin's elite some of these men and women were so light-skinned and socially respected that they were only officially labelled *gens de couleur* in the decade before the Revolution. Although Torbec was not as isolated as Aquin, its founding families, too, had been knit together by more than half a century of economic and social alliances. The parish's wealthiest and most active free families of colour in 1789 bore names that had belonged to the region's most prosperous early French colonists. While white immigrants despaired of the time it took to establish a plantation that could support their return to Europe, the descendants of Torbec's first generation restored dilapidated properties to profitability and built new estates as the years passed. Like Aquin's elite, Torbec's wealthy free families of colour saw themselves as island-born planters and their revolutionary careers cannot be understood outside this identity. In the nineteenth century, moreover, the deep creole roots of Torbec's free coloured planters were grafted to the sapling of Haitian nationalism.

MAP 1

TORBEC AND AQUIN PARISHES

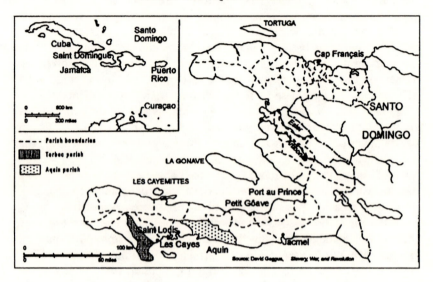

MAP 2

THE QUARTIERS OF CAYES, ST. LOUIS AND NIPPES

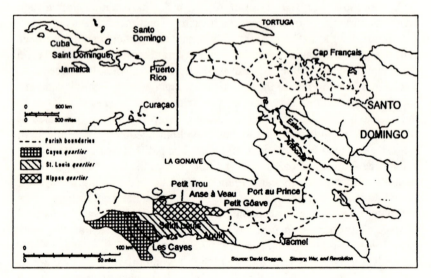

At the close of the eighteenth century Saint-Domingue's economy and the nature of colonial society were both changing in ways that threatened the social position of these established families of mixed ancestry. By the 1780s the colony's best agricultural lands had been claimed and developed, even in the southern peninsula, the last region of Saint-Domingue to be settled. Frenchmen who sailed west to become rich planters found few rural opportunities by the 1780s. Colonial cities, not sugar estates, absorbed the substantial increase in white immigration after 1763.

The sales of urban versus rural property in three neighbouring colonial districts from the 1760s to the 1780s reflect this shift[8] (See Map 2). From one decade to another the number of rural property sales increased from five per cent of all notarial activity (225/4882) to twelve per cent in a sample taken from the later decade (334/2679). However, over the same period notarized sales of urban property increased from 1.5 per cent (76/4882) of contracts to nine per cent (251/2679). The median value of rural property sales increased only about 20 per cent (6,600 to 8,000 livres) while the median value of urban property almost doubled (5,500 to 10,000 livres). While the average value of urban sales also doubled in this period (7,947 to 16,176 livres), the average value of rural property sales actually fell (24,296 to 19,034 livres).

These numbers reflect the saturation of Saint-Domingue's rural districts. In the 1760s arable land was still widely available in the colony's southern peninsula. But by the 1780s the best holdings had been consolidated into large plantations, which were more likely to be transferred by marriage

TABLE 1

SALES OF RURAL PROPERTY, 1760–69
PARTICIPATION OF FREE PEOPLE OF COLOUR IN EACH DECILE OF VALUE[9]

Per centile	Value of sale in colonial livres	% of these sales involving free people of colour	% of all free coloured sales
1–10	232–1,000	49 (11/23)	17
10–20	1,000–2,000	45 (10/22)	16
20–30	2,000–3,000	49 (11/23)	17
30–40	3,000–4,500	55 (12/22)	19
40–50	4,500–6,500	26 (6/23)	10
50–60	6,700–11,000	23 (5/22)	8
60–70	12,000–15,666	17 (4/23)	6
70–80	16,600–30,000	9 (2/23)	3
80–90	30,000–53,200	9 (2/22)	3
90–100	60,000–476,500	0 (0/22)	0
		Free people of colour participated in 28% (63/225) of valid cases	99

TABLE 2
SALES OF RURAL PROPERTY, 1780–89
PARTICIPATION OF FREE PEOPLE OF COLOUR IN EACH DECILE OF VALUE[10]

Percentile	Value of sale in colonial livre	% of these sales involving free people of colour	% of all free coloured sales
1–10	2–1,500	58 (19/33)	13
10–20	1,500–3,000	79 (26/33)	18
20–30	3,000–4,000	47 (16/34)	11
30–40	4,000–6,000	79 (27/34)	18
40–50	6,000–8,000	41 (14/34)	9
50–60	8,000–11,415	35 (12/34)	8
60–70	11,415–15,000	36 (12/33)	8
70–80	15,000–25,000	27 (9/33))	6
80–90	25,000–36,000	21 (7/33)	5
90–100	40,000–679,000	18 (6/33)	4
	Free people of colour participated in 44% (148/334) of valid cases		101

TABLE 3
SALES OF URBAN PROPERTY, 1760–69
PARTICIPATION OF FREE PEOPLE OF COLOUR IN EACH DECILE OF VALUE[11]

Percentile	Value of sale in colonial livre	% of these sales involving free people of colour	% of all free coloured sales
1–10	200–600	71 (5/7)	18
10–20	600–1,500	50 (4/8)	16
20–30	1,500–2,700	38 (3/8)	12
30–40	3,000–3,500	57 (4/7)	12
40–50	3,600–5,000	38 (3/8)	18
50–60	6,000–6,500	13 (1/8)	8
60–70	7,000–10,000	13 (1/8)	8
70–80	10,000–12,000	14 (1/7)	4
80–90	12,000–16,000	14 (1/7)	2
90–100	18,000–57,000	0 (0/8)	2
	Free people of colour participated in 30% (23/76) of valid cases		100

TABLE 4
SALES OF URBAN PROPERTY, 1780–89
PARTICIPATION OF FREE PEOPLE OF COLOUR IN EACH DECILE OF VALUE[12]

Percentile	Value of sale in colonial livre	% of these sales involving free people of colour	% of all free coloured sales
1–10	150–1,200	88 (22/25)	25
10–20	1,200–2,250	72 (18/25)	21
20–30	2,400–3,000	48 (12/25)	14
30–40	3,000–5,000	40 (10/25)	11
40–505	,000–10,000	24 (6/25)	7
50–60	10,000–12,000	32 (8/25)	9
60–70	12,000–18,000	24 (6/25)	7
70–80	18,000–24,000	8 (2/25)	2
80–90	25,000–40,000	8 (2/26)	2
90–100	40,000–180,000	4 (1/25)	1
	Free people of colour participated in 35% (87/251) of valid cases		100

contract, testament or lawsuit, than by sale. Most rural land sales involved smaller, less valuable parcels, making it difficult for new arrivals to establish viable plantations.

Nevertheless, while the rural real estate market was slowing and urban property sales were rising in volume and in price, free people of colour, paradoxically, were increasing their participation in rural sales and only just maintaining their place in the urban real estate market. In the 1760s, free people of colour participated in 28 per cent (63/225) of all rural property sales in this sample, but by the 1780s they were involved in 44 per cent (148/334) of such transactions. Moreover, this increased participation held steady across the entire range of sales, so even in the highest deciles of value, free people of colour were a far greater presence in the 1780s than they had been 20 years earlier (Figure 1; Tables 1 and 2). Over the same time period, free coloured participation in the urban real estate market remained consistent (Figure 2; Tables 3 and 4). In the 1760s they had been involved in 30 per cent of these transactions (23/76) and this rate grew to only 35 per cent in the 1780s (87/251).

These data reveal that capital was flowing into the free population of colour.[13] Yet by the 1780s this relative success in the rural economy was

FIGURE 1

SALES OF RURAL PROPERTY, 1760–69 vs 1780–89
PARTICIPATION OF FREE PEOPLE OF COLOUR IN EACH DECILE OF VALUE

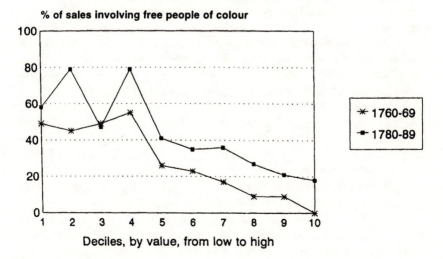

For details see Tables 1 and 2.

FIGURE 2

SALES OF URBAN PROPERTY, 1760–69 vs 1780–89
PARTICIPATION OF FREE PEOPLE OF COLOUR IN EACH DECILE OF VALUE

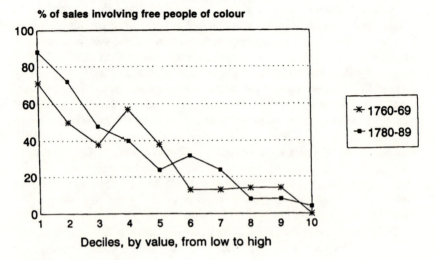

% of sales involving free people of colour

Deciles, by value, from low to high

For details see Tables 3 and 4.

mitigated by increasing racial tension. Saint-Domingue's administrators and high courts were writing laws to exclude or segregate persons of any African descent from white colonial free society. Notaries, priest and other officials were required to fix racial labels to all families of mixed European and African descent, and to demand proof of their freedom. African ancestry, however distant, became a permanent 'stain'. After 1769 men of colour could not serve as militia officers, even over other men of colour. Members of white militia units conducted deep-probing genealogical investigations of their colleagues, rejecting from their ranks men who were not 'pure' white. Families of colour were forbidden to take 'white' names and had to adopt 'African' names instead. Laws now formally segregated theatres, dance halls, and churches and barred people of colour from professions like goldsmith or law clerk. They were not to wear fine fabrics or ride in expensive coaches.[14]

The tensions behind this harsher racism were mostly urban, for it was in the cities that the independence of men and women of colour attracted the most negative attention. However, by the end of the century only fifteen per cent of Saint-Domingue's free people of colour lived in cities, compared to thirty per cent of colonial whites.[15] As land sale records suggest, Saint-Domingue's wealthiest and most politically self-confident free families of

MAP 3

SELECTED PROPERTIES IN TORBEC, CAYES, CAVAILLON AND AQUIN PARISHES, 1760–89

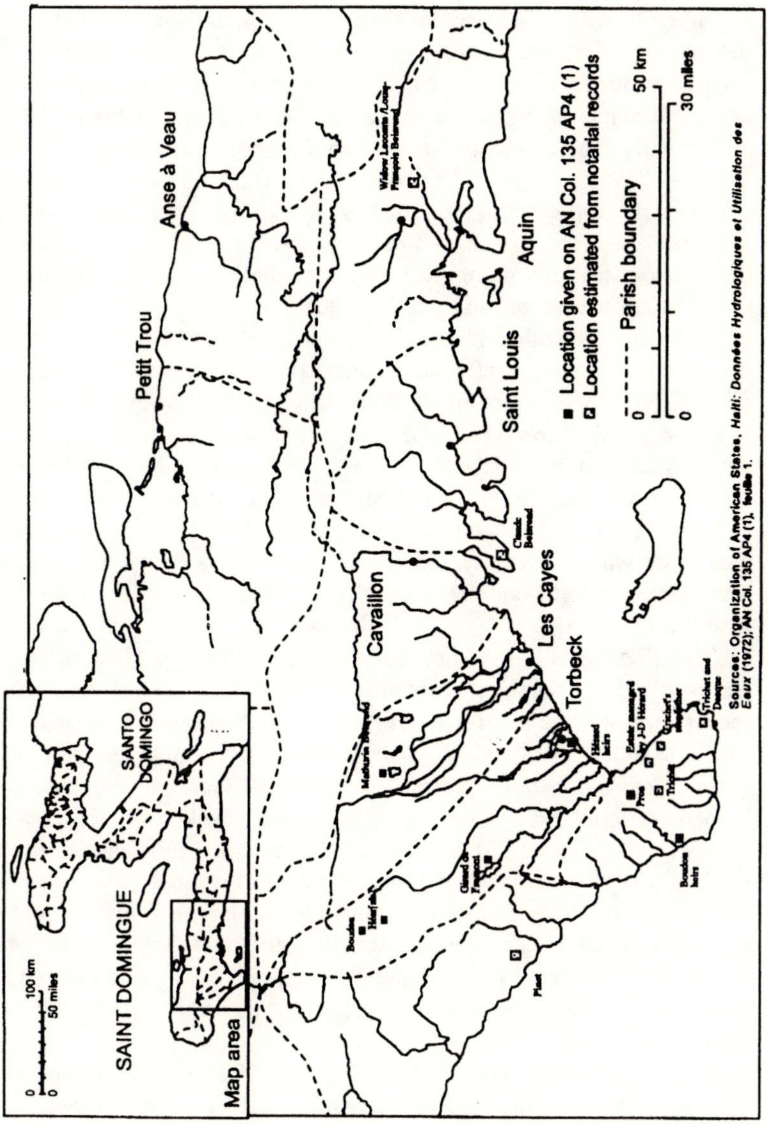

Sources: Organization of American States, *Haiti: Données Hydrologiques et Utilisation des Eaux* (1972); AN Col. 135 AP4 (1), feuille 1.

colour lived in the countryside. The careers of the leading free coloured planters of Torbec illustrate the roots of this leadership.

In 1720 French officials conducted a nominative census of the Cayes du Fond region, which was later divided between Torbec and Cayes parishes (see Map 3). Although the plain already had a plantation economy based on the labour of thousands of African slaves, the 1720 census did not categorize free men and women by their colour. Forty years later, when free people were increasingly labelled 'coloured' or 'white', many of the names on that early census were still prominent in Torbec parish. In the years from 1760 to 1769, 92 of the 277 names from 1720 were being used by families who would eventually be identified as 'free people of colour'.[16] This paper examines the origins of three such families, the Trichets, the Hérards and the Boisronds, illuminating the sources of their prosperity and suggesting the nature of their emerging political identity.

Like the two other families examined below, the Trichets of Torbec prospered through careful marriages, partnerships and by rebuilding dilapidated properties. Unlike their neighbours, however, the Trichets managed to avoid the racial labels that all persons of African descent were required to bear after 1773.[17] While other Torbec planters were publicly identified as 'mulatto' or 'quadroon' and had to prove their freedom at every turn, notarial records suggest that by the 1780s the Trichets were passing as white. Tellingly, the Trichets were not among those who urged Versailles to reform colonial racism on the eve of the French and Haitian Revolutions.

The 1720 census of Saint-Domingue's southern peninsula listed 115 slaves at the Trichet sugar plantation in the Torbec/Cayes plain.[18] With the second largest slave force in the region, the Trichets also claimed 109 cattle and 130 sheep. Although no documents have been found that link the generations, these early planters were almost certainly the ancestors of François Trichet, who, forty years later, was a well-respected resident of Torbec parish. The 1720 census did not provide racial labels, but these wealthy settlers were presumably what later generations would describe as 'white.' In the 1720s family arrangements that later colonists would scorn as interracial misalliances were socially accepted. Whether legitimized by marriage or not, these unions produced children who carried their father's name and often inherited his property, as well as their mother's possessions.[19]

In 1763 François Trichet, identified as a free *quarteron* (one-quarter African descent) by the notary, entered an indigo planting partnership with two free mulatto brothers, the Boudous (see Map 3). Trichet was married to a free mulatto woman named Victoire Claire Proa and the partners agreed to plant indigo on a plantation they purchased from a white militia captain named Alexandre Proa, probably the father or uncle of Trichet's wife.[20] The free coloured partners paid 53,200 livres for land and slaves – a sizeable sum – but their letters of credit covered nearly three-quarters of this price. Trichet, whose ties to Proa were probably responsible for the purchase, was to supervise the manufacture and sale of the indigo. This part of Torbec parish was well-known for its dye production, though over-cultivation and drought hurt the crop in the second half of the century.[21]

The five-year Trichet-Boudou partnership dissolved after eleven months, but Trichet bought out his former associates and soon sold some of this land to a free *quarteron* named Alexandre Proa, perhaps his brother-in-law, the son of the white man who had originally held the estate.[22] This younger Proa may have helped smuggle Trichet's indigo abroad, for he left Saint-Domingue for Jamaica in 1769 and died there. As much as two-thirds of the blue dye produced in Saint-Domingue's southern peninsula was illegally traded to that British colony. Julien Raimond and other planters in Aquin were also involved in this commerce.[23]

François Trichet continued to acquire land in Torbec parish throughout the 1770s and 1780s, buying large and small parcels from both free people of colour and from whites. In 1774 he paid a white planter only 15,000 livres for 279 acres (113 hectares) adjoining the property of his mother's second husband, Jean-Baptiste Raux (see Map 3). Trichet was already managing this neighbouring parcel for his step-father, who died by 1782. Trichet's mother left the plantation and nine slaves to 'Sieur François Joseph Trichet, her only son', giving him a good-sized estate, one of several he was building.[24]

In 1782 it was not only unusual for a man of colour to be given the respectful title 'Sieur', it was illegal.[25] But Trichet had social and economic connections with both whites and free people of colour that established him as a parish notable, and not only in his mother's eyes. In 1766, for example, friends and members of the neighbouring free mulatto Dasque family named him guardian of a younger Dasque brother, Jean Jacques. Significantly in this document the Dasques were identified by the notary as 'free mulattoes' while François Trichet bore no such label.[26]

Seventeen years later Trichet's ward was legally independent and an astute planter in his own right. Jean Jacques Dasques, like his two brothers, married well and had inherited his father-in-law's plantation, which bordered lands held by François Trichet. In 1783 he sold these indigo and cotton fields to his former guardian for 40,000 livres and the two formed a partnership to plant indigo (ses Map 3).[27] Trichet, who contributed 50 slaves to the enterprise, was to oversee the making of the dye, while Dasque, who put in 25 slaves, would grow food for the plantation on his own estate. Significantly, the partnership agreement identified Dasque as a free mulatto while Trichet was simply noted as a 'planter'.

Like partnership, marriage was an important route to success for free families of colour in Saint-Domingue's southern peninsula. Trichet's alliance with the Proa family had served him well and his own connections helped make his daughters attractive partners. In 1780, for example, Marie Françoise Gertrude Trichet married a young man named Jean François Pinet from the neighbouring Cotteaux parish, north-west of Trichet's lands (see Map 3). Bad health prevented Pinet's father from attending the ceremony, but the note he sent to Trichet made it clear that this was a good match for the groom.

> I am truly mortified and at the same time robbed of the pleasure I would have had in attending the marriage of my son and Mademoiselle your daughter … When I am able to mount my horse, I will have the pleasure of visiting you and the newly-weds whom I hope will be blessed by God and prosperous; this will be easy for them with your help.[28]

While Pinet's parents gave him two slaves, making the value of his property 3,950 livres, the Trichets gave their daughter slaves, land, and furniture totalling 15,600 livres. Jean François Pinet was his father's legitimate son, but he may have been a man of colour, since the notary did not identify the bridegroom as 'Sieur' in the marriage contract. His mother and two brothers were present, but none of these Pinets received honorific titles either. François Trichet, his wife and their daughter, however, were named 'Sieur', 'Dame' and 'Demoiselle' in the document.[29]

Four years later, Marie Françoise Trichet remarried. Pinet had died and in 1784 she wed a Frenchman. Jacques Manaut was a merchant born in Toulouse and this second marriage contract was signed in the business district of Les Cayes with at least two prominent white merchants attending.[30] All three whites were labelled 'Sieur' by the notary. The bride's parents, François Trichet and his wife, were not given these 'white' titles of respect. Yet the notary did not label them *quarteron*, as the law now required. Interracial marriages like this one were increasingly condemned by white colonial society, but in material terms this was an excellent match for Manaut, the French immigrant. Trichet's widowed daughter brought him a plantation, slaves, animals and furnishings valued at 24,150 livres.[31]

Another Trichet daughter married in 1784, also to a white man; this one from Cap Français, Saint-Domingue's leading city.[32] The entire Trichet clan attended the contract signing, including the bride's new French brother-in-law. As in the earlier 'white' wedding none of the bride's party, except Manaut, were given honorifics like 'Sieur' or 'Dame'. Yet once again the notary flouted the law by omitting the required racial labels. François

Trichet gave his daughter 15,000 livres and she had her own savings of about 3,000 livres. The groom was no penniless immigrant. Robert de Saint-Viart had an inheritance and collectable debts in Cap Français that he claimed were worth nearly twice his bride's property.[33] Yet Saint-Domingue's southern peninsula offered Viart de Saint-Robert the chance to build a plantation on nearly untouched soil. Marriage into one of Torbec's oldest planting families strengthened that opportunity. According to the marriage contract the groom already had a plantation near that of his new father-in-law.

For François Trichet these white sons-in-law helped maintain his family's place in the parish elite, despite the new requirements that racial labels be attached to all persons of any African descent. The notary's coded description of the wedding guests indicated that although the Trichets may not have been 'white' like Viart de Saint-Robert or Jacques Manaut, neither were they 'people of colour' with the low social status that designation increasingly denoted. In 1784 a number of François Trichet's free coloured neighbours in Torbec met or corresponded with Julien Raimond of Aquin, supporting his attempt to repeal these discriminatory regulations. The Trichets were not among this group.[34]

Like the Trichets, the Hérard family was linked in the 1720 census with the most prosperous households in the southern peninsula. The sugar plantation of 'Mrs Fesniers and Herards [sic] brothers' had 119 slaves, 150 cattle and 150 sheep, making it the region's largest in all three categories. The Hérards were also partners with the Fesniers in another sugar estate with 72 slaves, 72 cattle and 50 sheep. A third Hérard household, at Saint Louis, was an indigo plantation worked by 80 slaves in 1720.[35]

By the 1760s Jean Domingue Hérard, a free man of colour, was a prominent resident of Torbec parish. Hérard probably inherited lands in the Torbec plain, where their father had a sugar estate (see Map 3). Like François Trichet, he had ties to white planters and was highly regarded by other free people of colour. In 1764, though he had lands of his own, Hérard managed the estate of a white family descended from early settlers. In 1765 he was guardian to two mulatto daughters of a dead white planter. His sister Marie married into the Boisrond family (see below) and Jean Domingue's first marriage also allied him with Torbec's other elite free families of colour.[36]

In 1764 Hérard's daughter, Marie Elizabeth, married Alexis Girard, the illegitimate but recognized free coloured son of Monseigneur Girard de Fromont, the local white militia commander. Like the Trichets and Hérards, Girard de Fromont was from an old colonial family; his uncle or father had been attorney-general for the original colonial council at Léogane in 1707.[37] The militia officer was not present for his son's contract signing, but this

legal ceremony occurred in his plantation house and he had authorized
Alexis' use of his name. Jean Domingue Hérard dowered his daughter with
a horse and saddle, household furniture, 8,000 livres, and six slaves worth
about that sum again.[38]

If François Trichet sold his indigo to Jamaica through his brother-in-law,
Alexandre Proa, Jean Domingue Hérard had connections to Dutch Curaçao,
the other main destination for dye smuggled from Saint-Domingue.[39] Jean
Nicolas Fernandes, a free mulatto from Curaçao, lived on Hérard's Torbec
plantation. Notaries identified Fernandes as Hérard's brother and as the
uncle of his children although their family names differed. In 1764, five
months after Marie Elizabeth Hérard married Alexis Girard, Fernandes
married the free mulatto daughter of a dead white planter. For the occasion,
he and Jean Domingue Hérard returned to Girard de Fromont's plantation
for a second marriage contract signing.[40]

Jean Domingue Hérard's connection to Girard de Fromont served him
well in 1769, when he and other kin were nearly arrested for treason. Saint-
Domingue's militia had been dissolved in 1763, but Versailles re-
established the institution in 1769 over violent colonial opposition. For free
men of colour a critical aspect of the reform was that henceforth all militia
commissions were to be reserved for whites. Free men of colour would
continue to serve in the militia, but whites would command them.[41]

When Jacques Delaunay, a free man of colour, refused to attend the new
militia muster in Torbec, the provincial governor arrested him. This act
quickly brought Delaunay's neighbours out in protest, including Jean
Domingue Hérard, his son, George, and son-in-law, Alexis Girard. Hérard's
brother-in-law, François Boisrond, and one of his sons were also among
those who began to assemble in the hills in early February 1769, demanding
Delaunay's release. Within days they took as another free coloured planter
and ex-militia officer as a hostage. Jacques Bourry supported the reform,
unlike Delaunay. Although he would lose his militia commission, Bourry
was a master saddle maker who in 1765 held the royal monopoly on
butcheries and bakeries for the entire South province of the colony. After
Bourry was captured, royal authorities ordered the arrest of the Hérards,
Boisronds and others.[42]

At this point Girard de Fromont intervened. As the ranking militia
officer in the district he was in constant contact with the provincial
governor. He met with the angry men of colour at a hidden spot in the
mountains and convinced them to release Bourry. Jean-Domingue Hérard
may have been glad to agree to this for his wife and Bourry's wife were
sisters, and his daughter, Marie Claire Hérard, had recently married René
Bourry, a son or nephew of the hostage.[43] At the same time Girard de
Fromont convinced the provincial governor that Delaunay, Hérard and the

others – 'my mulattoes' – were innocent of sedition. They had been duped by white planters opposed to the reform.[44]

When the crisis had passed and the militia was re-established, the Hérards continued to acquire land and form connections with other successful families of colour. By 1781 Jean Domingue's son, Domingue, married a woman whose mother and sister were members of the Proa and Trichet clans. Domingue and his brother, George Nicolas Hérard, were both land owners, holding adjacent properties (see Map 3). Their father, Jean Domingue, had given George 106 acres (43 hectares) worth 7,500 livres in 1783.[45] Marie Claire Hérard and René Bourry remained together, selling a coffee plantation in the hills behind the Cayes plain to a white planter for 15,000 livres in the late 1770s; he resold it only four years later for half that sum.[46]

Pierre Hérard, another son of Jean Domingue, followed a different path, at least initially. He worked as a carpenter and boatwright, participating in the coastal traffic and perhaps contraband that was a vital part of the colonial economy. In April 1765 Pierre 'called Errard', rented a small vessel from a white wholesale merchant. This lease was to last four months but was formally dissolved after 31 days. Instead Errard purchased another boat outright for 300 livres and within two weeks had sold a similar vessel – perhaps the same one – to François Brilloin, a white merchant, for 2,000 livres.[47]

As a carpenter, Errard had apparently used his skill to transform the craft and realize a substantial profit. But this was only the beginning of his involvement with Brilloin, for the two now launched a formal partnership.[48] Although Brilloin owned Errard's vessel, the partners agreed to split costs and profits from their trade 'in personal items, commodities, different sorts of merchandise like flour, sugar, rum, etc.' Brilloin and four slave sailors would navigate the coast, sell their wares and acquire dyewood and mahogany. Back in the port of Les Cayes, Errard would work this wood and sell it.

Twenty years later, in 1785, 'Pierre Hérard known as Capitaine, free mulatto' was living in the town of Torbec. That year he bought a plot in the town from a free mulatto woman for 2,000 livres. The following year, however, he purchased 111 acres (45 hectares) in the Torbec hills near where other members of his family were established. The land cost 8,000 livres, but the two white men who sold him the parcel agreed that he could pay two-thirds of this price by 'work in his craft'.[49]

The growing colonial preoccupation with race created difficulties for planting families like the Hérards and Trichets, who had been in the southern peninsula since before 1720. If the Trichets emerged in the 1780s without racial labels, why were the Hérards designated 'free coloured'? The documents provide no clear answer to this question, which may have been determined by physical appearance. Social ties may have played a role in the Hérard's 'coloured' identity. Although Jean Domingue's first wife belonged to Torbec's free coloured elite, and his daughters and sons also married within this social orbit, his second wife was the daughter of a slave. Hérard and his second wife purchased his mother-in-law out of slavery in 1769. Had this socially incorrect marriage assured that these planters would be labelled *quarteron* while the Trichets were not? In 1789 a member of the Hérard family in the Torbec/Cayes region was listed among Julien Raimond's 1784 supporters against racial discrimination.[50]

The Boisrond family was Torbec's most conspicuous contribution to the free coloured political leadership of the revolutionary period. As with the Trichets and Hérards, the Boisrond name was prominent in the 1720s census. 'Beausire et Boisrond' operated a sugar plantation with 99 slaves, the third largest estate in the region. This plantation also had 100 head of cattle and 97 sheep. The other 'Boisrond' household was an indigo works with 89 slaves, the fourth largest in the plain. With 50 cattle and 100 sheep this too was a prosperous estate.[51]

By 1753 a free mulatto named François Boisrond owned land in the town of Torbec.[52] Like François Trichet and Jean Domingue Hérard, he enjoyed considerable local respect. In 1762 he stood as godfather of the bride at the marriage of two free mulattoes whose white fathers had died.[53] By this time he had married into the prosperous Hérard family. His wife, Marie Hérard, was the sister of Jean Domingue and through her François Boisrond acquired one-fifth of the Hérard sugar plantation in Torbec. In 1761 he paid his wife's sister 20,000 livres for her share in the sugar estate, whose total value was estimated at 50,000.[54]

François Boisrond was above all a planter, but he also worked as a builder and apparently trained his sons in this skill. In 1764 a white planter from a neighbouring parish paid 1,000 livres to put a young man in a five-year apprenticeship in Torbec with 'Sr François Boisrond and Claude François Boisrond his son both builders'.[55] As often happened before racial laws were strengthened, the notary named Boisrond 'Sieur' in this document and failed to mention that his client had any African ancestry. Nevertheless, in the 1769 militia unrest royal officials identified François Boisrond as one of the free men of colour who held Jacques Bourry hostage.

As Torbec lost inhabitants to the growing city of Les Cayes at the other corner of the plain, there was much that could be purchased and rebuilt. François Boisrond and his wife Marie Hérard had died by 1775, but the Torbec sugar plantation they reconstituted had dramatically increased in value. In 1775 their children sold this estate, valued at 50,000 livres in 1761, with its slave force for 500,000 livres to a white planter and royal judge.[56]

Although François Boisrond's creditors received much of this sum, profits from the sale helped launch the five Boisrond children into the careful marriages that were an important aspect of the family's success. One daughter married into another prominent Torbec family of colour and her husband, Pierre Braquehais, was a visible member of the free coloured political class of the 1790s.[57] The three Boisrond sons all married in the years after the sale of their parents' estate and these alliances carried them east into the parishes of Cayes, Cavaillon, Saint Louis, and Aquin. Here they emerged as planters and notables like their father, though in a different social climate.

In 1780, for example, Mathurin Boisrond sold an indigo plantation in Cayes parish for 76,000 livres to a white militia captain and planter. The land itself had come from his wife's family, but Boisrond had paid 20,000 livres to acquire additional water rights for the estate. This improvement brought him 10,000 livres in profit when the property was sold. A month later he sold another plantation that had belonged to his wife's family for 10,000 livres.[58]

Mathurin's brothers, Claude and Louis François Boisrond, moved east beyond Cayes from Torbec to Cavaillon parish where Claude Boisrond's wife owned land . Louis François, the youngest of the brothers, was living in Cavaillon in 1781 when he married Marie Rose Boissé, the widow LeComte of Aquin parish, still further east.[59] (see Map 3). The widow had an indigo plantation on Aquin's Grand Colline where most of that parish's wealthiest free families of colour lived. She was prosperous enough to give a young free coloured couple who were married on her plantation six male slaves and household furniture six months before her own marriage to Louis-François Boisrond. The Boisrond–Lecomte marriage contract did not list the property of the spouses, but the bride did reserve three slaves and 64,000 livres as her personal property, outside the marriage community.[60]

Within several years of this alliance, Louis-François Boisrond was numbered among Aquin's free coloured elite, answering court summons with other free coloured planters to nominate a guardian for a young orphan. In fact, in Aquin he found cousins on his mother's side, with their own claims to the Torbec sugar plantation his father had rebuilt twenty years before. In 1787 and 1788 the Boisronds and Julien Delaunay, a free coloured planter and master saddle maker whose wife descended from the Hérards of Torbec, settled some debts from the division of the old Hérard sugar estate.[61]

Louis-François' establishment and success in Aquin soon brought his two brothers into the parish. In 1784 Claude Boisrond and his wife sold the second of their two plantations at Cavaillon and purchased slaves and land on the banks of Aquin's Rivière Dormante for 25,000 livres. Within months they traded this property for a larger estate in the upper Aquin plain. That same year Mathurin Boisrond, too, purchased a plantation in Aquin.[62] Louis-François Boisrond bought land of his own in Aquin, since his wife planned to leave her indigo estate to her brother and sisters.[63]

Free coloured political consciousness was high in Aquin, where the Boisronds found other wealthy families whose French ancestry dated from the beginning of the century. As the Boisrond brothers reunited in Aquin, the mixed-blood planting elite of that parish wrote the colonial governor, then to Versailles, arguing that they should be regarded as citizens in the colony.[64] Julien Raimond and his wife left Aquin for France in 1784, taking with them Mathurin Boisrond's daughter, Ébé, bound for an Ursuline school in the Loire valley.[65] As he petitioned Versailles for civil reform, Raimond named the Boisronds among his Aquin supporters. The brothers maintained strong ties to Torbec and may have helped draw the Hérards and Bourrys from that parish into this movement.[66]

In March 1789, to support Raimond's efforts in France, Louis François Boisrond and other Aquin planters wrote to Versailles requesting representation in the approaching French Estates General.[67] Once the Revolution began Louis François became one of the most visible free men of colour in the colony through his transatlantic correspondence with Raimond. In the summer of 1790, as free coloured attempts to gain civil recognition were rejected by colonial whites, Boisrond gave Raimond what may have been Raimond's first sign that tensions in Saint-Domingue were moving faster than revolutionary legislation from France.

> It is not always possible to suffer the imperious vexations of the whites who claim the right to rule us by means outside the law. They refuse us the name of 'citizen' or 'planter'. We are only recognized as *'gens de couleur'* or by the insulting title 'enemies of the public welfare'.[68]

Four months later, in November 1790, as a free coloured planter named Vincent Ogé in the colony's North province demanded voting rights from the governor, Jacques Bourry, a son or nephew of the 1769 hostage, took the same position in the South. Ogé and Bourry both insisted that a recent ruling by the French National Assembly permitted financially qualified free men of colour to vote for a new Colonial Assembly. A committee of men of colour from Cavaillon parish, including Louis-François Boisrond's brother-in-law, Pierre Braquehais, had advanced this interpretation in July. When whites in Les Cayes threatened him, Bourry retreated to the hills, where six hundred free men of colour soon established a camp.[69] After repelling a white attack on 13 November 1790, the group surrendered peacefully to royal officials and its leaders were jailed in Port-au-Prince. They escaped in several months, when rioting in the capital opened the prisons there. By November 1791 these men, including Jacques Bourry and Jacques Dasque from Torbec, had become important figures in the free coloured struggle for civil rights.[70]

The Boisronds' revolutionary involvement was more pacific than that of their Bourry cousins. In 1791 one of the brothers presided over the assembly of Saint-Louis parish. In February 1793 Louis François Boisrond travelled to Cap Français as a member of an intermediary commission chosen to help Saint-Domingue move towards a new social and political system. Two years later he was elected to the Convention in Thermidor of the Year IV.[71]

This essay cannot conclude that the wealthy mixed-race families of either Torbec or Aquin parish were 'typical' of Saint-Domingue's free people of colour but it has demonstrated that these families had similar origins and many of the same economic and social strategies. The Trichets, Hérards and Boisronds of Torbec were descended from French colonists who controlled large plantations in the region's early days. In this colony brimming with newcomers after 1763 these families used their relatively deep roots to great advantage. They bought estates that other colonists had abandoned. They were carpenters, builders and master saddle-makers whose skills may have complemented their agricultural work. Moreover they formed partnerships and exploited family ties as they were able. They served as guardians for the free coloured children of dead white men. They maintained connections to Jamaica and Curaçao, where they might sell their crops illegally for greater profit. These strategies brought prosperity and consolidated their social rank in the parish.

Yet this landed rural class, whose economic presence was growing vis-à-vis whites, was threatened by growing racial discrimination. New laws and attitudes increasingly segregated Saint-Domingue's free population into European and non-European groups. By 1789 it was useless for Louis-François Boisrond or Pierre Hérard to argue that they were 'white', given the way colonial society had redefined that term. Because Frenchmen were 'white', the Boisronds and those like them could not fully claim this national identity either. Yet because 'coloured' was increasingly defined as non-European, that is to say, African, these families would not accept that label. What they could and did argue, however, was that they were 'citizens' and 'planters' – colons américains.[72] Events beginning in the metropole in 1789 gave them the opportunity to prove these claims.

Throughout a long civil and international struggle in the 1790s and early 1800s, the wealthy 'mulatto' families of Saint-Domingue's southern peninsula fought to maintain this 'French' identity. Yet after Napoleon's failed attempt in 1802 to restore slavery to the colony, it was Torbec's Louis Boisrond Tonnerre who gave words to a nascent Haitian nationalism. As secretary to the black general, Jean-Jacques Dessalines, Boisrond Tonnerre wrote the proclamation of Haitian independence in 1804 and much of the new country's 1805 Constitution. Born in Torbec parish in 1776, the son of Mathurin and nephew of Louis-François Boisrond, he was educated in France.[73] His virulent anti-colonial stance was a remarkable break from the pro-French sympathies of men like his father and uncle. His radical language has been ascribed to his youth, provocative personality and rapid rise to power as Dessalines' favourite secretary.[74]

Yet Boisrond Tonnerre's nationalism was surely fed by an awareness that his roots in this new Haiti were nearly a century old. In July 1790 his uncle Louis-François Boisrond had described white colonial racism as an attempt to oppress the 'island-born'.[75] During the Revolution Saint-Domingue's free coloured planters – 'American Colonists' – replaced racial labels with expressions that would allow them to be accepted as overseas Frenchmen. More than a decade later, confronted with the return of slavery, Boisrond Tonnerre took this creole identity a step further. On 1 January 1804, following Dessalines' orders, he addressed these words to the black and brown 'native army' (armée indigène) that had defeated Napoleon's troops.

> Citizens,
>
> It is not enough to have driven from your country the barbarians who have bloodied it for two centuries; it is not enough to have restrained the ever-evolving factions, each in its turn deceived by the mirage of liberty that France held before your eyes; a final act of national authority is necessary to guarantee forever the reign of liberty in the country of our birth; the inhuman regime that has so long held our spirits in the most debasing torpor must be stripped of any hope of resubjugating us; we must, in the end, be independent or die.[76]

NOTES

1. The best of the existing original research is Yvan Debbasch, *Couleur et liberté: Le jeu du critère ethnique dans un ordre esclavagiste* (Paris, 1969). See also Gabriel Debien, 'Gens de couleur libres et colons de Saint-Domingue devant la constituante, 1789–Mars 1790', *Notes d'histoire coloniale – XVIII* (Montreal, 1951); Gwendolyn M. Hall, *Social Control in Slave Plantation Societies: A Comparison of St. Domingue and Cuba* (Baltimore, 1971), and her 'Saint Domingue' in David Cohen and Jack Greene (eds.), *Neither Slave Nor Free* (Baltimore, 1972). The best of the overview articles is Michel-Rolph Trouillot, 'Motion in the System: Coffee, Colour and Slavery in Eighteenth-Century Saint-Domingue', *Review*, 5 (1982), pp.331–88. In this category also see Robert L. Stein, 'The Free Men of Colour and the Revolution in Saint Domingue, 1789–1792', *Histoire Sociale – Social History*, 14 (1981), pp.7–28; Laura Foner, 'The Free People of Colour in Louisiana and St. Domingue: A Comparative Portrait of Two Three-Caste Slave Societies', *Journal of Social History*, 3

(1970), pp.407–30; and Valery Quinney, 'The problem of civil rights for free men of colour in the early French revolution', *French Historical Studies*, 7 (1971), pp.514–47.

2. John Garrigus, 'Blue and Brown: Contraband Indigo and the Rise of a Free Coloured Planter Class in French Saint-Domingue', *The Americas*, 50 (Oct. 1993), pp.233–63.

3. Descriptions of free coloured activity in the colony and in Paris can be found in Debbasch, *Couleur et liberté*, pp.141–95. Françoise Thésée, 'Les assemblées paroissiales des Cayes à St. Domingue (1774–1793)', *Revue de la Société haïtienne d'histoire et de géographie*, 40, No.137 (December 1982), pp.5–179, offers the best account to date of local revolutionary politics in Saint-Domingue. On Raimond's role, see David Brion Davis, *The Problem of Slavery in the Age of Revolution, 1770–1823* (Ithaca, 1975), p.143, or Debien, 'Gens de couleur libres'. On free coloured identity during the French Revolution, see Julien Raimond, *Correspondance de Julien Raimond, avec ses frères, de Saint-Domingue, et les pièces qui lui ont été adressées par eux* (Paris: Imprimerie du Cercle Social, 1794), pp.16, 19, 34, 51–52. On Raimond's background and career, see John D. Garrigus, 'Julien Raimond', in Gad Heuman and David Barry Gaspar (eds.), *Brown Power in the Caribbean* (forthcoming, Duke University Press).

4. See Michel-Rolph Trouillot, 'Motion in the System: Coffee, Colour and Slavery in Eighteenth-Century Saint-Domingue', *Review*, 5 (1982), p.354.

5. Pierre de Vassière, *Saint Domingue, (1629–1789): La société et la vie créole sous l'ancien régime* (Paris, 1909), pp.40–3; Moreau de Saint-Méry, *Description*, pp.1241–4, 1327.

6. This new parish, Port Salut, existed in name only. Religiously, socially and administratively Torbec parish remained largely undivided. Moreau de Saint-Méry, *Description*, pp.1334–5. For this reason I include Port Salut as part of Torbec.

7. The confusion about Cayes and Torbec stems from the fact that Cayes was the name of a city, a parish and also the multi-parish administrative district, or *quartier*, that included Torbec. For a historical account of Torbec, see Moreau de Saint-Méry, *Description ... de la partie française de l'isle Saint-Domingue* (repr. Paris, 1959 [Philadelphia, 1797]), pp.1304–8, 1326–7, 1332; even Moreau ignored parish boundaries in order to describe the rich sugar plain shared by Torbec and Cayes. For anti-militia violence in 1768 and 1769 see Archives Nationales Colonies (henceforth AN Col.) F3182, or Charles Frostin, *Les révoltes blanches à Saint-Domingue aux XVIIe et XVIIIe siècles* (Paris, 1975); for Julien Raimond's pre-revolutionary supporters see André Maistre de Chambon, 'Acte notarié rélatif aux doléances des "gens de couleur" de Saint-Domingue, (29 juillet 1789)', *Mémoires de la Société archéologique et historique de la Charente* (June, 1931), pp.7–8; on the tensions between whites and free men of colour in 1790, see Françoise Thésée, 'Les assemblées paroissiales des Cayes à St. Domingue (1774–1793)', *Revue de la Société haïtienne d'histoire et de géographie*, 40, 137 (Dec. 1982), p.68; for battles in Torbec in 1792 see Archives Nationales (henceforth AN) Dxxv 112, dossier 891, piece 32, 'Extrait des pièces déposées aux archives de l'assemblée coloniale de la partie française de Saint-Domingue', and Carolyn Fick, *The Making of Haiti: The Saint Domingue Revolution From Below* (Knoxville, TN, 1990), pp.142–50.

8. These were the neighboring *quartiers* of Cayes, Saint Louis and Nippes. A *quartier* was a multi-parish district and this sample includes both Torbec and Aquin parishes.

9. This data is taken from the 4,882 notarial deeds surviving from the *quartiers* of Cayes, Nippes and Saint Louis in the period 1760–69. This data set includes all such records from these districts for this period stored in France's Archives Nationales, Section OutreMer [henceforth ANSOM], in Aix-en-Provence. All notarial sources in this paper are from this ANSOM collection, unless noted otherwise.

10. For the period 1780–89, 2,679 notarial deeds from the *quartiers* of Cayes, Saint Louis and Nippes were studied. This includes 1,339 notarial contracts from the parish of Aquin, all such surviving documents for this period. In addition 882 contracts from the Cayes *quartier* and 476 contracts from Nippes were sampled.

11. This data from the same set of notarial records analysed in Table 1.

12. This data is from the same set of notarial records analysed in Table 2.

13. Free people of colour sold to white buyers in half (77/149) of the 1780s land sales involving members of this class. More than a quarter of the transactions (41/149) were sales from

whites to free people of colour, while a fifth (31/149) were sales between free people of colour. Michel-Rolph Trouillot suggests that whites may have been buying up land to grow coffee. See his analysis of land tenure and Saint-Domingue's free population of colour in 'Motion in the System', *Review*, 5 (Winter 1982), pp.353–63.

14. Gwendolyn M. Hall, *Social Control in Slave Plantation Societies: A Comparison of St. Domingue and Cuba* (Baltimore, 1971), p.77; AN Col. F3273, p.783; AN Col. F391, pp.129–30, ms. 'Mémoire sur la police des gens de couleur libres;' Moreau de Saint-Méry, *Loix et constitutions des colonies françaises de l'Amérique sous le Vent*, vol.5 (Paris, 1784–90), pp.767, 807. For the most complete treatment see Yvan Debbasch, *Couleur et liberté* (Paris, 1967), pp.22–131.

15. For urban attitudes, see Moreau de Saint-Méry, *Description*, pp.31–3, 105, 109. For urban population, see David P.Geggus, 'Urban Development in 18th Century Saint-Domingue', *Bulletin du Centre d'histoire des espaces atlantiques*, 5 (1990), pp.210, 212.

16. ANSOM G1509 No.17, 'Extrait du recensemens général du quartier du Fonds de L'isle à Vache'. There was one household headed by 'Claude, mulatto'. There were only 265 households listed in 1720, but a number of these were partnerships listing several family names like that of 'Mrs Fesniers et Herards freres' – two free men with 119 slaves. The data on the 1760s comes from the notarial records described above.

17. Moreau de Saint-Méry, *Loix et constitutions*, vol.5, pp.448–9; Yvan Debbasch, *Couleur et liberté*, p.69.

18. ANSOM G1509 No.17, 'Extrait du recensemens général du quartier du Fonds de L'isle à Vache'.

19. The census of 1720 counted 194 free men in the Cayes plain, with only 76 free women, ANSOM G1509 No.17. On intermarriage, see Debbasch, *Couleur et liberté*, p.47. For one example of such an alliance, see Garrigus, 'Blue and Brown', *Americas*, (1993), p.248.

20. 3 février 1763, Berton reg. 129, Cayes, association; 30 décembre 1764, Berton reg. 130, Cayes, vente.

21. Trichet's main plantation was in the mountains, near the source of the Marchaterre river, whose indigo reputation was discussed by Moreau; *Description*, p.1337; this location may have spared him the worst effects of the drought. By the time Moreau de Saint-Méry visited this region in the 1780s, part of Torbec had been split off into the new parish (1784) of Port-Salut, whose border is shown on Map 3; *Description*, pp.1334–5.

22. In 1764 Alexandre Proa lived with Victoire Claire Proa's mother; 30 décembre 1764, Berton reg. 130, Cayes, vente; 18 décembre 1764, Berton reg. 129, Cayes, résiliation de société.

23. 4 février 1781, Scovaud reg. 1588, Cayes, convention. For fuller development of the indigo smuggling theme, see Garrigus, 'Blue and Brown', *Americas* (1993), pp.239–46. Two-thirds was the claim of Hilliard d'Auberteuil and Venault de Charmilly; Hilliard d'Auberteuil, *Considerations sur l'état présent de la colonie française de Saint-Domingue, ouvrage politique et législatif* vol.1 (Paris, 1776) pp.58, 279, 281–3; Frostin, *Les révoltes blanches*, pp.274–6.

24. 27 septembre 1768, Legendre reg. 1212, Cayes, vente; 6 mai 1781, Scovaud reg. 1588, Cayes, vente; 7 novembre 1781, Scovaud reg. 1588, Cayes, vente; 22 novembre 1782, Scovaud reg. 1589, Cayes, dép't de vente privé; 6 octobre 1782, Scovaud reg. 1589, Cayes, quittance; 22 novembre 1782, Scovaud reg. 1589, Cayes, donation.

25. Moreau de Saint-Méry, *Loix et constitutions*, vol.5, pp.448–9. By the late 1770s use of these titles in legal documents was cited in court cases to prove that a family was considered white. See AN Col. E71, dossier 'Chapuiset', 'Réflexions sommaires sur la possession d'état des Chapuizet', (Cap Français, 1779). By the same logic, whites who were not given these titles sued for defamation of character; see the 1785 case of Pamelard and wife, in ANSOM Receuil de Mémoires, Colonie Tome XVIII, Bibliothéque Moreau de Saint-Méry 95 No.11, p.2.

26. 13 janvier 1766, Legendre reg. 1207, Cayes, nomination de tuteur; 11 mai 1766, Legendre reg. 1207, Cayes, nomination de tuteur; 15 mai 1766, Clouet du Bruc reg. 395, Cayes, nomination de tuteur. The name Dasque also appeared on the 1720 census.

27. 22 avril 1783, Scovaud reg. 1590, Cayes, vente et société. In 1772 Jean Jacques Dasque and his two brothers had purchased a plantation and formed a partnership to plant coffee. In 1787

Charlot and Pierre Dasque sold this failed coffee estate to a white man. Jean Jacques had already left the partnership.23 mai 1787, Carré reg. 337, Cayes, vente.

28. Letter annexed to 30 octobre 1780, Scovaud reg. 1587, Cayes, mariage.
29. 30 octobre 1780, Scovaud reg. 1587, Cayes, mariage.
30. In 1801 Manaut was listed as a member of the reconstituted masonic lodge 'Frères Sincèrement Réunis' in Les Cayes. Elisabeth Escalle and Mariel Gouyon Guillaume, *Francs-Maçons des Loges Françaises 'aux Amériques' 1770–1850* (Paris, 1993), pp.127–30 and 657.
31. 24 janvier 1784, Scovaud reg. 1591, Cayes, mariage; 20 décembre 1785, Scovaud reg. 1592, Cayes, quittance.
32. 28 septembre 1784, Scovaud reg. 1591, Cayes, mariage.
33. There is reason to doubt this claim. Viart was from the Limonade parish outside Cap Français and Moreau de Saint-Méry noted that in 1764 the Viart plantation in Limonade was 'nearly abandoned and beyond repair'. *Description*, p.201.
34. Gabriel Debien, *Gens de couleur libres et colons de Saint-Domingue devant la constituante, 1789–Mars 1790* (Montreal, 1951), p.8.
35. ANSOM G1509 No17. The name 'Hérard' appeared in the census without the accent.
36. 15 octobre 1765, Bugaret reg. 323, Cayes, bail. Hérard worked for the Farin family, which had come to Saint-Domingue from the French Caribbean colony of Saint-Christophe. Moreau de Saint-Méry, *Description*, pp.1396, 1486, The sisters of Hérard's wife, Marie Catherine Duteil, had married into the prominent free coloured Bourry family. 19 mai 1764, Berton reg. 130, Cayes, marriage; 10 mai 1769, Ladoué reg. 1144, Cayes, testament.
37. Moreau de Saint-Méry, *Description*, p.1494.
38. 22 mai 1764, Berton reg. 130, Cayes, mariage; 30 juin 1763, Berton reg. 129, Cayes, transaction. Hérard's daughter was four months pregnant at the ceremony and the marriage contract specified that this union was to legitimize the child. Of the 118 notarized marriage contracts surviving from the period 1760–69 from this region, nearly 85 per cent were signed either in the notary's office or at the home of the bride or of her parents.
39. Garrigus, 'Blue and Brown', *Americas* (1993), pp.244–5. It is possible that Hérard had relations in Jamaica, as well. His first wife's mother was Anne Thomas, a free black woman from Jamaica. In 1819 a merchant named Jacques Herard [*sic*] was a member of the French Masonic lodge in Kingston, Jamaica. See Escalle and Mariel Gouyon Guillaume, *Francs-Maçons des Loges Françaises 'aux Amériques' 1770-1850* (Paris, 1993), p.535.
40. 19 mai 1764, Berton reg. 130, Cayes, mariage; 17 octobre 1764, Berton reg. 130, Cayes, mariage.
41. For a review of these events, see John D. Garrigus, 'Catalyst or Catastrophe? Saint-Domingue's Free Men of Colour and the Savannah Expedition, 1779–1782', *Review/Revista Interamericana*, 22 (1992), pp.109–25. Also, Frostin, *Révoltes blanches*, pp.297–341.
42. Both the names Bourry and Delaunay were in the 1720s census, cited above. Like François Trichet, Jacques Bourry was frequently described as 'Sieur' by notaries; he was a landowner and the father of ten children. 18 April 1765, Bugaret reg. 321, vente, Cayes. His sons or nephews figured prominently among Torbec's politically active men of colour in 1790 and 1791. See Julien Raimond, *Correspondance*, pp.39, 50. For the arrest, see AN Col.F3 182, correspondence between the provincial governor d'Argout in Les Cayes and the colonial governor Rohan in Port-au-Prince in early February 1769.
43. Jacques Bourry and Jean Domingue Hérard had both married daughters of Anne Thomas. The marriage between René Bourry and Marie Claire Hérard took place sometime before their grandmother Anne Thomas dictated her last testament on 10 May 1769, Ladoué reg. 1144, testament, Cayes.
44. AN Col. F3 182, letters of 4–6 February, 1769.
45. 31 mai 1781, Scovaud reg. 1588, Cayes, mariage; 5 avril 1783, Carré reg. 334, Cayes, vente.
46. 16 février 1783, Scovaud reg. 1590, Cayes, vente.
47. 21 avril 1765, Bugaret reg. 321, Cayes, bail; 22 mai 1765, Bugaret reg. 321, Cayes, vente; 3 juillet 1765, Bugaret, reg. 321, Cayes, vente et declaration; 17 juillet 1765, Bugaret reg. 321, Cayes, vente et procuration; 26 juillet 1765, Bugaret reg 322, Cayes, vente.
48. 28 juillet 1765, Bugaret reg. 322, Cayes, association.

49. 25 mai 1785, Scovaud reg. 1593, Cayes, dép't; 9 décembre 1785, Scovaud reg 1593, Cayes, vente; 25 mai 1786, Scovaud reg. 1593, Cayes, vente.
50. 8 janvier 1769, Legendre reg. 1215, Cayes, affranchissement. Seventeen years later Jean Domingue was dead, but his widow and free black mother-in-law were still alive. 13 février 1786, Scovaud reg. 1593, Cayes, vente; André Maistre de Chambon, 'Acte notarié', *Mémoires de la société archéologique et historique de la Charente*, (1931), pp 7–8.
51. ANSOM G1509 No 17.
52. 26 juillet 1784, Scovaud reg. 1591, Cayes, vente. By the 1760s there were no white Boisronds among the clients of Torbec and Cayes notaries. But Charles Gellée's mother, whose own mother was rumored to be of African descent, was named 'Marie Catherine Boiron (sic)'. She gave birth to Charles Gellée in 1728 in Cayes. Escalle, *Francs-Maçons*, p.499.
53. 22 novembre 1762, Legendre reg. 1201, Cayes, mariage.
54. 13 septembre 1787, Barnabé de Veyrier, Aquin, convention entre héritiers.
55. 29 juillet 1764, Berton reg. 130, Cayes, apprentissage.
56. 11 janvier 1785, Scovaud reg. 1592, Cayes, quittance.
57. 13 septembre 1787, Barnabé de Veyrier, reg. 54, Aquin, convention. Julien Raimond, *Correspondance*, pp.26, 28, 31.
58. 21 novembre 1780, Scovaud reg. 1589, Cayes, vente and quittance; 20 décembre 1782, Scovaud reg. 1589, Cayes, vente.
59. 25 avril 1781, Paillou reg. 1451, Aquin, mariage.
60. 28 septembre 1780, Paillou reg. 1451, Aquin, mariage.
61. 12 avril 1784, Paillou reg. 1452, Aquin, nomination de tuteur; 13 septembre 1787, Barnabé de Veyrier reg. 54, Aquin, convention; 8 août 1788, Barnabé de Veyrier reg. 55, Aquin, ratification. Julien Delaunay may have been the brother of Jacques Delaunay, the Torbec's ex-militia captain who was arrested in 1769. A Jacques Delaunay was a free mulatto indigo planter in Aquin in 1760 and 1765; 14 octobre 1760, Daudin reg. 429, Aquin, inventaire; 15 janvier 1765, Daudin reg. 432, Aquin, exchange. In 1765 Julien Delaunay of Aquin visited Torbec to buy some land for his mother-in-law from Jacques Bourry, using a letter of credit signed by François Boisrond. 22 juillet 1765, Legendre reg. 1206, vente, Cayes.
62. 20 juin 1780, Scovaud reg. 1587, Cayes, vente; 12 avril 1784 Scovaud reg. 1591, Cayes, vente; 28 juin 1784, Scovaud reg. 1591, Cayes, vente; 26 juillet 1784, Scovaud reg. 1591, Cayes, vente; 19 avril 1784, Paillou reg. 1452, Aquin, vente; 9 avril 1784, Paillou reg. 1452, Aquin, vente; 27 juillet 1784, Paillou reg. 1452, Aquin, echange; 23 mai 1785, Paillou reg. 1452, Aquin, dép't; 14 octobre 1784, Paillou reg 1452, Aquin, ratification.
63. In 1784, 3 years after her marriage to Boisrond, the widow LeComte drew up a testament that gave 14,375 livres to each of her 4 siblings, and left slaves to other family members, including Claude Boisrond's daughter and Pierre Braquehais, who had married her Boisrond sister-in-law. She was in perfect health and she made her husband executor of the will. 15 février 1784, Paillou reg. 1452, Aquin, testament. Nineteen months later she was ill and redrew her will, this time simply dividing her indigo plantation among her four Boissé siblings to avoid a court battle over payment of the money. 12 septembre 1785, Paillou reg. 1452, Aquin, testament. Lecomte-Boisrond's three sisters were, like her, widows of local free coloured planters. Louis-François Boisrond's own land purchases occurred about the same time. 11 septembre 1784, Monneront reg. 1411, Aquin, vente; 7 septembre 1788, Monneront reg. 1414, Aquin, vente.
64. Debbasch, *Couleur et liberté*, pp.121–5.
65. 2 mars 1784, Paillou reg. 1452, Aquin, procuration; Julien Raimond, *Correspondance*, p.89.
66. Debien, *Gens de couleur libres*, p.8; André Maistre de Chambon, 'Acte notarié rélatif aux doléances des "gens de couleur"', p.9.
67. Gabriel Debien, *Gens de couleur libres*, p.13.
68. In Raimond, *Correspondance*, pp.16–17; judging by this collection, Boisrond was Raimond's most faithful correspondent, see pp.15–28, 28–31, 42–7, 53–8.
69. Julien Raimond, *Correspondance*, pp.25–6, 50–1. Beaubrun Ardouin, *Etudes sur l'histoire d'haïti*, vol.1 (Port-au-Prince, 1958), p.53, names André Rigaud as the leader of this camp and gives its size at five hundred men.

70. For example, the white provincial assembly late in 1791 printed a copy of letter from Port-au-Prince to from Jacques Bourry to Jacques Dasque. Bourry wrote that he had been working with men of colour in Miragoâne parish in the West province on a concordat with the whites that would give civil rights to qualified men of colour. He sent greetings to his friends at 'la ravine sêche, du Fond de March-à-Terre, de la ravine du sud'. AN Dxxv 112, dossier 890, piece 73 'Extrait des minutes déposées aux archives de l'Assemblée provinciale et provisoirement administrative du Sud. Extrait des Minutes déposées aux Archives du Greffe prévotal de Tiburon'. (slnd).
71. Julien Raimond, *Mémoire sur les causes des troubles et des désastres de la colonie de Saint-Domingue, Présenté aux comités de Marine et des Colonies, dans les premiers jours de juin dernier, par les Citoyens de couleur; d'après l'invitation qui leur en avoit été faite par les comités* (Paris, 1793), p.4; AN Col. F3196, dossier 424.
72. As Drexel Woodson has noted, 'By the 1780s, whites used *américain* and *créole* as synonyms, both terms opposed to *métropolitain* or *européen* in the dichotomy that disclosed place of birth for whites'. Drexel Woodson, 'Which Beginning Should be Hindmost?: Surrealism in Appropriation of Facts About Haitian "Contact Culture"', in Brakette F. Williams (ed.), *Contact Culture: In Search of Hemispheric Americana* (forthcoming). See Moreau, *Description*, p.34. Radical white colonists also claimed this title in the Revolution; see Frostin, *Révoltes blanches*, p.388.
73. According to Haitian tradition, this most famous member of the Boisrond family took his name from the threatening weather that accompanied his birth; Buteau, 'Preface', p.6. It is more likely that 'Tonnerre' came from the French town where Julien Raimond's brother Jean and his nephew Pierre Julien were living in 1789 and 1790, perhaps for schooling; AN Dxxv 111 dossier 880, piece 3; 17 janvier 1791, Monneront reg. 1419, Aquin, transfer de procuration. The Raimonds had taken Boisrond Tonnerre's sister Ébé to a school in France in 1784 and in May 1791 Louis François asked Julien Raimond to watch over all Boisrond children in France, since he no longer trusted the agent previously charged with this trust. In July 1791, expecting Raimond's return to the colony, Boisrond asked his friend to bring his niece Ébé back to Aquin. Predicting the end of racial strife, he noted 'I will ask (for the return of) all my other children (from France), to raise them here'. Raimond, *Correspondance*, pp.46, 89. Haitian tradition does note that Boisrond Tonnerre was educated in France. Buteau, 'Preface', p.6.
74. Pierre Buteau, 'Preface' to Boisrond Tonnerre, *Mémoires pour servir à l'histoire d'Haïti* (Port-au-Prince: Editions des Antilles, 1991), pp.5–17.
75. Raimond, *Correspondance*, p.19.
76. 'Procès-verbal de la proclamation de l'Indépendance d'Haïti' in Boisrond Tonnerre, *Mémoires pour servir à l'histoire d'Haïti* (original edition, 1804) (Port-au-Prince, 1991), pp.28–9.

Patronage, Property and Persistence: The Emergence of a Free Black Elite in Spanish New Orleans

KIMBERLY S. HANGER

The origins of antebellum New Orleans' large, influential, and propertied free black population, unique to the United States South, can be found in the Spanish colonial period. During the Spanish regime in Louisiana demographic, economic, political and military conditions meshed with cultural and legal traditions to favour the growth and persistence of a substantial group of free people of colour. Interpersonal relations in this small circum-Caribbean community ameliorated prejudice, facilitated familiarity among persons of all races, nationalities and classes, and enabled individuals to advance, always within acceptable limits, on their own merit or with the aid of kin and patronage connections. Only when Louisiana's plantation system matured and slavery intensified with profitable sugar and cotton cultivation in the initial years of United States rule, did officials and planters together restrict manumissions and free black activities.[1]

This essay looks at the progenitors of antebellum New Orleans' creoles of colour and the strategies they and their white allies utilized to create and perpetuate a free black elite in colonial New Orleans.[2] Before the United States Congress abolished the external slave trade to Louisiana in 1804, free blacks and slaves entered the colony willingly or by force from Africa, Europe, and throughout the Americas.[3] Once the slave trade was cut off, however, more and more Louisiana blacks were native born (creoles). Many of those blacks identified as creoles of colour in the nineteenth century had parents or grandparents of various ethnic makeup who gained their freedom in Louisiana during the Spanish regime of the eighteenth century.

Indeed, it was during the three and a half decades of actual Spanish rule in Louisiana (1769–1803) that free persons of African descent in New Orleans made their greatest advances in terms of demographics, privileges, responsibilities and social standing. In desperate need of allies and labourers, Spanish authorities fostered growth of a free black population.

Not all slaves sought freedom, a status that free persons of colour and whites often experienced differently, but those who did yearn for liberty were more likely to attain it under Spain's dominion than under that of France or the United States. African Americans astutely availed themselves of conditions present in Spanish New Orleans not only to gain freedom, but also to attain decent living standards and advance their social status, or at least that of their children.[4]

THE SETTING: COLONIAL NEW ORLEANS

Founded in 1718 on the site of a long-established native American portage point where the Mississippi River comes closest to the shores of Lake Pontchartrain, New Orleans was Louisiana's principal urban centre and port. The furs, hides, timber and agricultural products of the Mississippi Valley region flowed through the city *en route* to the West Indies, the North American colonies and then states, New Spain, and occasionally Europe. New Orleans also served as the entrepôt for slaves and various goods such as flour and cloth that colonials could not supply or manufacture themselves. France held Louisiana and its capital city of New Orleans from 1699 to 1763, when it ceded the colony to Spain under provisions of the Treaty of Paris in that year. Spain did not actually take control of Louisiana until 1769 and governed it until 1803.

Under French and Spanish rule Louisiana's value was mainly strategic. Both Bourbon monarchies viewed Louisiana as useful primarily within the context of larger geopolitical considerations: neither wanted Britain to seize it. Although Spain, like France, considered Louisiana an economic burden, the Spanish crown hoped to utilize it as a protective barrier between mineral-rich New Spain and Britain's increasingly aggressive North American colonies. Spain thus actively endeavoured to attract settlers and slaves to the region, not only to defend it, but also to balance the somewhat hostile French population remaining in Louisiana and to promote agricultural and commercial growth.[5]

In Louisiana, as in many areas of Spanish America, the crown fostered the growth of a free black population in order to fill middle-sector roles in society, defend the colony from external and internal foes, and give African slaves an officially approved safety valve. The labour shortage dilemmas that plagued New Orleans throughout the colonial period were for the most part solved by Africans, both slave and free. Free blacks were especially suited for the skilled, petty commercial and transportation jobs that whites accepted reluctantly and mistrusted their black slaves to carry out. In addition to playing an essential role in the New Orleans economy, free black men also performed vital defensive and public service acts. Their militia formed part of Spain's circum-Caribbean defence system. On a more daily basis they repaired breaks in the levee, fought fires and chased runaway slaves. Free people of African descent also contributed to New Orleans' rich cultural diversity and participated in the region's complex cross-cultural exchange networks.[6]

DEMOGRAPHIC CHARACTERISTICS OF SPANISH NEW ORLEANS

Although census figures conflict and provide only approximate accuracy, they point to a growing population over the Spanish period of New Orleans' history (Table 1). White males consistently outnumbered white females; the opposite held true for slaves and free blacks. During the period the white population of New Orleans almost doubled, while the slave population grew 250 per cent. As a result of restrictions on slave importations, the number of slaves in New Orleans decreased in the 1790s, but then multiplied in the early 1800s in response to the growing demand for slave labour on sugar and cotton plantations and the lifting of import bans.[7] The number of free blacks increased sixteenfold, and this group reportedly was under-counted throughout the era![8] Also significant, the percentage of free persons of colour in the total, free and non-white populations increased under Spanish rule (Table 2). Manumission, reproduction, and immigration (particularly from Saint-Domingue in the 1790s and early 1800s) contributed to this rise in the number and proportion of free people of African descent.

Among free blacks females outnumbered males two to one, a proportion that paralleled the sex ratio of those being manumitted (about 58 males for every 100 females). It was lower, however, than the sex ratio for the city's slaves, which hovered around 82 and rose to 95 in 1805 (refer to Table 1). Thus, compared to their proportion of the total New Orleans slave population, bondwomen secured freedom more frequently than did bondmen. Both unconditional and conditional (for service or money) manumission favoured female slaves in late eighteenth-century New Orleans. Although for the Spanish period as a whole, the majority of slaves continued to receive liberty by way of acts instituted by the master – as they had under French rule – a rising proportion initiated manumission proceedings themselves or with the help of a relative or friend.[9]

PURCHASING FREEDOM: EXPENDITURE OF RESOURCES

Slaves attained free status in a number of ways. Some ran away and joined the maroon communities that proliferated in the swamps surrounding New Orleans; others escaped from plantations to the city, where they tried to pass as free or sought passage to another territory.[10] Avenues to freedom deemed more legitimate by the dominant society included manumission initiated by masters (during their lifetimes or on their deathbeds) and manumission initiated by slaves or third parties (self-purchase either with the master's approval or forced before a tribunal). In keeping with its aim of encouraging growth of a free black population in Louisiana, the Spanish crown implemented a practice common in its American colonies known as *coartación*: the right of slaves to purchase their freedom for a stipulated sum of money agreed upon by their masters or arbitrated in the courts. Confronted with a reluctant owner, the slave, a relative, or a friend could request a *carta de libertad* (certificate of manumission) in front of a government tribunal. Two and sometimes three assessors declared the slave's monetary value, and upon receipt of that sum, the tribunal issued the slave his or her carta. Thus, under Spanish law slaves did not have to depend upon the generosity of masters to attain freedom, but rather relied on their own efforts and the aid of a usually favourable legal system.[11]

Even within an environment conducive to manumission, slaves often struggled long and hard to become free. Purchase of a carta represented a major investment for the slave or a third-party white, free black, or other slave. In Louisiana the price of freedom increased during the Spanish period (Figure 1) and rose even higher in the antebellum era as officials closed the foreign slave trade and restricted opportunities for manumission. Many people of colour laboured long years and used most of their scarce resources to free themselves or friends and kin, indicating the premium they placed on freedom.

Upon request, masters usually allowed slaves to purchase themselves and their family members. In 1791 a white man and his wife manumitted their moreno slave Michaut for 1,000 *pesos* (the peso was equivalent to the dollar at the time and was the monetary unit upon which the dollar was based). At the time Michaut had already deposited two instalments of 500 and 100 pesos with his owners, and he swore to pay the remaining 400 pesos at the rate of five pesos per month.[12] Even though he would now be working as a free man, it would probably be several years before Michaut finished paying for his carta and started building an estate for himself and his family. María Luisa, a thirty-two-year-old parda slave, paid her master 500 pesos in 1772 for her carta and that of her four children, ages seven, five, two and a half, and three months. A more complex kin group purchase involved the morena Magdalena, fifty-three years old, who bought her own liberty for 350 pesos and within the next few days purchased cartas for her twenty-year-old son Francisco (300 pesos), twenty-three-year-old daughter Lileta (350 pesos), and Lileta's two young sons for 150 pesos each.[13] In 1775 the thirty-nine-year-old morena Francisca Montreuil reimbursed her master, don Roberto Montreuil, 800 pesos for her freedom and that of her parda daughter Naneta, more commonly known in later documents as Ana Cadis. Francisca also registered her obligation to pay Montreuil an additional 300 pesos within one year; he cancelled the note one year and two days later. By 1777 the morena libre Francisca Montreuil had accumulated the 300 pesos needed to purchase from her former master the carta of her son Carlos, a twenty-year-old pardo blacksmith.[14]

When Francisca died in 1803, she possessed an estate valued at 10,459 pesos, which when debts of 3,157 pesos 3 *reales* (eight reales to the peso) were subtracted, left 7,301 pesos 5 reales to be divided among her three living children (Carlos, María Genoveva, and Agata) and her three living grandchildren by her deceased daughter Naneta. A native of Louisiana and the natural daughter of Francisco Rancontre and Susana, Francisca was about seventy years old when she died. Among her substantial estate were five slaves worth 2,650 pesos, one slave who was promised his freedom, a house and lot in New Orleans worth 2,825 pesos, two plantations along Bayou Road worth 1,735 pesos, livestock, furniture, and household goods.[15]

Francisca's daughter Naneta died three years before her, in 1800, and like her mother left a large estate acquired during her quarter century of freedom. Naneta had married Pedro Bahy (Bailly), also a recently freed pardo, in 1778 and brought a dowry of 350 pesos in silver and four cows worth forty pesos given her by her mother Francisca. Naneta's father was a white man, don Pedro Cadis. She gave birth to five legitimate children, two of whom died before they reached the age of ten, and all of whom had leading white citizens and officials as their godparents. Naneta was left to care for her family, properties, and slaves while her husband spent over two years in prison in Cuba, convicted of espousing radical French ideals and of conspiring to overthrow the Spanish government in 1794. Pleading for the welfare of her children, Naneta successfully petitioned the Spanish crown to release her husband in 1796. These children, second-generation free blacks, benefited greatly from the business acumen of their parents and grandmother when they inherited their estates in the early 1800s.[16]

As seen from the above cases, relatives and friends often paid the price of a slave's freedom. After soliciting don Joseph Villar on many occasions, the parda libre Marion finally convinced him to liberate her son Janvier, a nineteen-year-old creole pardo, for 400 pesos and her daughter Luisa, a creole grifa about twenty years of age, for 200 pesos.[17] When she wrote her will in 1798, the free morena Janeton, a native and citizen of New Orleans, instructed her executor, don Francisco de la Rua, to collect the money owed her by another white man and use it to purchase the freedom of her youngest child María. In addition, la Rua was to give María what remained from the estate so that she could use it to earn money with which to purchase the freedom of her three other slave siblings.[18] Why Janeton did not try to collect the debt and manumit her children while she was still alive is unclear.

Like whites and free blacks, slaves paid masters to issue cartas for loved ones, but most likely such purchases involved much greater personal and material sacrifice. When slaves used scarce resources to manumit others, they placed a desire to liberate fellow bondpersons above their own freedom in true acts of compassion, consideration, and selflessness. Examples include the parda slave Margarita, who gave her master 200 pesos to manumit her cuarterón son Pedro, two years of age.[19] Don Carlos Delachaise's moreno slave Francisco requested the carta of his eighteen-month-old morena daughter, who along with the child's mother were also slaves of Delachaise. Francisco paid 100 pesos.[20] When the mulata libre María Angela Tribiño was baptized in March 1795, the priest noted that her mother, a morena slave, had purchased the child's freedom two months prior.[21]

Sometimes free blacks purchased slave relatives but did not free them. At age twenty-six the parda Naneta Chabert was freed by her master without conditions in 1772. One year later she purchased two slaves, her mother and grandmother. Three months later Naneta manumitted the mother, but she never freed the grandmother. Perhaps enslavement by caring kin held advantages for the elderly, or possibly the grandmother died soon after the purchase. In her will dated one day before she died in April 1786, Chabert did not mention her grandmother but noted that her mother lived in Mobile. Chabert's goods consisted of one plantation near New Orleans and another between Baton Rouge and Pointe Coupée on the Mississippi River; she also owned four slaves, one of whom cared for her mother in Mobile. Chabert owed various sums to three white men, one white woman, one free black woman, and one male slave. It is interesting to note that Chabert did not leave her estate to her mother, but rather to her goddaughter and her goddaughter's husband.[22]

OWNERSHIP OF SLAVES

As seen in the Chabert case, free blacks purchased and freed or kept slave kin, but they also owned slaves for purposes of service and speculation, just as their white neighbours did. The holding of African slave property by free people of colour was customary throughout the Americas and most colonial governments guaranteed the property rights of their free black citizens. Ownership of black slaves fostered free black identification with white society and thus dissipated white fears of racial collusion. The pattern of free black ownership of slaves in Spanish Louisiana closely resembled that of other Spanish, Portuguese, and French American colonial regions where there were few legal restrictions on manumission. In these areas free blacks primarily owned slaves to help them in their trades in both cities and fields. As long as slave prices remained low, free people of colour who could afford bondpersons used them. In addition, as noted above, free blacks often could afford to purchase their slave relatives and free them with few constraints, and thus did not need to hold them as slaves.[23]

New Orleans free blacks purchased rising numbers of slave labourers into the 1790s, with a slight dip in the 1800s as prices rose (Table 3). Comparison of free black purchases of slave non-kin with those of kin reveals the prevalence of the former, a trend that increased over time. Analysis of the notarial records also indicates that almost two-thirds of the slaves free blacks acquired were females. In addition, the gap between gender ratios in the free black population and that of free black purchasers closed until the ratios were almost on parity. Initially, a disproportionately large percentage of slave buyers were free morenas and pardas, but with each decade the percentage of female purchasers declined while that of males increased, until by the early 1800s the percentage of purchasers by gender almost mirrored sex ratios among free blacks. Census and purchasing data show that in 1777 females comprised 67.9 per cent of the free black population in New Orleans but purchased 77.8 per cent of the slaves bought by free people of colour from 1771 through 1773. Respective proportions for the 1780s were 71.6 per cent and 75.8 per cent; for the 1790s 62.4 per cent and 64.8 per cent; and for the 1800s 60.2 per cent and 60.4 per cent. The percentage of males in the free black population in 1777 (32.1 per cent) and in the universe of free black buyers 1771–73 (22.2 per cent) rose to 39.8 per cent and 39.6 per cent respectively in the first years of the nineteenth century. Why female purchasers were so prevalent in the early years of Spanish rule is not clear; perhaps they had access to greater cash or credit resources than males did.

Given the total available slaves purchased and free black buyers by gender and phenotype, it appears that free morenas and pardas purchased greater numbers of female and fewer male slaves than would be expected, whereas free morenos and pardos preferred male slaves. It is most likely that intended use of the slave based on occupational gender roles, along with higher prices for male slaves, influenced this pattern. Free black women used slaves to perform domestic chores and peddle their trade goods; free black men were more likely to buy slaves who could assist them in their trades and care for their houses. Both men and women augmented their income by hiring out skilled slaves, and they bought and sold slaves for speculative purposes. As an example, take María Teresa Cheval, a free parda tavern-keeper: she purchased a morena *bosal* (a slave newly imported from Africa) from one man for 90 pesos and sold her the next day to another man for 300 pesos![24]

In addition to procuring bondpersons through purchase, free people of colour acquired slave property by way of testamentary and *inter vivos* acts. Heirs rarely contested these generous bequests to free blacks, and Spanish colonial courts usually upheld the deceased's wishes as long as there existed a written, witnessed last will and testament. According to the December 1779 will of Henrique Mentzinger, who was a sergeant in the white militia, the pardito libre Juan Baptista, two years old, was to receive Mentzinger's twenty-six-year-old morena slave named Fatima. In addition, Mentzinger left to the parda libre Luison, eight years of age, his eight-year-old moreno slave named Manuel. Both Juan Baptista and Luison were the children of the free morena Gabriela, Mentzinger's former slave and probable common-law mate. Mentzinger bequeathed Gabriela 200 pesos.[25]

Doña Magdalena Brazilier's will stipulated that María Luisa, a free parda about seven or eight years old, was to receive two slaves – Batista (twenty years old) and Luisa (eighteen years old) – along with Brazilier's residence in New Orleans and all her clothes, jewellery, household goods, kitchen utensils, and furniture. María Luisa was the daughter of Brazilier's *mulata mestiza* slave named Maneta. In the will Brazilier freed seven of her slaves, many of them other children of Maneta, but she did not manumit Maneta. The transition of Maneta's children to free status was probably made smoother with this gift of property and the assistance of their brother Poiquon, a free pardo whom Brazilier had manumitted prior to making her will.[26]

Upon his death in 1791 don Marcos de Olivares, a native of Coruña in Spain, bestowed upon his natural daughter, the free parda María Josepha de los Dolores, ownership of a morena slave and her two children, along with another morena slave. Olivares also bequeathed her 2,000 pesos, two houses, furniture, clothing, silver and various household effects. Thirteen years earlier Olivares had given his then four-year-old daughter perhaps the most precious gift: her freedom. In his testament don Marcos donated to María Josepha's mother, the free morena Mariana Voisín, a morena slave, a small house and land, and 1,000 pesos and instructed her to administer their daughter's inheritance until she reached majority. Other free persons of colour, including María Josepha's grandmother, also benefited from Olivares' generosity.[27]

Free persons of colour, as well as whites, donated slave property to friends and kin in their wills. Near death in 1793, the fifty-six-year-old free morena criolla Mariana Meuillon designated her natural son as her only heir. Bautista Meuillon, a twenty-five-year-old free pardo, thus acquired his mother's silverware, two lots and houses in New Orleans, a large tract of land upriver from the city, and a morena bosal named Mariana. The last two items Mariana had received from don Luis Meuillon, her likely consort, who had freed her and Bautista without conditions in 1777. Several people owed Mariana money, including one white woman, four free black women, and one free black man.[28] Unmarried and without heirs, the morena libre Margarita Momplessir stated in her testament that she owned thirteen *piezas de esclavos*: the morena Juli, her ten children (ages twenty-two years to eight months), and the three children of Juli's oldest daughter, Clarisa (six to one years of age). Momplessir distributed this slave family to free and slave female friends and relatives: Clarisa to Catalina, a morena slave belonging to the estate of don Francisco Momplessir; one of Clarisa's daughters to a pardita libre named Eufrosina Dimitry, daughter of don Andrias Dimitry; and the remaining slaves to the free cuarterona Francisca Momplessir. She also donated 100 pesos to each of the three children of another free black woman.[29]

Though not as common as testamentary bequests, *inter vivos* donations of slaves to free people of colour occasionally appeared in the notarial registers. Among these benefactors was don Francisco Raquet, who in 1782 donated two young morena slaves and two pieces of land to Adelaida, free cuarterona, daughter of the free parda Francisca Lecler, alias Raquet. In his will dated twenty years later don Francisco recognized the now twenty-four-year-old Adelaida as his natural daughter; donated 3,000 pesos to her, 400 pesos to her mother Francisca, and 1,000 pesos to each of Adelaida's two sons; and named as heir to his plantation and twelve slaves Adelaida's daughter named Adelaida Dupry.[30] Apparently don Francisco preferred his granddaughter to his grandsons. His generosity improved the material well-being of three generations of free black women.

CONTRIBUTING FACTORS TO MATERIAL SUCCESS

Free people of African descent in colonial New Orleans acquired slave, real and personal property by working for wages, operating successful business enterprises, and receiving inheritances or donations from whites, slaves, and other free blacks. Within their own lifetimes or over generations some free blacks amassed sizeable estates, although they were generally much smaller than those recorded for wealthy white New Orleanians. No matter how much or what they owned, however, most free people of colour actively endeavoured to protect and expand their resources in order to improve their own material conditions and social standing and that of their kin and friends. Numerous court cases attest to their struggle to protect their rights within a society that exploited them as non-whites but also gave them some advantages over slaves.

Although free blacks generally acted upon every opportunity presented them, several factors influenced their capacity to acquire enough goods in order to provide economic security for themselves and their families, or in other words, to accumulate wealth that was then passed on to their descendants. First, free blacks who acquired marketable skills either before or after being freed tended to prosper. Throughout the Americas skilled blacks found it easier to purchase freedom and to continue to earn a living as a free person. Many slaveholders allowed their slaves to rent themselves out, taking a portion of their *jornales* (daily wages) and permitting them to keep the remainder.[31] The free morena Helena poignantly revealed the impact that possessing a skill high in demand could have on attaining and retaining free status. Helena tried to convince the court that appraisals of her slave son were excessive because he knew no trade and his master had readily admitted that the slave was a thief and drunkard. In her plea Helena provided several examples of skilled slaves who had purchased their freedom at the amount her son was appraised and pointed out that an unskilled moreno slave could never earn such exorbitant sums.[32]

A free person of colour's ties to and reputation in the white community constituted a second factor in the succeed/fail equation. Much of the wealth that free blacks in Spanish Louisiana possessed was passed on to them by whites and other free blacks through intricate kinship and friendship networks.[33] Associations with whites – whether sexual, familial, friendship, or business – benefited free people of colour, women in particular. In New Orleans' corporate society, advantages accrued to those free people of colour who were linked by kin and patronage to leading white families. The importance of such connections can be demonstrated by an example of what could happen when they were threatened. As the free pardo Pedro Bahy quickly discovered, alienating influential whites could damage one's status. When a prominent white man, don Luis de Lalande Dapremont, brought charges of criminal activity against Bahy (husband of Naneta Cadis discussed earlier), he threatened the livelihood of Bahy and his family. Bahy claimed that the charges were false and entered out of spite; Dapremont had just recently lost a suit that Bahy had brought against him for collection of a debt. Bahy also stated that the mistrust engendered by these charges had seriously affected his retail business because white patrons from whom Bahy had borrowed funds and goods were beginning to harass him for payment and refused to extend him additional credit. A militia officer and loyal servant of the king, Bahy had earned the distinction of a *buen vasallo* (good subject) meriting the favour of local *jefes* (leaders). The court eventually dropped Dapremont's charges against Bahy, thereby restoring his favourable reputation, at least for the moment.[34]

Whites occasionally formed business partnerships with free people of colour. Pedro Viejo jointly owned a small dry goods store with the morena libre Juana. A native of Guinea, Juana was a former slave of Luis Poirson and the legitimate daughter of two slaves. Half of the enterprise belonged to her, and she designated Viejo as her only heir.[35] Antonio Sánchez and María Juana Ester, a free cuarterona, were partners in another retail business. Born in New Orleans to the parda libre Victoria Rouden and an unknown father, María Juana had one natural daughter named Francisca, also a free cuarterona. In her will María entrusted Sánchez with selling her share of the partnership's goods and placing its proceeds in her daughter's possession. Included in the estate inventory were farm and carpentry implements, wagons, ox teams (all of them named), cows, horses, lumber, a canoe, slaves, and two farms.[36]

Kinship ties to white persons as well as patronage gave some free people of colour added economic leverage. Some white fathers publicly acknowledged their free black consorts and offspring and donated personal and real property to them. In his 1794 will don Pedro Aubry declared that he was single but that he had two natural children – Pedro Estevan and María Genoveva – by the morena libre María Emilia Aubry, all his former slaves. As his only heirs, the children received a farm seven leagues from New Orleans, two slaves, livestock, furniture and household goods.[37] When don Francisco Hisnard died on 28 July 1798, he left a will written three months prior in which he declared that he was single but recognized his three natural children by the free morena Mariana Grondel, more commonly called Hisnard: Clemencia (about twenty-three or twenty-four years old), Eufrosina (twenty-two), and Sofía (eleven), all free pardas. Don Francisco instructed his executors to divide the proceeds from the sale of his goods among his only heirs, his three natural daughters. In addition, the three women came into possession of their mother's estate, Grondel having died one year before Hisnard and naming him executor of her estate. Clemencia, Eufrosina, and Sofía inherited property totalling 1,852 pesos from their mother and 468 pesos 5 reales from their father. Eufrosina had served as the former slave and long-time consort of Louisiana's *auditor de guerra* (military legal counsellor to the governor) don Nicolás María Vidal, for whom she bore three daughters and one son. They moved to Pensacola, Florida, following the cession of Louisiana to the United States, where Vidal died in 1806. One of their daughters, María de la Merced, 'caused an international incident in Pensacola when she appealed to Andrew Jackson as territorial governor to intercede with Spanish officials to recover documents regarding her late father's estate.'[38] Kinship ties with propertied whites and other free blacks enabled some free persons of colour to wield greater influence.

In some cases, however, patronage placed free blacks in positions of dependency much like slavery. Mary C. Karasch found that in early nineteenth-century Rio de Janeiro 'since so many freedpersons were women, many continued to work as servants for their previous owners and to maintain old patterns of dependency.' Other scholars note that throughout the New World 'newly "freed" persons were typically enveloped in conditions of lingering servitude resulting from provisos in their manumission papers or from debts incurred in self-purchase'.[39] Such a continuing dependent relationship involving a benefactor and a recently manumitted slave transpired in New Orleans between don Antonio Pascual y de Regas and Angélica. Pedro Visoso manumitted his morena slave Angélica, about thirty years old, for 400 pesos paid by don Antonio. Angélica in turn contracted with don Antonio to serve him the rest of his life and travel with him wherever he should go, but she retained all the rights of a free person.[40] These arrangements, while exploitative, also offered a newly manumitted person who had few skills or assets protection from the many uncertainties and possible downward mobility freedom could impart.

Indeed, a third factor that could help a free person of colour succeed materially was that of being born a free person or having free kin. Free persons of colour passed their goods to lineal and lateral kin and to friends, thereby contributing to the well-being of others. Both the Spanish and French practised partible inheritance, whereby children received at least somewhat equitable portions of their parents' estates. Even illegitimate children could inherit up to one-third and consorts up to one-fifth of the estate, although parties often left larger shares without having their testaments contested by other heirs. Second or third generation free blacks usually inherited the accumulated riches, no matter how meagre, of past generations, and slaves who had well-established free black friends or relatives stood a better chance of being 'rescued' from slavery than those with no ties to the free black population. For example, Juan Bautista Hugón, born free and a captain of the free pardo militia when he died in 1792, purchased the freedom of three out of five of his children (one son and two daughters; another daughter was born free) and their mother during his lifetime, at a cost of 650 pesos. On the day of his death Hugón's goods consisted of a house and land in New Orleans, one slave, furniture, and clothes. He donated to a morena slave named Magdalena (most likely one of his consorts) a bed, a stoneware fireplace ornament, one pig, and the chickens on the patio of his house. Hugón also requested that his testamentary executor purchase his fifth child's *carta de libertad*. Hugón's goods sold at public auction for 1,095 pesos. After paying for the carta, outstanding debts, and burial and court costs, the executor turned over 227 pesos, 5 reales to Hugón's children.[41]

Testaments and estate inventories like Hugón's illuminate the extent of property free blacks could accumulate during their lifetimes and bestow upon relatives and friends when they died. They also reveal intricate kinship and patronage ties among free blacks, whites and slaves. The childless parda libre María Francisca Riche distributed her estate among her closest kin and long-time friends, as well as the poor. A natural daughter of the free morena Carlota Riche, native of Pointe Coupée, and resident of New Orleans, Riche donated ten pesos to indigent patients at Charity Hospital and one hundred pesos and a harness decorated with silver to doña Julia Bauvais of Pointe Coupée (Riche had served as Bauvais' nurse when she was a child). She ordered her executor to sell her household goods and a morena slave and spend the proceeds to liberate her brother and sister, Pedro and María Luisa. In turn, the siblings were to use what funds remained to purchase the cartas of María Luisa's two daughters, and these nieces were to inherit Riche's estate.[42]

Unlike Riche, the free morenas Janeton Laliberté and María Belair had living children, and their estates can be traced down through at least two generations during the Spanish period. A native of Senegal, Laliberté wrote her will in 1771 and noted that thirty years earlier she was married to a moreno named Gran Jacot (also known as Luis) and that they had a daughter named María Juana. She later married another free moreno, but this union produced no children. Laliberté willed to her daughter her half lot in New Orleans, a plantation downriver from the city at English Turn and located adjacent to lands of Pedro Tomás, her son-in-law, and four cows with their calves. Thirty years later María Juana Tomás wrote her will. Her marriage to Pedro Tomás had produced eight children, six of whom were still living, the oldest forty-four years and the youngest twenty-five. Tomás' only property consisted of the half lot and house inherited from her mother, and she left this to her children and the one son of one of her dead children.[43]

Prior to her marriage to the pardo libre Luis Daunoy, María Belair had two natural daughters, Carlota and Martona, to each of whom she willed one-fifth of her estate when she died in 1794. The rest of her estate she left to her and Daunoy's legitimate son also named Luis. María's property consisted of her dowry (500 pesos) and half the goods communally owned with her husband, which included a half lot and cabin in New Orleans. Martona Belair followed her mother to the grave one year later and left her one-fifth share of María's estate to her six natural children, ranging in age from thirteen years to twenty months. Martona made her living as a dry goods retailer and during her lifetime had acquired much more property than her mother. Appraisers valued her estate – furniture, household goods, personal clothing, a half lot and house in New Orleans, a promissory note and dry goods for her business – at 1,572½ pesos. Martona owed one white woman and eight white men (most of them wholesale merchants) 553 pesos, thus leaving 1,019½ pesos for her six children. In addition, Martona held as guardian one female slave (valued at 400 pesos) for two of her minor children and another female slave (valued at 350 pesos) for one of her other minor children. Two white men, probably the respective fathers, had donated the slaves to the children.[44]

TABLE 1

NEW ORLEANS POPULATION, YEAR BY STATUS BY GENDER

Year	Whites			Free Blacks			Slaves		
	M	F	Total	M	F	Total	M	F	Total
1771[a]	—		1803	—	—	97	—	—	1227
1777[b]	1104	632	1736	101	214	315	518	633	1151
1788[c]	1310	1060	2370	233	587	820	956	1175	2131
1791[d]	1474	912	2386	324	538	862	871	918	1789
1805[e]	—	—	3551	—	—	1566	—	—	3105

TABLE 2

PROPORTION OF FREE PEOPLE OF COLOUR IN THE TOTAL, FREE, AND NON-WHITE POPULATIONS, NEW ORLEANS

Year	% of Total Population	N	% of Free Population	N	% of Non-W Population	N
1771[a]	3.1	3127	5.1	1900	7.3	1324
1777[b]	9.8	3202	15.4	2051	21.5	1466
1788[c]	15.4	5321	25.7	3190	27.8	2951
1791[d]	17.1	5037	26.5	3248	32.5	2651
1805[e]	19.0	8222	30.6	5117	33.5	4671

a   Lawrence Kinnaird, *Spain in the Mississippi Valley, 1765-1794*, 3 vols. (Washington, DC, 1946-49), II:196.
b   AGI PC 2351, 12 May 1777.
c   AGI PC 1425, 1788.
d   Census of New Orleans, 6 Nov. 1791, Louisiana Collection, NOPL.
e   Matthew Flannery, comp., *New Orleans in 1805: A Directory and a Census Together with Resolutions Authorizing Same now Printed for the First Time* (New Orleans, 1936).

TABLE 3

FREE BLACK PURCHASES OF NON-KIN AND KIN SLAVES, NEW ORLEANS, 1771-1803

Years	Purchase of Non-Kin		Purchase of Kin	
	FW	FFB	FW	FFB
1771–73	7	–	3	–
1781–83	58	3	12	–
1791–93	106	11	15	–
1801–3	92	7	–	–

FW=From White   FFB=From Free Black

Sources: Notarial Records

FIGURE 1

MEAN VALUE OF SLAVES PURCHASING FREEDOM, NEW ORLEANS

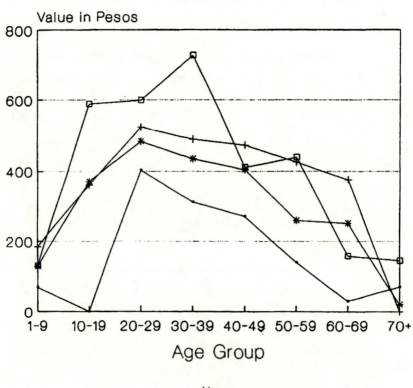

Value in Pesos

Age Group

Years

—•— 1771-1773   —+— 1781-1783

—*— 1791-1793   —□— 1801-1803

Sources: Notarial Records.

Marriage contracts that specify dowries hint at the material well-being of free blacks earlier in their life cycles than do wills and estate inventories.[45] On 10 January 1779 Pedro Langlois wed Carlota Adelaida, both pardos libres, and on 23 January they entered into a marriage contract. Langlois declared his possessions as three slaves and cash totalling 1,800 pesos. A widow with a young child, Carlota Adelaida declared both the property she brought from her former marriage and her daughter's inheritance. This included land, slaves, and debts worth a net total of 1,350 pesos. While Langlois administered his new wife's and step-daughter's possessions, he could not alienate them without their consent.[46]

In a second example the husband, cuarterón libre Francisco Alexandro Colombe, was marrying for the second time and made clear in the prenuptial agreement that half of his goods – valued at 3,000 pesos – belonged to the three children from his previous marriage. His new wife, parda libre Henriqueta Toutant, also carefully delineated the possessions her family – in particular her wealthy white father don Bartolomé Toutant Beauregard – had bestowed on her. Hard currency, jewellery, clothes, furniture and household utensils valued at 1,200 pesos comprised Toutant's dowry.[47] The cuarterona libre María Constancia's dowry was also appraised at 1,200 pesos and included 540 pesos worth of stamped silver (which she had acquired 'through personal work in an honest manner'), 360 pesos worth of clothes and furniture, and a young female slave valued at 300 pesos. She entered into a marriage contract with Carlos Lavibarière, a free pardo, but their marriage is not recorded in the sacramental records for St. Louis parish.[48] When Augustín Malet, the natural son of Mr Rocheblase and the morena libre Juana Malet, wed Jacinta Demasillière, the natural daughter of don Joseph Wiltz and the morena libre Theresa Dufaut, in 1785, he brought 1,400 pesos in cash and a half lot in New Orleans worth 300 pesos. Demasillière's dowry consisted of 1,100 pesos in cash given her by her mother. Fifteen years later Malet, an officer in the free pardo militia and a wood dealer, wrote his will. He and Demasillière had produced three offspring, ages fourteen, eight and seven, whom Malet named as his heirs. A fourth son who would have been ten years old must have died in the interim. Malet's goods included slaves, lands, houses, furniture and personal effects, which the three children named in the will and at least one sister born after the will was written shared equally.[49]

Although many free people of colour increased their material worth between the time of their marriage and that of their death, some experienced a decline in wealth and status. Among them was Luison Brouner (Mandeville), a parda libre who in many documents is recorded as a mestiza. Brouner was freed in 1770 at age twenty-three. Into her marriage to pardo libre Francisco Durand in 1785 Brouner brought a plot of land and a house with a separate kitchen in New Orleans, much furniture, personal clothing and five slaves. Brouner was the natural daughter of Mr Mandeville and María Juana, an *india mestiza libre*, and had had a common law relationship with don José López de la Peña, which had produced four natural daughters, prior to her marriage to Durand. Brouner and Durand had no children. When she wrote her will in 1794, Brouner's holdings had been reduced to one slave, plus a half interest in a slave and plantation near Baton Rouge that her godmother, the parda libre Naneta Chabert, had donated to

Brouner and Durand. Brouner owed her former white consort 400 pesos, an amount somewhat offset by the 200 pesos that one of her daughters owed her.[50] It is most likely that Brouner had dispersed the majority of her properties over her lifetime or had faced some misfortune, thus indicating that wills made near the end of a lifetime were sometimes not representative of one's maximum material value.

A list of losses incurred in the first great fire to sweep colonial New Orleans (March 1788) is another useful source for estimating at least the real and personal property holdings of the city's free blacks and for comparing them with those of white men and women. In September 1788 a list of 496 claims for damage to buildings and interior furnishings (plus ten claims on government property) totalling more than 2.5 million pesos was submitted to the Spanish crown. Fifty-one of these claimants were free black women, and their average estimated loss to real and personal property was 1,770 pesos. Free black men made up only twenty-one of the claimants, with an average loss of 1,723 pesos. Another sixty-seven of the claimants were white women (average loss of 2,880 pesos), and the remaining 357 claims were made by white men. The white male average claim of 6,090 pesos was more than double that of white females and about three and a half times greater than that of free black women or men.[51] Clearly, white men possessed the vast majority of material wealth in late eighteenth-century New Orleans, and while there were more free black women holding property than free black men (which one would expect given the demographic makeup of the city), the men possessed more valuable or larger amounts of property.

CONCLUSION

Many of those who made up antebellum New Orleans' free creole of colour elite could trace their ancestry and foundations for their prosperity back to free blacks living in the Spanish colonial era. During this period free people of colour used patronage and kinship networks, inheritance patterns and individual talent to improve their economic and social standing in the community, or at least that of their children. They acquired marketable skills and forged favourable relationships with influential whites and free blacks. Inheritance from propertied white and free black *vecinos* (citizens or residents), in particular, augmented one's material standard of living. Even with the advantage of inheritance, though, privileged free people of colour had to employ all their energy, skills and business acumen in order to maintain and increase their property holdings. Efforts to free friends and family members from bondage, along with race discrimination on the part of many whites, placed additional constraints upon the ability of free blacks to prosper, despite their utmost attempts. Nevertheless, the numerous documents remaining from the Spanish period of New Orleans' history indicate that free people of colour did struggle to attain success as defined by the dominant society and in the process did help to create a Creole of Colour elite.[52]

NOTES

Research for this article was made possible through the generous assistance of the Program for Cultural Cooperation Between Spain's Ministry of Culture and United States Universities, Alfred G. Beveridge Grant for Research in the History of the Western Hemisphere, the American Philosophical Society, the Oklahoma Foundation for the Humanities, the University of Tulsa Faculty Development Summer Fellowship Program, and the University of Tulsa Faculty Research Grant Program.

1. It was during the antebellum period that creoles of colour began to identify themselves as such and that the term 'creole' acquired its modern, distinctive meaning in Louisiana: a white or black person who claimed French or Spanish ancestry, spoke French and practised the Catholic religion. During the eighteenth century colonials applied the term creole more broadly to all persons born in the Americas, especially to those of African descent; 'creole of colour' is not found in existing documents from the colonial period. Rather, correspondence, censuses, militia rosters, sacramental records, notarial registers and other official documents from New Orleans' Spanish era grouped free blacks into two general categories based on phenotype: *moreno* (dark-skinned, primarily of African ancestry) and *pardo* (light-skinned, primarily of European ancestry). Although free blacks had special privileges and rights, as did other racial, status and occupational groups within the corporate societies of Spain and Spanish America, they cannot be viewed as one monolithic group. Some maintained associations and cultural identity more closely with slave society, especially those who were newly freed or whose spouses or relatives remained enslaved. Second-generation free blacks or those with white relatives or greater wealth tended to associate more frequently with white society. Nevertheless, even materially prosperous, Louisiana-born blacks who were several generations removed from slavery by the turn of the century, did not identify themselves as creoles of colour. They were starting to coalesce as a separate socio-economic group, but it was their offspring who, when faced with a cultural and material threat from incoming Anglo-Americans, began to emphasize their distinctive traits and common cause, just as their white creole counterparts did. For a discussion of division, cohesion and identity among free blacks in slave societies, see Arnold A. Sio, 'Marginality and Free Coloured Identity in Caribbean Slave Society', *Slavery and Abolition*, 8 (1987), pp.166–82.
2. This essay looks at elite status as defined by wealth. Status and prestige for free blacks, as for whites, can also be measured in terms of militia service (especially for officers) and frequency of being requested to stand as godparents. Future work by this author will examine these factors.
3. Gwendolyn Midlo Hall, *Africans in Colonial Louisiana: The Development of Afro-Creole Culture in the Eighteenth Century* (Baton Rouge, 1992).
4. Throughout this essay I use the inclusive somatic terms 'free black' and 'free person of colour' to encompass anyone of African descent, that is, any free non-white person whether he or she be pure African, part white, or part Native American. The exclusive terms *pardo* (light-skinned) and *moreno* (dark-skinned), preferred by contemporary free blacks over *mulato* and *negro*, are utilized to distinguish elements within the non-white population. Occasional references delineate further between *grifo* (offspring of a pardo[a] and a morena[o], and in some cases of a pardo[a] and an india[o]), *cuarterón* (offspring of a white

and a pardo[a]), and *mestizo* (usually the offspring of a white and an Amerindian but in New Orleans sometimes meaning the offspring of a pardo[a] or moreno[a] and an india[o]).

The term creole of colour was not used in Louisiana during the Spanish period and acquired its distinct meaning in the nineteenth and twentieth century. Colonial documents sometimes refer to a person, usually someone of African ancestry, as a 'creole of Jamaica', 'creole of Martinique', 'creole of Louisiana', etc., meaning a native of that particular place. Throughout the New World, creole was applied to anyone of European or African ancestry born in the Americas.

5. For a survey of Louisiana's colonial history, see Bennett H. Wall (ed.), *Louisiana: A History* (2nd ed., Arlington Heights, IL, 1990) and David J. Weber, *The Spanish Frontier in North America* (New Haven, 1992).

6. A more in-depth look at free people of African descent is provided by Kimberly S. Hanger, 'Avenues to Freedom Open to the New Orleans Black Population, 1769–1779', *Louisiana History*, 31 (1990), pp.237–64; '*Personas de varias clases y colores*: Free People of Color in Spanish New Orleans, 1769–1803' (Ph.D. dissertation, University of Florida, 1991); and 'A Privilege and Honor to Serve: The Free Black Militia of Spanish New Orleans', *Military History of the Southwest*, 21 (1991), pp.59–86. See also Virginia Meacham Gould, 'In Full Enjoyment of Their Liberty: The Free Women of Color of the Gulf Ports of New Orleans, Mobile, and Pensacola, 1769–1860' (Ph.D. dissertation, Emory University, 1991); Hall, *Africans in Colonial Louisiana*; Daniel H. Usner, Jr., 'The Frontier Exchange Economy of the Lower Mississippi Valley in the 18th Century', *William and Mary Quarterly*, 44 (1987), pp.165–92; and Usner, *Indians, Settlers, and Slaves in a Frontier Exchange Economy: The Lower Mississippi Valley Before 1783* (Chapel Hill, 1992).

7. Paul F. Lachance, 'The Politics of Fear: French Louisianians and the Slave Trade, 1786–1809', *Plantation Society in the Americas*, 1 (1979), pp.162–97 examines Louisiana's slave trade policy in the context of the French Revolution.

8. Census counts were very low for free blacks. The Spanish government conducted most censuses for military service or tax reasons and thus also undercounted women as well. See Cecilia Wu, 'The Population of the City of Querétaro in 1791', *Journal of Latin American Studies*, 16 (1984), pp.277–307.

9. Hanger, 'Personas de varias clases y colores,' ch. 2.

10. Hall, *Africans in Colonial Louisiana*, pp.201–36, 317–42.

11. Hans W. Baade, 'The Law of Slavery in Spanish Luisiana, 1769–1803', in Edward F. Haas (ed.), *Louisiana's Legal Heritage* (Pensacola, 1983), pp.43–86; Herbert S. Klein, *African Slavery in Latin America and the Caribbean* (New York, 1986), pp.194–5.

12. Acts of Francisco Broutin, Orleans Parish Notarial Archives (hereafter cited OPNA), no.7, f.253, 24 May 1791.

13. Acts of Andrés Almonester y Roxas, OPNA, f.251, 10 Sept. 1772; Acts of Carlos Ximénez, OPNA, no.2, f.229, 231, 5 May 1792 and f.234, 235, 237, 7 May 1792. The documents do not indicate from where Magdalena obtained the funds to purchase so many family members. She could have earned the money, or a free black or white relative or even her mistress could have supplied the funds anonymously. The slaveholder, doña María Julia de la Brosse, legitimate wife of don Francisco Carrière and childless, let several other slaves purchase their cartas at the same time. Two months later she wrote her will and donated to Magdalena, now a free morena, a fully outfitted bed and to Magdalena, her three daughters, and another former slave all the clothes of her use, divided equally five ways (Acts of Ximénez, OPNA, no.2, f.331, 6 July 1792).

14. Acts of Almonester y Roxas, OPNA, f.4, 5, 8 Jan. 1775 and f.17, 19, 10 Jan. 1777.

15. Court Proceedings of Narciso Broutin, OPNA, no.59, f.1028–76, 28 June 1803; Court Proceedings of Ximénez, OPNA, f.246–63, 28 May 1804. A natural child was one who was illegitimate but recognized by his or her parents.

16. Acts of N. Broutin, OPNA, no.2, f.13, 29 Jan. 1800; Acts of Almonester y Roxas, OPNA, f.25, 25 April 1778; Black Baptisms, book 2, f.290, 17 July 1782, book 3, f.51, 31 May 1784, and book 4, f.220, 15 April 1791; Archivo General de Indias, Papeles de Cuba (hereafter cited AGI PC), legajo 211-A, f.160, 1796. For more on Bahy (or in its French version, Bailly) see Hanger, 'Conflicting Loyalties: The French Revolution and Free People of Color in

Spanish New Orleans', *Louisiana History*, 34 (1993), pp.5–33.
17. Acts of Juan Bautista Garic, OPNA, no.9, f.595, 597, 29 Dec. 1778.
18. Acts of F.Broutin, OPNA, no.47, f.460, 15 Nov. 1798.
19. Acts of Garic, OPNA, no.10, f.78, 1 Feb. 1779.
20. Acts of Pedro Pedesclaux, OPNA, no.17, f.312, 24 April 1793.
21. Black Baptisms, book 5, no.750, 8 March 1795.
22. Acts of Garic, OPNA, no.3, f.28, 1 Feb. 1772; Acts of Garic, OPNA, no.4, f.264, 16 Sept. 1773 and f.358, 23 Dec. 1773; Acts of Rafael Perdomo, OPNA, no.7, f.189, 21 April 1786.
23. Mary C. Karasch, *Slave Life in Rio de Janeiro, 1808–1850* (Princeton, 1987), pp.211, 335–70.
24. Acts of Pedesclaux, OPNA, no.17, f.295, 18 April 1793 and f.297, 19 April 1793; Hanger, '*Personas de varias clases y colores*', pp.203–7.
25. Acts of Almonester y Roxas, OPNA, f.683, 22 Dec. 1779 and f.684, 23 Dec. 1779.
26. Acts of F. Broutin, OPNA, no.15, f.344, 14 Nov. 1792.
27. Acts of Garic, OPNA, no.9, f.91, 27 Feb. 1778; Acts of Pedesclaux, OPNA, no.13, f.764, 18 Dec. 1791. Olivares was buried on 20 Dec. 1791 (White Funerals, Book 2).
28. Acts of Garic, OPNA, no.8, f.67, 21 Feb. 1777; Acts of N. Broutin, OPNA, no.25, f.108, 4 May 1793.
29. Acts of Ximénez, OPNA, no.19, f.76, 2 April 1803 and f.152, 11 Aug. 1803.
30. Acts of Leonardo Mazange, OPNA, no.5, f.283, 18 March 1782.
31. For examples, see Karasch, *Slave Life in Rio*, pp.362, 364.
32. 'Elena Negra libre sobre darle la Libertad a su hijo Esclabo de Dn. Henrique Despres por el precio de su estimación', Spanish Judicial Records, Record Group 2, Louisiana State Museum Historical Center (hereafter cited SJR), 12 Aug. 1780.
33. Free and slave persons of African descent could inherit property from whites. According to the *code noir*, which governed slaves and free blacks in Louisiana under French rule, free blacks could not inherit property. Louisiana judges rarely enforced this provision of the code, and when Spain established its rule in Louisiana, Spanish codes replaced French ones (Baade, 'The Law of Slavery in Spanish Luisiana', pp.43–86). In 1774 the free morena Angélica Perret tested the extent of Spanish law regarding free black inheritance rights. She petitioned to obtain the goods and property that Juan Perret had left her in his will. One of Perret's white grandchildren requested that the court deny Angélica's petition based on Article 52 of a royal French edict pertaining to persons of African descent, which stated that free or not, they could not receive property from whites. The judge ruled in favour of Angélica ('Angélica v. Heirs of Juan Perret', SJR, 25 May 1774).
34. 'Criminales seguidos de oficio contra el Pardo libre Pedro Bailly', SJR, 7 Oct. 1791. Bahy was tried and convicted on similar charges in 1794 (Hanger, '*Personas de varias clases y colores*', ch. 7).
35. Acts of Almonester y Roxas, OPNA, f.389, 1 Sept. 1775.
36. Court Proceedings of N. Broutin, OPNA, no.53, f.225–98, 11 June 1802. As an aside, it is interesting to note that the will listed each of the oxen by name.
37. Acts of F.Broutin, OPNA, no.30, f.328, 23 Dec. 1794.
38. 'Testamentaria de don Francisco Hisnard que falleció en el Puesto de Opellousas,' SJR, 27 Aug. 1798; Acts of Pedesclaux, OPNA, no.40, f.81, 6 Feb. 1802; Acts of N. Broutin, OPNA, no.4, f.544, 31 Dec. 1802; William J. Coker and Thomas D. Watson, *Indian Traders of the Southeastern Spanish Borderlands: Panton, Leslie & Company and John Forbes & Company, 1783–1817* (Pensacola: University of West Florida Press, 1984), pp.330–49; Jack D.L. Holmes, 'Do It! Don't Do It!: Spanish Laws on Sex and Marriage', in Haas (ed.), *Louisiana's Legal Heritage*, p.23.
39. David Cohen and Jack P.Greene, 'Introduction', in Cohen and Greene (eds.), *Neither Slave Nor Free: The Freedmen of African Descent in the Slave Societies of the New World* (Baltimore, 1972), pp.12–13; Karasch, *Slave Life in Rio*, p.363.
40. Acts of F.Broutin, OPNA, no.15, f.370, 371, 14 Dec. 1792.
41. Acts of Garic, OPNA, no.7, f.17, 25 Jan. 1776 and no.12, f.534, 25 Nov. 1779; 'Autos fechos por fin y Muerte de Juan Bta Hugón', SJR, 8 Aug. 1792.
42. Acts of Pedesclaux, OPNA, no.12, f.47, 21 Jan. 1791. Riche's household goods included

(besides the silver harness): a walnut armoire, a bedstead with two feather mattresses and two Spanish moss mattresses, two feather pillows, four pairs of sheets, one linen mosquito net, two woolen blankets, one cotton blanket, four chairs, eight pots, one frying pan, and her personal clothing.

43. Acts of Garic, OPNA, no.2, f.181, 1 June 1771; Acts of N. Broutin, OPNA, no.3 f.367, 24 Nov. 1801.

44. Acts of Pedesclaux, OPNA, no.21, f.728, 1 Aug. 1794; 'Autos fechos por fallecimiento de Martona Belair', SJR, 15 Aug. 1795.

45. Marriage contracts, like wills, indicate that on average free blacks were not as prosperous as whites and females possessed fewer assets than males. For the Spanish period there were a total of ten marriage contracts between free blacks recorded in the notarial registers. Of these, one listed property for both parties but no assessed value for this property. Three other contracts did not include property the male party brought to the marriage. The average value of goods for free black women was 787 pesos (N=9), while the average for free black males was almost twice that amount (1,487 pesos; N=6). A sample of twenty marriage contracts negotiated between white partners (where six did not include property assessments for the groom) shows an average of 3,270 pesos brought by women – more than four times that of free black brides – and 4,113 pesos brought by men – almost three times that of free black grooms.

46. Black Marriages, book 1, no.11, 10 Jan. 1779; Acts of Almonester y Roxas, OPNA, f.57, 23 Jan. 1779. For a discussion of dowry rights under Spanish law see Edith Couturier, 'Women and the Family in Eighteenth-Century Mexico: Law and Practice', *Journal of Family History*, 10 (1985), pp.294–304 and Ann Twinam, 'Honor, Sexuality, and Illegitimacy in Colonial Spanish America', in Asunción Lavrin (ed.), *Sexuality and Marriage in Colonial Latin America* (Lincoln, 1989), pp.118–55.

47. Acts of F.Broutin, OPNA, no.25, f.144, 22 May 1793. The couple wed four days prior (Black Marriages, book 1, no.65, 18 May 1793).

48. Acts of Almonester y Roxas, OPNA, no.1, f.224, 15 June 1781. Marriages absent from the sacramental records were not all that rare. For example, the union of Pedro Bahy with Naneta Cadis does not appear in the records, even though their marriage contract was registered in a notarial act and the baptismal records of their children state that they were legitimate offspring. Other documents also indicate that Bahy and Cadis were officially married.

49 'Liberation of Luison, Mulatresse', SJR, 9 May 1770; Black Marriages, book 1, no.25, 1 April 1785; Acts of Rodríguez, OPNA, no.4, f.297, 2 April 1785; Acts of N. Broutin, OPNA, no.2, f.165, 23 June 1800; Black Baptisms, book 7, f.65, 6 March 1802.

50. Black Marriages, book 1, no.27, 27 Sept. 1785; Acts of Ximénez, OPNA, no.6, f.27, 27 Jan. 1794. In 1799 Brouner's youngest daughter Clarisa (Clara) López de la Peña instituted proceedings before an ecclesiastical tribunal to prove that she was of Indian descent and to have her daughter Luisa's baptismal record transferred from *el Libro de los Negros y Mulatos* to *el Libro de los Blancos*. Luisa's natural father was don Luis Declouet, a lieutenant in the fixed infantry regiment of Louisiana. The court granted Clarisa's request (Proceedings by Clara López de la Peña, Records of the Diocese of Louisiana and the Floridas, on microfilm at Louisiana Historical Center, Roll 8, 14 Sept. 1799).

51. 'Relación de la perdida que cada Individuo ha padecido en el Incendio de esta Ciudad...', Archivo General de Indias, Audiencia de Santo Domingo, legajo 2576, f.532, 30 Sept. 1788. The document gives phenotype and status for free blacks but not for whites; yet other documents indicate that some individuals who were not identified as free blacks were such. For example, in a separate petition for damage remuneration, María Methode is identified as a parda libre, whereas in the 'Relación' she is not. Thus, the 'Relación' may include more free blacks and fewer whites than those who appear.

52. Further analysis of these documents and comparisons with white wealth accumulation might make for an even stronger case.

The Limits of Privilege: Where Free Persons of Colour Stood in the Hierarchy of Wealth in Antebellum New Orleans

PAUL LACHANCE

No less than six times in her seminal article on three-caste societies in Saint-Domingue and Louisiana, Laura Foner describes free persons of colour, the intermediate group between whites and slaves, as 'privileged'.[1] The same adjective appears three times in Ira Berlin's chapter on the free people of colour of Louisiana and the Gulf ports in *Slaves without Masters*.[2] Loren Schweninger contrasts the economic losses of former free persons of colour in post-Civil War Louisiana with 'their unique and privileged prewar status'.[3] This view extends beyond historians who refer literally to 'privileges'. In a critique of romantic notions about early nineteenth-century New Orleans that is harsher than most in its portrayal of free persons of colour, Joseph Tregle nevertheless remarks that they 'enjoyed a status ... probably unequaled in any other part of the South'.[4]

Among its connotations, 'privileged' refers to special advantages in the opportunity to accumulate property. According to Ira Berlin, a shortage of white men in Spanish Louisiana permitted free men of colour to enter skilled trades and crafts. 'Some of the free Negro carpenters and joiners, shoemakers and tailors, coopers and painters opened their own shops. The most successful of these often purchased slaves, and a few even pushed their way into the planter class. Their powerful economic position further guaranteed their unencumbered legal status.'[5]

Other historians, remarking on the shortage of white women and frequency of interracial unions in the Spanish period, trace free coloured fortunes back to donations and bequests from white males to their concubines and children.[6] Laws enacted in the decade after the Louisiana Purchase deprived free persons of colour of all political rights and circumscribed their civil liberties, but left intact their right to own property.[7] Thus they were able to participate to some extent in the extraordinary demographic and economic growth of New Orleans under American domination.

Leonard Curry, David Rankin and Loren Schweninger have compiled empirical data on occupations and property ownership of free persons of colour in antebellum New Orleans. Curry, whose study of free blacks in cities of the North as well as of the South spans the first half of the nineteenth century, declares that 'no city provided more favorable employment opportunities to free blacks than New Orleans'. From occupations listed in the 1850 manuscript census, he determined that it had the highest percentage of free black males employed as artisans, professionals and entrepreneurs, and the lowest in 'low opportunity' occupations like labourer, mariner, gardener, servant and waiter. New Orleans alone contained more than a quarter of all free men of colour employed as professionals, managers, artists, clerks and scientists in the fifteen largest cities in the United States.[8]

Rankin's doctoral dissertation contains the most thorough analysis to date of information in tax and census records on property held by free persons of colour in New Orleans between 1850 and 1870. Whether measured per capita or as a proportion of total assets, a small fraction of the city's wealth was in their hands. Questioning his own data, however, Rankin cites cases of tax assessors who undervalued free coloured property and of wealthy free persons of colour who did not reveal their full worth to census takers. 'For a variety of reasons,' he concludes, 'free Negro wealth may have been considerably larger than the census reveals.'[9]

Schweninger identifies, in addition to wealthy free black planters in rural parishes of Louisiana, several of the richest free persons of colour in New Orleans on the eve of the Civil War: Eulalie d'Mandeville Macarty, undoubtedly the beneficiary of cohabitation with a wealthy white businessman, but whose personal fortune of over $150,000 was made in part in her own wholesale dry goods business in the 1840s; Pierre Casenave, an undertaker whose income increased from $10,000 to $40,000 per year between 1850 and 1857; Bernard Soulié, a merchant and real-estate broker whose holdings doubled in value from $50,000 to $100,000 in the 1850s; and François Lacroix who made $242,600 from speculation in city properties. 'By 1860, five of the ten wealthiest free persons of colour in the South – Bernard Soulié, Francis Ernest Dumas, François Lacroix, grocer J. Camps, worth an estimated $86,000, and landlord François Edmund Dupuy – claimed the Crescent City as their place of residence.'[10]

The evidence is convincing that New Orleans offered to free persons of colour possibilities of acquiring property which their counterparts in other cities must have envied. Biographical sketches of rich individuals and national comparisons do not, on the other hand, reveal how free coloured wealth compared to that of whites in New Orleans society itself, or how much of it was concentrated in the hands of an elite, nor how the economic standing of free persons of colour developed over the antebellum period.

These are the topics covered in this essay which demonstrates that, in the hierarchy of wealth of New Orleans, free persons of colour were obviously privileged only in comparison to slaves.

Data in this essay are taken from wills, inventories and marriage contracts. These sources reveal the degree to which different elements of the population, including free persons of colour, benefited from the increase in wealth in New Orleans over the antebellum period. For every tenth year from 1810 to 1860 this author recorded the value of assets in all extant inventories of testate and intestate successions. The other database consists of all marriage contracts drawn up in census years and in three clusters of years: 1804–20, 1835–40, and 1855–60.[11]

Documents generated by the legal complexities surrounding the transmission of wealth are biased in the sense that they only concern property owners, among whom the rich are over-represented. The wealthier an owner, the more likely he was to give instructions in a will on disposition of his estate after he died, to leave property that needed to be inventoried, or to have a notary draft a marriage contract providing legal proof of assets owned by both parties on the eve of marriage and specifying how separate and community property were to be divided on dissolution of the union by death or divorce.

To give some idea of the extent to which the sources used in my article exclude much of the population, marriage contracts were found for one in every four couples whose names were entered in the marriage registers of Catholic churches between 1804 and 1820; and the ratio of contracts to marriages declined to only one in fifteen in 1850.[12] Mortality records for New Orleans recorded 3,825 deaths of adults in 1850 and an average of 3,839 per year from 1856 to 1860. Assuming at least 15 per cent of the adults who died were slaves, the estates of around 10 per cent of free adult decedents were inventoried. In 1850 only 20 per cent of these successions were testate; in 1860, 37 per cent.[13] Under-representation of individuals with little property and the absence of the propertyless inevitably make a society described through marriage contracts and inventories appear richer than it was.

Nevertheless, such documents remain useful for comparing the relative economic standing of subgroups of a population. Inventories have often served this purpose. Indeed, ingenious methods have been devised to control for their biases and use them to generalize about the wealth of the entire living population.[14] Marriage contracts automatically control for biases of age and gender found in inventories. They give information about property owned by individuals at a younger age than succession records, and males and females are equally represented. Where marriage contracts exist in sufficient number to allow for quantitative analysis, as they do in antebellum New Orleans, they provide an independent measure of trends detected in inventories.

A first indication of relative economic standing is the percentage of documents concerning transmission of wealth for a particular group (Table 1). Is it smaller or larger than the proportion of the group in the total population?

TABLE 1

NUMBER AND PERCENTAGE OF FREE PERSONS OF COLOUR IN FREE POPULATION OF NEW ORLEANS AND IN DOCUMENTS REVEALING WEALTH, 1810–60

Year	Free Population N	Free persons of colour N	(%)	Inventories N	(%)	Wills N	(%)	Marriage contracts N	(%)
1810	11,281	4,950	(43.9)	8	(14.5)	6	(11.4)	0	(0.0)
1820	19,821	6,237	(31.5)	11	(12.4)	7	(13.2)	3	(6.0)
1830	31,717	11,607	(36.6)	22	(19.1)	7	(15.2)	12	(21.4)
1840	81,307	19,376	(23.8)	36	(23.4)	16	(23.2)	10	(18.5)
1850	112,015	10,237	(9.1)	33	(9.0)	10	(13.5)	11	(13.9)
1860	166,159	11,133	(6.7)	20	(6.2)	8	(7.1)	3	(5.2)

Sources: Population statistics are derived from aggregate returns of the federal census of the United States: *Third Census, 1810: Population*, p.82; *Fourth Census, 1820: Population*, p.81; *Fifth Census, 1830: Population*, pp.104–5; *Sixth Census, 1840: Population*, p.256; *Seventh Census, 1850: Population*, p.474; *Eighth Census, 1860: Population*, p.195. Databases of New Orleans succession inventories, wills, and marriage contracts.

Notes: Population figures are for urban areas of Orleans parish in 1810 and 1820 and of Orleans and Jefferson parishes from 1830 on.

In 1810 free persons of colour made up 44 per cent of the free population in New Orleans, the culmination of an upward trend since 1769 when the first census after the effective Spanish take-over of Louisiana enumerated 99 free persons of colour, just 5 per cent of the free population of the city. Although probably undercounted in the 1769 census,[15] there is no doubt as to their substantial increase over the Spanish period. In the New Orleans census of 1805, the first after the Louisiana Purchase, free persons of colour numbered 1,566, soon to be augmented by over 3,000 of the same race and condition among 10,000 Saint-Domingue refugees who arrived by way of Cuba in 1809.[16] The free coloured population continued to grow in the next decade; but unable to keep pace with the sizeable white immigration into Orleans Parish after the War of 1812, it declined to 31 per cent of the total free population in 1820.

In 1810 and 1820, the proportion of inventories, wills, and marriage contracts for free persons of colour did not equal even half their proportion of the free population (Table 1 and Figure 1).

FIGURE 1

FREE PERSONS OF COLOUR AS PERCENTAGE OF FREE POPULATION AND OF
INVENTORIES, WILLS AND MARRIAGE CONTRACTS

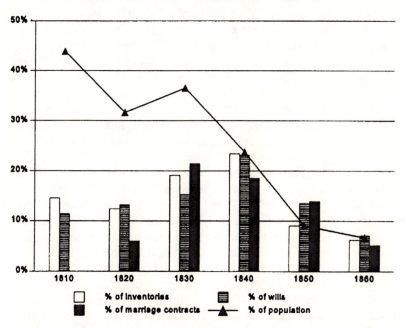

Source: Censuses and data sets cited under Table 1.

Most of the testators and individuals whose estates were inventoried in these
years had come of age in the Spanish period. The older a free person of
colour, the more likely he or she had been born in slavery. In that light, to
already account for over 10 per cent of inventories and wills in the city at
the beginning of the nineteenth century can be considered remarkable
economic progress. Nevertheless, the proportion of wills and inventories for
free persons of colour did not catch up with their proportion of the free
population until 1840. The formation of a viable free coloured community,
begun under Spanish domination, was completed under American
domination.

The increase in the proportion of inventories and wills for free persons of
colour from 15 and 11 per cent respectively in 1810 to 23 per cent of both
types of documents in 1840 shows that discriminatory legislation in the
territorial period (1804–12) did not prevent their economic advance.[17]
Although they decreased from 44 to 24 per cent of the free population of
New Orleans between 1810 and 1840, the demographic decline was relative.
The number of free persons of colour in the city actually quadrupled from

4,950 in 1810 to 19,376 in 1840.[18]

From that apogee, the free coloured population shrank to 10,237 persons in 1850. In the last decade of the antebellum period, it climbed again to 11,133; but at the same time the number of whites increased from 101,778 to 155,026, reducing non-whites to less than seven per cent of the free population of New Orleans on the eve of the Civil War. The percentage of inventories and wills for free persons of colour also fell sharply from 1840 to 1860; yet it stayed closer to their proportion of the free population than it had been from 1810 to 1830. Irish and German immigrants, who began to arrive in large numbers in the 1830s and who displaced free persons of colour from various trades in the 1840s and 1850s, had a less immediate effect on their ability to accumulate enough wealth to warrant wills and inventories in proportion to their numbers.

The trend in marriage contracts, drawn up for persons from younger age cohorts than those whose wealth is reported in wills and inventories, is distinctive. The absence of contracts for free persons of colour in 1810 reflects their extremely low marriage rate at the outset of American rule, 1.9 per thousand, another sign a free coloured community had not yet matured.[19] Cohabitation, often interracial, was still the norm at the beginning of the nineteenth century. Only 5 of 65 free children of colour baptized in the first four months of 1810 were legitimate.[20] A dramatic change in matrimonial behaviour underlay the sharp increase in the percentage of marriage contracts for free persons of colour from 1820 to 1840. The number of entries in Catholic marriage registers for free Negroes and mulattoes jumped from 8 per year in the first decade of the nineteenth century to 53 per year in the third decade, and their marriage rate climbed to 3.2 per thousand in 1820 and 3.3 per thousand in 1830.[21]

The increase in the percentage of marriage contracts for free persons of colour is also evidence of an upward trend in property ownership in the generation that came of age in the middle decades of the antebellum period. Although marriage contracts for free persons of colour decreased from 21 to 19 per cent of all contracts between 1830 and 1840, they did so over a decade when non-whites declined from 36 to 24 per cent of the free population. The ratio of the percentage of contracts for free persons of colour to their percentage of the free population actually increased from 0.58 in 1830 to 0.78 in 1840.

Similarly, a further decline in the percentage of free coloured marriage contracts from 19 per cent in 1840 to 14 per cent in 1850 was less than the reduction of the group from 24 to 9 per cent of the free population in the same decade. Free persons of colour accounted in 1850 for a higher percentage of both marriage contracts and wills than they did of the free population. By 1860, though, the percentage of both marriage contracts and inventories fell below this reference point, indicative of deterioration in the economic condition of free persons of colour in the last decade of the antebellum period.[22]

Inventories and marriage contracts not only reflect trends over time in the proportion of whites and free persons of colour who succeeded in accumulating property; they also reveal the amount of wealth acquired by each racial group, a second and equally important measure of their relative economic standing. Although the aggregate value of inventoried property did not quite keep pace with the tenfold increase in the population of New Orleans from 1810 to 1860, it still reflects impressive economic growth (Figure 2).

FIGURE 2

TOTAL ASSETS IN INVENTORIES AND POPULATION GROWTH
OF NEW ORLEANS, 1810–60

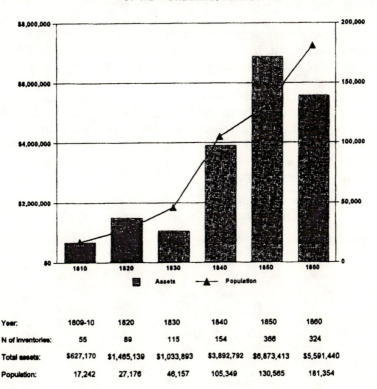

Year:	1809-10	1820	1830	1840	1850	1860
N of inventories:	55	89	115	154	366	324
Total assets:	$627,170	$1,465,139	$1,033,893	$3,892,792	$6,873,413	$5,591,440
Population:	17,242	27,176	46,157	105,349	130,565	181,354

Source: Censuses cited under Table 1 and data base of succession inventories.

Note: Number of inventories and assets for 1810 are the average for 1809 and 1810.

From around $600,000 in 1810, wealth reported in inventories increased to nearly $7,000,000 in 1850 before slipping to $5,500,000 in 1860.

The doubling in value of inventoried wealth between 1810 and 1820 coincides with a spurt of economic growth once the War of 1812 ended; and the sharp jump in total estate from $1,034,000 in 1830 to $3,893,000 in 1840 fits characterizations of the 1830s as a boom decade.[23] A comparable increase from 1840 to 1850 occurred in a period described by one historian as a 'long hard depression' following the banking crises of 1837 and 1839,[24] while the apparent decline of inventoried assets in the last antebellum decade clashes with the renewed growth suggested by the increase in the value of commerce passing through New Orleans from $48 million in 1850 to $129 million in 1860.[25] It should be remembered, though, that inventories do not reflect so much immediate economic conditions as the accumulation of wealth over preceding decades. Moreover, the chance occurrence of two estates worth over a million dollars pushed total assets above the trend line in 1850.[26]

Free persons of colour had so small a share of the aggregate value of inventoried assets that, if it were shown on Figure 2, it would be barely discernible. The statistics are provided in Table 2. From one census year to the next, inventories of free persons of colour listed property worth between $22,000 and $115,000, just 1 to 5 per cent of the value of assets in all inventories, the best year being 1830. From then to the last decade of the antebellum period, one observes an uninterrupted decline in the free coloured share of inventoried wealth in New Orleans. Also noteworthy is

TABLE 2

PERCENTAGE OF INVENTORIES AND OF VALUE OF INVENTORIED ASSETS
HELD BY FREE PERSONS OF COLOUR

Inventories for f.p.c.	Total assets		Value of assets held by f.p.c.		Ratio of share of assets to inventories	
	(A)	(B)	(C)	(D)	(E)	(E/B)
Year	N	%	$	$	%	%
1810	8	14.5	627,170	22,131	3.5	24.1
1820	11	12.4	1,465,139	22,657	1.5	12.1
1830	22	19.1	1,033,893	51,426	5.0	26.2
1840	36	23.4	3,892,792	115,437	3.0	12.8
1850	33	9.0	6,873,413	71,129	1.0	11.4
1860	20	6.2	5,591,440	53,562	1.0	15.5

Source: Database of succession inventories.

Notes: Statistics for 1810 are the average for 1809 and 1810. The ratio of the percentage of inventoried assets for free persons of colour to the percentage of inventories for the group is obtained by dividing the fifth by the second column of figures.

that the proportion of total assets held by free persons of colour ranged from 11.4 to 26.2 per cent of the proportion of inventories for the group, pointing to lower average wealth than whites.

It was not as straightforward as anticipated to compare findings from inventories with statistics cited in other studies of free coloured property-holding in antebellum New Orleans. At the high end, former free persons of colour claimed during the Reconstruction that they had been taxed on around $15 million in property in the last three decades of the antebellum period, a figure taken at face value by Robert Reinders and considered by Rankin to be less implausible than it might appear on first sight.[27] At the low end, Richard Tansey identified 283 free persons of colour with real estate appraised at $724,000 in the tax records for New Orleans in 1860.[28] Studies by Schweninger and Curry based on census data in 1850 and 1860 report from 263 to 650 free coloured owners of over $2 million in real estate.[29]

Samples I have taken of tax and census records in 1860 offer no support for the high estimate of $15 million, but confirm a discrepancy in the total value of free coloured real estate in these two sources that is of the same magnitude as in the findings of Tansey, Schweninger and Curry. Their figures can be reconciled if free persons of colour were taxed on as little as a third of the value of their holdings. My samples also indicate taxation of half as many free persons of colour as the number who reported real estate in the census. If it were the poorer half who largely escaped taxation, the effect on the aggregate value of appraised assets would have been minimal.[30] Assuming that free persons of colour owned lots and buildings worth $2,317,300 in 1860 (Schweninger's figure), they still held a minute portion of the total value of real estate in New Orleans: 3.7 per cent of $62,681,212 reported in the census of 1860, 2.8 per cent of tax assessments on $83,702,710 in realty for the same year.[31] Although greater than the free coloured share of the total value of real estate in inventories from 1860, 1.9 per cent, the proportions observed in the census and tax records are still below the 6.7 per cent of the free population of New Orleans who were free persons of colour.[32]

The 1860 tax rolls also assessed slaves, animals and vehicles of transportation, capital, income and household furniture; and the 1860 federal census reported the value of personal as well as real property. David Rankin found 1,328 free persons of colour in the manuscript census of New Orleans who owned either or both types of property, worth in total $2,287,465.[33] He compares this sum with the total value of taxable property in the city: $121,030,650. The combined value of real and personal property in the census was $105,175,542.[34] Depending on which basis of comparison is used, free persons of colour held 1.9 or 2.2 per cent of the city's wealth, in either case more than their 0.9 per cent of total inventoried assets, real

estate plus other forms of property, but again less than their percentage of
the free population in 1860.

One factor limiting the free coloured share of total wealth in inventories
is that none of the very rich free persons of colour found in systematic
searches of census records happened to die in 1860 or in any other census
year. That itself is a sign of how exceptional such individuals were. Adding
to the inventory data for a particular year one or two free persons of colour
worth more than a hundred thousand dollars would make little difference in
aggregate statistics. In 1860, for example, an additional $200,000 in assets
for free persons of colour would increase their share of total inventoried
assets from 0.9 to 4.4 per cent. That would still be less than the 6.2 per cent
of inventories for free persons of colour and their 6.7 per cent of the free
population.

It follows that free coloured property holders were on average less
wealthy than whites. The racial disparity in Figure 3 is striking. Depending
on the decade, the average value of property listed in white inventories was
five to ten times greater than in inventories for free persons of colour. The
variation was mainly due to fluctuations in average white wealth from
$10,564 to $32,011 per year. By contrast, average free coloured wealth

FIGURE 3

AVERAGE VALUE OF ASSETS LISTED IN INVENTORIES BY RACE

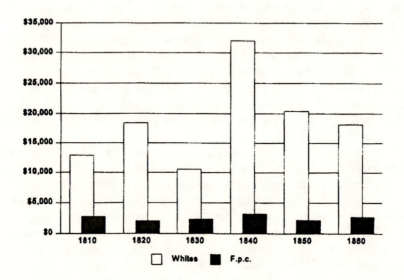

Source: Data base of succession inventories.

FIGURE 4

AVERAGE VALUE OF PROPERTY DECLARED IN MARRIAGE CONTRACTS BY
PERIOD, GENDER AND RACE

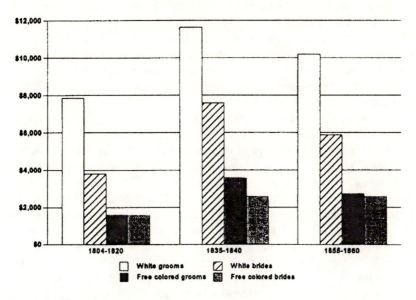

Source: Data base of marriage contracts

varied within the lower and narrower range of $2,060 to $3,207 per year.

Allowance made for the younger age at which marriage contracts were drawn up, the average declarations of property in these documents changed over time in much the same fashion as in inventories (Figure 4). The value of assets listed in marriage contracts increased in the 1830s for grooms and brides of both races and then, except for free women of colour, fell at the end of the antebellum period. White grooms declared three to five times more than free men of colour, while white brides brought two to three times more to their marriages than free women of colour.

Gender differences in declarations of wealth were greater between white than between free coloured spouses. This was in part a consequence of white men marrying later in life than free men of colour while white women married at a younger age than free women of colour. White bridegrooms had more time to accumulate property before marriage, and white brides less.[35] In addition, free men of colour were concentrated in occupational sectors with limited possibilities of enrichment. Rankin's analysis of occupations of free men of colour in the 1850 and 1860 censuses of New Orleans shows that only 2 per cent were professionals and 5 to 7 per cent were businessmen. Over 77 per cent were skilled labourers.[36] The occupations of 153 males are ascertainable in marriage contracts signed between 1804 and 1819; and they have been determined for 97 other males from city directories published in 1811 and 1822.[37] Professionals brought on average three-and-a-half times more to their marriages than artisans. Merchants involved in international commerce brought seven times more than artisans and three times more than retailers, the type of entrepreneurial activity in which free coloured businessmen were most often involved. As artisans and shopkeepers, their average declarations were only slightly larger than those of their brides.[38]

The relative economic disadvantage of free men of colour is also apparent in inventories. While over three-quarters of white inventories were for males, close to two-thirds of those for free persons of colour were for females. The excess of white males in the census was exaggerated in inventories. From 1820 to 1860, there were 13 to 18 per cent more inventories for white males than their 55 to 71 per cent of the adult white population. Likewise, in 1820 and 1840, free women of colour accounted respectively for 13 and 8 per cent more inventories than their proportion of adult free persons of colour in the census. Conversely, in 1830, 1850, and 1860, there were 5 to 8 per cent fewer inventories for females that their percentage of the free coloured population, which might be related to the loss of one special economic advantage over free men of colour as consensual unions with white men dwindled towards the end of the antebellum period.[39]

The average value of inventoried assets was higher for free women of colour than for free men of colour in every year except 1810, although they almost caught up in 1860. Among whites, by contrast, average inventoried wealth was higher for men in every year except 1820 and 1860 (Figure 5); and 1820 is anomalous. In that year, the average value of white female inventories was pulled up from $3,354, one-fifth the male average of $17,418, to $24,405 by an inventory of two plantations and 297 slaves worth $255,962, occasioned by the death of Marie Charlotte Dussuau, the wife of a rich sugar planter.[40]

In general, the difference in the average value of male and female property was less in white inventories than in marriage contracts. Between marriage and death, laws governing ownership and transmission of property in Louisiana, along with the tendency of husbands to die first, accentuated by the large gender difference in age at marriage among whites, worked to the advantage of women of that race.

Classification of inventories by level of wealth reveals its distribution and the size of fortunes of the richest element of both races (Table 3).

In 1810 and 1820, the proportion of free coloured estates worth between

FIGURE 5

AVERAGE VALUE OF ASSETS IN INVENTORIES BY PERIOD, GENDER AND RACE

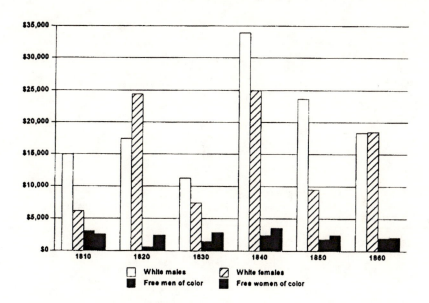

Source: Data base of succession inventories

$10,000 and $100,000 was not much greater than the proportion worth more than $100,000 for whites; it was the same in 1830 and 1840; and it was smaller in 1850 and 1860. Only 6 of 138 inventories for free persons of colour in census years, 4.3 per cent, listed more than $10,000 in total assets. By comparison, 25.1 per cent of white inventories in the data set exceeded

TABLE 3

INVENTORIES AT DIFFERENT LEVELS OF WEALTH BY PERIOD AND RACE (%)

$	1810–20		1830–40		1850–60	
	Whites	F.p.c.	Whites	F.p.c.	Whites	F.p.c.
<100	2.9	7.4	1.4	3.4	1.9	1.9
100-999	30.2	44.4	24.2	32.8	25.0	28.3
1,000-9,999	45.9	40.7	39.3	58.6	50.2	67.9
10,000-99,000	16.3	7.4	29.9	5.2	19.3	1.9
>100,000	4.7		5.2		3.6	
Total	100.0	100.0	100.0	100.0	100.0	100.0
N	172	27	211	58	637	53

Source: Database of succession inventories.

TABLE 4

MARRIAGE CONTRACTS AT DIFFERENT LEVELS OF WEALTH
BY PERIOD, GENDER, AND RACE (%)

$	1804–20		1835–40		1855–60	
Grooms:	Whites	F.m.c.	Whites	F.m.c.	Whites	F.m.c.
<100	5.9	17.2	9.2	8.6	12.9	
100-999	12.9	34.5	13.3	20.0	14.4	25.0
1,000-9,999	59.6	48.3	46.8	57.1	43.2	75.0
10,000-99,000	21.0		29.5	14.3	28.8	
>100,000	0.7		1.2		0.7	
Total	100.0	100.0	100.0	100.0	100.0	100.0
N	272	29	173	35	139	4

Brides:	Whites	F.w.c.	Whites	F.w.c.	Whites	F.w.c.
<100	3.2	5.6	1.7	2.7	4.6	10.0
100-999	17.4	38.9	2	24.0	13.8	20.0
1,000-9,999	72.4	55.6	70.7	70.7	65.5	60.0
10,000-99,000	6.7		18.0	2.7	16.1	10.0
>100,000	0.3		0.4			
Total	100.0	100.0	100.0	100.0	100.0	100.0
N	344	36	239	75	261	10

Source: Database of marriage contracts.

$10,000; 4.1 per cent exceeded $100,000; and 0.3 per cent (3 inventories) exceeded $1,000,000.

Using $10,000 as the threshold of elite status, far fewer free persons of colour than whites crossed it prior to marriage (Table 4). Only in the middle of the antebellum period did 14 per cent of free men of colour entering into marriage contracts declare over $10,000. The percentage of white bridegrooms who did so increased from 22 per cent between 1804 and 1820 to around 30 per cent between 1835 and 1840 and again between 1855 and 1860. Free women of colour who declared over $10,000 in marriage contracts increased from none to 3 to 10 per cent over the three periods; but the proportion never equalled that of white brides. A few whites were already worth over $100,000 when they married, but no free persons of colour were.[41]

The types of belongings mentioned in inventories above $10,000 bespeak modest affluence. Free women of colour left silver place settings, jewellery and mahogany furniture.[42] A few free persons of colour had enough surplus wealth to make small investments. Jean-Baptiste Ambroise, owner of a cigar shop on Bienville street, held promissory notes of $4,000 and $2,000 and four shares of capital stock in the City Bank of New Orleans with a nominal value of $400.[43] All six free coloured inventories from census years worth more than $10,000 listed slaves and real estate. Nevertheless, none approached the quantity or quality of different types of property listed in white marriage contracts and inventories worth more than $100,000. The richest estate I found for a free person of colour was worth $27,556.[44]

Not only was the white elite much wealthier than the free coloured elite, it also had a much larger proportion of the total value of property belonging to its own racial group. The six inventories worth over $10,000 that comprised the richest 4.3 per cent of free coloured estates in census years contained 22.5 per cent of their total assets. In comparison, the 44 inventories that made up the richest 4.3 per cent of white inventories accounted for 61.8 per cent of total white assets. Smaller coefficients of variation in the average assets of free persons of colour also reflect a less unequal distribution of wealth.[45]

In conclusion, free coloured property owners were demonstrably less wealthy than whites in antebellum New Orleans. The free coloured economic elite fell short of the white elite in the amount of property it acquired and its share of its group's wealth. Improvement over time was observed in the percentage of marriage contracts, wills, and inventories for free persons of colour relative to their presence in the free population; but it took place primarily in the first decades of the nineteenth century. The 1840s and 1850s were a period of economic decline for free persons of colour. Their average wealth diminished somewhat in comparison to the level it had reached in 1840; and their aggregate wealth shrank as the size of their community contracted. Although average white wealth was also less in 1850 and 1860 than it had been in 1840, it continued to be two to four times greater than the average declarations of assets by free persons of colour in marriage contracts and ten times greater than their inventoried estates; and aggregate white wealth increased substantially in the years leading up to the Civil War.

These findings show the limits to whatever special advantage free persons of colour in antebellum New Orleans enjoyed in the pursuit of wealth. They never rivalled whites in the amount of property they were able to acquire. If occupational and economic opportunities of free persons of colour were more favourable in a three-caste society than in the two-caste pattern prevalent in other regions of the United States, both racial systems were highly discriminatory. To be sure, historians have usually characterized free persons of colour in antebellum New Orleans as privileged to set off by contrast the worse conditions of free Afro-Americans elsewhere.

Recognizing their position at the bottom of the hierarchy of wealth in New Orleans does not undercut this argument. On the contrary, if free persons of colour were objects of discrimination and at a marked disadvantage even in the city where they were most successful in acquiring property, then the title of Berlin's book, *Slaves without Masters*, is only more apt.

NOTES

1. Laura Foner, 'The Free People of Colour in Louisiana and St. Domingue: A Comparative Portrait of Two Three-Caste Societies', *Journal of Social History*, Vol.3 (1970), pp.406, 407, 408, 416, 420, 430.
2. Ira Berlin, *Slaves Without Masters: The Free Negro in the Antebellum South* (New York, 1976 [1974]), pp.117, 129, 130.
3. Loren Schweninger, 'Antebellum Free Persons of Colour in Postbellum Louisiana', *Louisiana History*, Vol.30, No.4 (1989), p.346.
4. Joseph Tregle, 'Early New Orleans Society: A Reappraisal', *Journal of Southern History*, Vol.18 (1952), p.34.
5. Berlin, *Slaves Without Masters*, pp.113–14. Note that Berlin uses the term 'free Negroes' rather than 'free persons of colour'. Historians also often refer to this social group as 'free blacks'. If I prefer 'free persons of colour', it is because it was the most commonly used expression in antebellum New Orleans. The French equivalent was *couleur libre*. When mention was made of 'free blacks', it was usually to distinguish them from 'free mulattoes'. According to the federal censuses of 1850 and 1860, which identified individuals of complete and partial African ancestry in this way, four out of five of those who were free were 'mulattoes'. J.D.B. DeBow (comp.), *Statistical View of the United States* (1854; rpr. New York 1970), p.74; *Eighth Census, 1860: Population*, p.194.
6. For example, Foner, 'Free People of Colour in Louisiana and St. Domingue', pp.410–11; and Thomas Fiehrer, 'The African Presence in Colonial Louisiana: An Essay on the Continuity of Caribbean Culture', in Robert Macdonald and John Kemp (eds.), *Louisiana's Black History* (Baton Rouge, 1979), pp.19–25. Actually, as Kimberly Hanger makes very clear in her essay in this volume and as most historians would readily admit, the economic progress of free persons of colour in the Spanish period was due to a combination of patronage and extraordinary efforts by free persons of colour themselves. Before accumulating property, many first literally purchased their own freedom.
7. Donald Everett, 'Free Persons of Colour in New Orleans, 1803–1865' (Ph.D. dissertation, Tulane University, 1952), pp.55–74.
8. Leonard Curry, *The Free Black in Urban America, 1800–1850: The Shadow of a Dream* (Chicago, 1981), pp.29, 22–6, 260–1.
9. David Rankin, 'The Forgotten People: Free People of Colour in New Orleans, 1850–1870' (Ph.D. dissertation, The Johns Hopkins University, 1976), pp.107–21.
10. Schweninger, 'Antebellum Free Persons of Colour', p.351. See also his monograph, *Black Property Owners in the South, 1790–1915* (Chicago, 1990), pp.102–3, 117–18.
11. These are the databases labelled 'New Orleans Marriage Contracts', 'New Orleans Wills', and 'Succession Inventories', created from documents in the Notarial Archives and the City Archives of New Orleans and described in Charles Patch (comp.), *Gulf Coast Historical Database Group* (New Orleans: Historic New Orleans Collection, Feb. 1993), pp.6–9, 13, 15, 18. In addition to inventories from census years used for the figures and tables in this article, several inventories for testate successions in intervening years are cited below in discussion of types of possessions owned by free persons of colour.
12. The fraction of marriages for which contracts were drawn up was determined by comparing

contracts from 1804 to 1820 located in the Notarial Archives, Civil District Court, New Orleans, La. with entries in corresponding years in the marriage registers of St. Louis Cathedral and the Ursulines Chapel and Church of St. Mary, located in the Archives of the Archdiocese of New Orleans, New Orleans, La. [hereafter Archiocesan Archives]. In 1850, 71 of 82 marriage contracts were for whites. *The Seventh Census of the United States: 1850* (Washington, 1853), p.475, lists 1,056 'married whites' in Orleans parish for the year ending 1 June 1850.

13. The number of inventories and wills in 1850 and 1860 in my data sets, found mainly in the City Archives, New Orleans Public Library, New Orleans, La. [hereafter City Archives], are compared with age-specific statistics on mortality in 1849 and 1850 in DeBow, *Statistical View*, pp.109, 398, and from 1856 to 1860 in Stanford E. Chaillé, *Life and Death in New Orleans from 1787 to 1869, and more especially during the five years 1856 to 1860* (New Orleans, 1869), p.57. In the 1850 census, slaves were 14.2 per cent of the population of New Orleans; in the 1860 census, 8.4 per cent. I allow for 15 per cent of adult deaths partly because a higher proportion of slaves were adults than in the free population and partly because slave mortality may also have been higher.

14. See in particular Gloria Main, 'The correction of biases in colonial American probate records', *Historical Methods Newsletter*, Vol.8, No.1 (1974), pp.10–28; and Daniel Scott Smith, 'Underregistration and bias in probate records: An analysis of data from eighteenth-century Hingham, Massachusetts', *William and Mary Quarterly*, 3d ser., Vol.32, No.1 (1975), pp.100–10.

15. Virginia Gould, 'In full enjoyment of their liberty: The free women of colour of the gulf ports of New Orleans, Mobile, and Pensacola, 1769–1860' (Ph.D. dissertation, Emory University, 1991), p.81.

16. Paul Lachance, 'The 1809 immigration of Saint-Domingue refugees to New Orleans: Reception, integration, and impact', in Carl Brasseaux and Glenn Conrad (eds.), *The Road to Louisiana: The Saint-Domingue Refugees, 1792–1809* (Lafayette, 1992), pp.247–8.

17. Berlin maintains that the contribution of two free Negro battalions to the American victory in the Battle of New Orleans halted the loss of status of free persons of colour in the first years of American rule. *Slaves Without Masters*, pp.128–9.

18. My population figures, which include parts of New Orleans in Jefferson parish, are slightly higher than those based exclusively on Orleans parish. Although this makes a difference of less than one per cent in the proportion of free persons of colour in the free population of New Orleans in a particular year, it has the merit of being consistent with the location of some inventoried assets in Jefferson parish.

19. The marriage rate of 1.9 per thousand is based on the average number of marriages of free persons of colour in 1809, 1810, and 1811 in Book I (Jan. 1777–29 July 1830) of Negro and Mulatto Marriages at St. Louis Cathedral in the Archdiocesan Archives. This average is divided by the number of free persons of colour enumerated in the 1810 census and multiplied by 1,000. For the sake of comparison, the white marriage rate, calculated in the same way, was 10.4 per thousand in 1810. Since Protestant marriages were not entered in Catholic marriage registers, the actual marriage rates were somewhat higher, but not by much in 1810 when both the white and free coloured populations were still largely Catholic. The free coloured marriage rate appears to have been lower in the first decade of the nineteenth century than in the 1790s. See rates cited in my article, 'Intermarriage and French Cultural Persistence in Late Spanish and Early American New Orleans', *Histoire sociale–Social History*, Vol.15 (1982), p.68, esp.note 55.

20. This statistic is based on entries in the months and year indicated in the St. Louis Cathedral Baptismal Register of Negroes and Mulattoes, Vol.11 (Sept. 1809–Jan. 1811), in the Archdiocesan Archives.

21. These numbers and rates are based on entries for free persons of colour in Books II (1 Aug. 1830–31 Oct. 1835) and III (1 Nov. 1845–31 Dec. 1839) of Negro and Mulatto Marriages as well as in Book I, cited in n.19 above, and in the non-white register of St. Mary's Italian Church covering the years 1805 to 1880, all located in the Archdiocesan Archives.

22. Robert Reinders, 'A Social History of New Orleans, 1850–1860' (Ph.D. dissertation, University of Texas, 1957), pp.185–90, argues that the economic position of free persons of colour in New Orleans remained 'fairly firm' in the 1850s despite a clear deterioration in legal and social status. For evidence of economic decline as well, see Schweninger, *Black Property Owners*, pp.81–4.

23. Total assets include property in rural areas of Orleans parish (and Jefferson parish after 1830) located on the outskirts of the city proper. The estates of four wealthy planters happened to be inventoried in 1820. Subtracting the value of rural assets, aggregate urban assets increased in more regular fashion than total assets as shown in Figure 2. They were worth $380,000 in 1810 (the average for 1809 and 1810), $467,000 in 1820, and $986,000 in 1830. By 1830, urban assets represented 95 per cent of total assets, and at least 98 per cent from 1840 on.

24. Merl Reed, 'Boom or Bust–Louisiana's Economy during the 1830's', in Mark T. Carleton *et al.* (eds.), *Readings in Louisiana Politics* (Baton Rouge, 1975), p.136. The article originally appeared in *Louisiana History*, Vol.4 (1963), pp.35–53.

25. These are the figures for the combined value of exports ($38 million in 1850, $107 million in 1860) and imports ($10 million and $22 million respectively), as given in Robert Greenhaigh Albion, *The Rise of New York Port, 1815–1860* (New York, 1939), pp.390–3, and cited as the source for Table 10 in Appendix 1 by Thomas Redard, 'The Port of New Orleans: An Economic History, 1821–1860' (Ph.D. dissertation, Louisiana State University, 1985), Vol.2, pp.229–31.

26. An additional factor was higher than average mortality in 1850, 8,086 deaths in a population of 130,565, compared to 7,341 deaths in a population of 181,354 in 1860. There were 745 more deaths and 42 more inventories in 1850 than in 1860. Nevertheless, without the two millionaires who died in 1850, total inventoried assets would have been greater in 1860. The median value of inventories in 1860 was $3,562, compared to $1,927 in 1850.

27. New Orleans *Tribune*, 29 October 1867; deposition of Oscar Dunn, U.S. Congress, House, *Testimony Taken by the Sub-Committee of Elections in Louisiana*, 2 Pts., House Misc. Doc. No.154, 41st Congress, 2d sess., 1870, Pt.1, p.179. The *Tribune* was a newspaper edited by former free persons of colour. Oscar Dunn, born a free Negro in New Orleans in 1826, was lieutenant governor of Louisiana in 1869. Both sources are cited in Rankin, 'Forgotten People', pp.111–13. The figure of $15 million is mentioned in Robert Reinders, *End of an Era: New Orleans, 1850–1860* (Gretna, La., 1989 [1964]), p.23.

28. Richard Tansey, 'Out-of-state Free Blacks in Late Antebellum New Orleans', *Louisiana History*, Vol.22, No.4 (1981), pp.384–5.

29. Schweninger, *Black Property Owners*, p.114; Curry, *Free Black in Urban America*, pp.39, 267–71. Curry found 650 free black owners of real estate with a total value of $2,354,640 in the 1850 census of New Orleans. According to Schweninger, the 1850 census lists '311 prosperous businesspeople and landholders [who] owned $2,188,000 in realty; a decade later, 263 owned $2,317,300'. The difference in the number of property holders and value of real estate in 1850 could be due to Schweninger's limitation of his search to blacks owning at least $100 worth of property.

30. In my sample of 487 tax bills from 1860, 10 free persons of colour were assessed on $17,700 in real estate. Among all 18,612 tax bills, this is equivalent 382 free persons of colour taxed on $676,452. In a separate sample of 391 households in the 1860 census, containing 2,416 persons, 11 free persons of colour owning $27,100 in real estate were found. That is equivalent, among 168,675 persons enumerated in Orleans parish in 1860 (the part of New Orleans located in Jefferson parish is not included in the sample), to 683 owners of real estate worth $1,683,023. The samples were drawn from records of the New Orleans Comptroller's Office, Tax Ledgers for 1860, CC419, City Archives, and from the microfilm of the Eighth Census of the United States, 1860, free schedules for Orleans Parish and the City of New Orleans (National Archives Microcopies, M653, rolls 415–422).

31. 'Recapitulation of the Assessment of the Twelve Districts of New Orleans, for the Year 1860', in the *Comptroller's Report, Embracing a Detailed Statement of the Receipts and Expenditures of the City of New Orleans, from 1 July 1860 to 1 January 1861* (New Orleans,

1861), copy located in City Archives. The higher aggregate value of real estate in assessment rolls than in the census is due to taxation of corporate wealth, while the census reports only property belonging to individuals.

32. Strictly speaking, since the statistics from tax and census records are for Orleans parish, the point of comparison should be the 7 per cent of residents of that parish who were free persons of colour; but I cite the figure of 6.7 per cent to be consistent with population figures used elsewhere in my essay, which include parts of New Orleans in Jefferson as well as in Orleans parish.

33. David Rankin, 'The Impact of the Civil War on the Free Coloured Community of New Orleans', *Perspectives in American History*, Vol.11 (1977–78), p.396; 'Forgotten People', p.111.

34. *Statistics of the United States (Including Mortality, Property, &c,) in 1860, compiled from the original returns and being the final exhibit of the Eighth Census, under the Direction of the Secretary of the Interior* (Washington, 1866), p.303.

35. In marriage contracts from 1804 to 1819, the average age at first marriage was 32 for white males and 21 for white females, 28 for free men of colour and 25 for free women of colour. See Paul Lachance, 'L'effet du désquilibre des sexes sur le comportement matrimonial: comparaison entre la Nouvelle-France, Saint-Domingue et la Nouvelle-Orléans', *Revue d'histoire de l'Amérique française*, Vol.39, No.2 (1985), p.220.

36. Rankin, 'Forgotten People', pp.108–9, Tables 2 and 3. Curry, *Free Black in Urban America*, pp.15–36, and Appendix B, pp.258–66, also analyses data on occupations of free persons of colour in the 1850 census. Contrary to the impression created by Curry's grouping of artisans, entrepreneurs, and professionals into one block of 'high occupational achievement and economic opportunity', Rankin's breakdown shows that, in New Orleans, the vast majority of free men of colour in this category were skilled labourers.

37. Thomas H. Whitney (comp.), *New Orleans Directory, and Louisiana and Mississippi Almanac for the Year 1811* (New Orleans, 1810); John Adems Paxton (comp.), *The New Orleans Directory and Register* (New Orleans, 1822).

38. See my discussion of the ethnicity and average wealth of spouses in different occupational sectors in 'The Foreign French', in Arnold Hirsch and Joseph Logsdon (eds.), *Creole New Orleans: Race and Americanization* (Baton Rouge, 1992), pp.123–5.

39. For whites, the percentage of males in the adult population and the percentage of inventories for males were, respectively, 71 and 85 per cent in 1820, 68 and 83 per cent in 1830, 67 and 80 per cent in 1840, 64 and 78 per cent in 1850, and 55 and 73 per cent in 1860. Among free persons of colour, females were 69 per cent of the adult population and represented 82 per cent of the inventories in 1820. The respective figures are 69 and 64 per cent in 1830, 60 and 69 per cent in 1840, then 66 and 58 per cent in 1850, and 63 and 58 per cent in 1860. See Table 6 in my article, 'The Formation of a Three-Caste Society: Evidence from Wills in Antebellum New Orleans', *Social Science History*, Vol.18, No.2 (1994), p.224, for the census data from which the percentages of the domninant sex in each racial group were calculated and the sex ratios (males per 100 females) to which they correspond. This article provides evidence of a sharp decline in the frequency of interracial unions in New Orleans between 1810 and 1860.

40. Inventory of Marie Charlotte Dussuau, 12 May 1820, drawn up by the notary Michel de Armas, in the City Archives as well as in the minutes of Armas for 1820.

41. The difference that accumulation of wealth over a lifetime made in the proportion of property owners attaining higher levels of wealth is evident from a comparison of inventories and marriage contracts at different levels of wealth. While less than 1 per cent of white grooms and brides had assets greater than $100,000, 4 to 5 per cent of white inventories exceeded this amount.

42. Inventories of Charlotte Leclair alias Gentilly, 17 May 1820; Iphigénie Carries, 27 Oct. 1840; Michaella Charlot alias Arnoult, 23 Sept. 1840; Rose Noisette, 30 Sept. 1858; and Madelaine Clémence Oger, 16 Nov. 1859. Copies located in City Archives. See Rankin, 'Forgotten People', pp.121–3, for descriptions of homes, clothing and furniture of affluent free persons

of colour, and the following pages for a style of life and types of cultural expression that presuppose material well-being.

43. Inventory of Jean-Baptiste Ambroise, 15 Jan. 1836, in City Archives.

44. Inventory of Fanchonette Robert, 6 July 1859, succession No.15,684, in City Archives. Among inventories in census years used for statistical analysis in this article, the richest was that of Iphigénie Carries, 27 Oct. 1840, whose assets totalled $15,886. The sum of her assets by the notary Boudousquié, $15,568.56, does not include items worth $318 mentioned in a memorandum.

45. From one census year to the next, coefficients of variation for average inventoried wealth of free persons of colour ranged from 0.77 to 1.39; for whites, they ranged from 2.29 to 6.68. From one cluster of years to the next, they ranged from 0.75 to 1.41 for average declarations in marriage contracts of free persons of colour, and from 1.65 to 2.23 for those of whites.

Acquisition and Loss on a Spanish Frontier: The Free Black Homesteaders of Florida, 1784–1821

JANE G. LANDERS

Poised between the North American and Caribbean worlds, Spanish Florida was buffeted by the revolutions of the late eighteenth century, as well as by annexation plots, invasions and Indian wars in the early nineteenth century. The dangers of the age created hardships for many, but also, on occasion, avenues for upward mobility, which in a more stable time might not have been available. This essay examines how free blacks in Spanish Florida acquired, exploited and retained or lost land and other property despite great political and economic challenges on a volatile frontier.

Many of the black citizens of Florida had once been considered property themselves and in the English areas from which they fled had few opportunities to hold property. But Spanish law (which was grounded in Roman law) guaranteed slaves the right to a *peculium*, or personal property, and custom supported that right.[1]

Sevillian notarial registers of the fifteenth and sixteenth centuries record enslaved blacks lending money to their freed counterparts.[2] And despite the generally depressed economic and social position of free blacks in early modern Spain, the same registers show at least some black property owners renting houses to other free blacks, as well as to Europeans.[3] Because Spain transferred its legal institutions and socio-economic customs, first to the Atlantic Islands and then across the Atlantic to the Americas, free persons of African descent also became propertied in the 'New World'.

In theory, all land in the Americas belonged to Castile and its monarch might grant usufruct of it to faithful vassals or corporate groups as suited. Spanish political, religious, and social values all promoted the creation of ordered and well-governed communities which would redound to the prestige of the state. Spain granted land to its vassals in proportion to their perceived social standing, making sure that even the least noteworthy received sufficient arable land to sustain his family and animals. Moreover, persons of other ethnic and racial backgrounds might, under specified conditions, become Spanish vassals and once incorporated into the Spanish community, would have the same property rights as free Spaniards.[4]

Believing that 'to govern is to populate' and drawing on medieval Reconquest patterns, Spain followed a policy of *repoblación*. Lands vacated by war, conquest or epidemic created a dangerous vacuum into which enemies might filter. The Crown, therefore, filled these *tierras baldías* with loyal settlers who, in gratitude, were to defend royal interest as indeed their own. In addition to land grants, incentives for relocation included municipal *fueros* (charters specifying exemptions and privileges), royal subsidies and tax relief.[5]

With these understandings of property and frontier expansion, Spanish citizens had settled Florida since 1565, concentrating themselves near the walled city of St. Augustine, but eventually establishing large cattle and wheat ranches in the rich lands of the Apalachee Indians near present-day Tallahassee and in the north central savannahs near present-day Gainesville. These seventeenth-century Florida estates were owned by important families connected to the royal government, and while free blacks worked on them as overseers and ranch-hands, it is doubtful that in the seventeenth century any persons of African descent acquired substantial rural property.[6] One exception might be Diego de Espinosa, described in various documents as mulatto, who built a sizeable cattle ranch complete with fortified house in the Diego Plains, twenty miles north of St. Augustine, and whose economic success may have been made possible by a white father.[7] However, in general, the free population of African descent was small in Spanish Florida's early years and had less leverage, and property, than it later would.

Notarial records for the so-called first Spanish period (1565–1763) are scattered and fragmentary, so it is impossible to determine whether property patterns visible in the eighteenth century had earlier origins. Occasional references to free black property ownership in St. Augustine surface from other types of documents. The free black, Isabel de los Rios, sold sweets and baked goods from her St. Augustine home and the free black militia member, Captain Chrispin de Tapia, operated a grocery store/tavern in his home.[8] It seems probable that free blacks concentrated in, or near, the city of St. Augustine, where employment and community life were possible, rather than disperse themselves in a dangerous frontier. Indian and pirate attacks threatened even the large spreads with resident work forces to protect them, and smaller family farmsteads would have been all the more vulnerable.[9]

In 1670 the frontier was made even more dangerous when the English established Charles Town in Carolina, 'only ten days journey from St.

Augustine'. This challenge to Spanish hegemony triggered almost a century of Anglo/Spanish imperial conflict over what is today the south-eastern United States. Throughout the end of the seventeenth century and the early eighteenth century, Spain struggled to hold her claimed possessions, but after repeated English and Indian attacks which devastated many Indian nations as well as the Spanish mission system and most productive enterprises in Florida, Spain's grip was severely weakened.[10]

The geopolitical turmoil also had important demographic repercussions. Not only were most of the south-eastern Indian nations destabilized or forced to migrate from traditional homelands, but groups of runaway slaves from Carolina and later, Georgia, began appearing in St. Augustine, where they claimed to be seeking conversion into the 'True Faith'. Florida's governors emphasized their religious duty, but clearly recognized that by accepting and sheltering the fugitives they were weakening the English plantation economies to the north. In 1693 the Crown granted freedom to all the runaways, 'the men as well as the women…so that by their example and by my liberality others will do the same'.[11] And others did in sufficient numbers that they eventually composed a sizeable community.

After a period of indecision over their status and what to do with the African refugees, a newly-installed governor, Manuel de Montiano, decided that all fugitive slaves of the English were not only free, but should be settled on lands of their own. In 1738 the governor granted the black refugees homesteading lands two miles north of St. Augustine on which they created a village called Gracia Real de Santa Teresa de Mose.[12] The grateful freedmen and women submitted a memorial to the King in which they vowed to be 'the most cruel enemies of the English', and to 'shed their last drop of blood in defense of the Great crown of Spain and the Holy Faith'.[13] The black homesteaders understood full well that Mose served as a military buffer against the English, but they had the strongest interest of all in repelling Spain's enemy.

This is the first reference to free blacks living autonomously outside the urban context of St. Augustine, but in creating Mose, the governor drew on an approved model – the mission village or *reducción*. This Caribbean institution was approved by Queen Isabela on the grounds that congregating the Indians into villages nearby Spanish settlements would facilitate the religious instruction of the residents, while making sure that they provided required labor or tribute. Refugee Indian villages already encircled St. Augustine following the British raids of 1700–4, and Spanish governors treated Mose as another of those villages, supplying the black village with the same subsidies and goods, and with some of the same Franciscan priests.[14]

Among the approximately 100 free men, women and children living at

Mose were skilled carpenters, masons and agriculturalists. Together they cleared the land, planted new fields and erected homes, a church and a fort. Governor Montiano commended the industry of the settlers and the progress he witnessed at Mose. It is clear the black settlers had fulfilled all the Spanish expectations of living a 'vida política', that is an orderly and community-focused life.[15] However, Mose's progress was short-lived for in 1740 General James Oglethorpe led a combined land and sea attack on St. Augustine which overran Mose, forcing the ruined black homesteaders to withdraw to the safety of St. Augustine.[16]

In 1752 many of the original settlers and some new African runaways who had since claimed sanctuary in St. Augustine re-established Mose. Once again, the Mose settlers built homes, a fort, a church and guardhouses, and planted their fields, but continued Indian and British raids through the 1740s and 1750s made life difficult on the frontier. Some blacks associated with the first Mose settlement or, allied to the Mose group through marriage, chose to remain behind in their town houses, although little is known of their property holdings since notarial records are missing.[17]

Spain finally lost Florida to the English challengers in 1763 by the provisions of the Treaty of Paris which ended the Seven Years War. This turn of events led to a mass evacuation of Europeans and allied Indians and Africans from Florida. Over 3,000 individuals joined in an exodus to Cuba and Campeche. Although the emigrants lost their property holdings when Spain evacuated the province, the Crown granted those who wanted them, including the free black homesteaders of Mose, replacement lands and subsidies in Matanzas, Cuba. Mose's founders struggled for years to break in new homesteads at San Agustín de la Nueva Florida (popularly called Ceiba Mocha), but inadequate water and infrastructure caused many to abandon their lands and migrate back to Havana.[18]

While black Floridians struggled on the Matanzas frontier, Great Britain worked to develop Florida along the lines of successful Anglo/Caribbean and Southern plantations. The British governors of Florida issued generous land grants to encourage white settlement and British homesteaders established flourishing new rice and indigo plantations in the colony with the help of vast numbers of slaves, many of them imported directly from Africa.[19] Soon blacks outnumbered whites in the colony, and after Loyalists from South Carolina and Georgia transplanted their operations and work forces to Florida, the black/white ratio was approximately three to one.[20]

The British plantation model severely curtailed freedom for blacks in Florida, eventually requiring them to wear silver armbands engraved 'free'. Some free blacks supported themselves selling produce, fish, game and crafts in the public market, or by their skills as ironsmiths, butchers and masons, and a few industrious free blacks like Jacob Stewart managed to acquire homes in St. Augustine. But more free blacks found their opportunity in armed service for the British – on land and sea. This meant that most free blacks could not set down roots and develop their own homesteads as they did later under Spanish administration of the colony. [21]

After a British interregnum of twenty years, the Treaty of Versailles retroceded Florida to Spain in 1784. English settlers who chose to remain in Florida could do so and keep their property if they swore loyalty oaths to Spain and many took this option rather than abandon holdings they had worked hard to develop. Some Floridanos – persons born in Florida under the first Spanish regime – returned from Cuba to reclaim their original homesteads.[22] If that proved impossible, the Spanish government granted the returnees other properties of comparable value. But after twenty years many former Floridians preferred to stay in Cuba and Spanish administrators complained frequently about problems of under population in the vast province, which by 1784 was bordered by the fledgling United States of America. Spain's frontier commander called this neighbour 'a nation, as ambitious, as it is industrious'.[23]

Spain worried about its own weakness in the face of such ambition and also about the failure of the United States to control its citizens on the turbulent southern frontier. For several years after the cession, assorted 'banditti' stole cattle, slaves, and other moveable property from planters and farmers thinly spread south of the St. Mary's River. In an effort to stabilize the province Florida's new governor, Vicente Manuel de Zéspedes, offered amnesty to those who would desist and deported those who would not, but opined that 'the best fortification would be a living wall of industrious citizens'.[24]

Spain tried to increase Catholic immigration into Florida by offering tax exemptions and royal subsidies to critical industries, and by approving the unlimited introduction of slaves. Despite these encouragements, uncertainty about land tenure frustrated Spanish efforts to maintain a stable population in Florida. The governors warned repeatedly that the Crown would have to clarify the land titles of non-Spaniards so that those living in the province would not depart, and so that new settlers might be attracted.[25]

Spain's failures to repopulate the frontier created an opportunity for an unexpected group of new immigrants. They were fugitive slaves of the Loyalists who during the chaos of the American Revolution and the subsequent retrocession of Florida to the Spanish government, escaped from bondage and fled to St. Augustine to claim religious sanctuary. Governor Zéspedes doubted the religious motivation of the supplicants but the seventeenth-century sanctuary decree was still in effect and the governor was required to honour it. However, he also attempted to stabilize and account for the refugee population by ordering that all Negroes and mulattoes without a known owner, or papers attesting to their free status, present themselves, clarify their status and obtain a work permit, or be apprehended as slaves of the Spanish King.[26]

More than 250 petitioners presented themselves to be registered and they came to form the nucleus of the free black community in 'second-period' Spanish Florida (1784–1821). This group included skilled carpenters and masons, hostlers, hunters and fishermen, sailors and soldiers, ranch foremen, butchers, shoemakers and tanners, and field hands. Many of the newcomers quickly found employment in town. Others became paid labourers on the plantations and farms of Anglo, Spanish and Minorcan homesteaders. Those who hired them were responsible for the good behaviour of their black employees and were required to notify authorities of any problems. But their work contracts specified that all the men were free, as were their wives and children.[27]

Within a few years the freedmen and women had begun to work the Spanish system. They usually had their children baptized quickly, and as soon as they had learned the required doctrines, they too were baptized, taking the Spanish names of their godparents. Some couples had their consensual unions validated in religious ceremonies. The men began to enlist in volunteer militia units and hire on to do public works for the government – cutting lumber, building bridges and repairing fortifications. Some participated in building the new Cathedral, donating everything from chickens to timber to cash. They learned the legal system and went to court to advance their positions or petition for redress of grievances.[28]

When, in 1790, Spain finally adopted a revised land policy (based on the British 'headrights' system), free blacks quickly tested their rights. According to the new policy, foreigners who wished to move to Florida were required to swear allegiance to the Spanish Crown but previous requirements to convert to Catholicism were dropped. Each incoming head of household would receive one hundred acres for himself and fifty for every person attached to his household, of whatever race. The *nuevo poblador*, or new homesteader, had ten years in which to hold and develop the land after which time he received full title.[29] Within a few months after the new policy was announced approximately 300 Anglo immigrants crossed Florida's northern border to take up these grants, bringing with them about 1,000 slaves.[30]

As soon as they could, free blacks also petitioned for land as new settlers. In general, the need to hold the frontier and make it productive overrode any racial qualms the governors may have had, and all legitimate land requests were approved unless the land in question were already occupied. Petitioners carefully described the land they wanted and the governor would request a recommendation from the royal engineer. The engineer would often comment on the industry of the applicant and the benefits to the plaza of having the land settled, whereupon, the governor would grant the request. If problems later arose and the land became unproductive or uninhabitable due to danger from Indian attacks, for example, the owners appeared to request exchanges for new land, and these too, would usually be granted.[31]

Prince Witten, his wife, Judy, and their children, Polly and Glasgow, are examples of how talented and determined free blacks might rise within the Spanish system. After several failed attempts, in 1786 the family escaped from slavery in Georgia and requested sanctuary in St. Augustine.[32] Witten was a skilled carpenter and Judy was a laundress and both quickly found employment in the city. As they earned a free living the Witten family also began to adapt to the social norms of St. Augustine. The parents and children were baptized and the renamed Wittens, Juan Bautista and María Rafaela, were married in the Cathedral after twenty-one years of cohabitation. The elder Wittens became godparents of numerous children in the community over the next years, as did Polly and Glasgow, now María Francisca and Francisco Domingo.[33]

The Wittens also became property holders. A census from 1793 shows the Wittens living in a house in town, with prominent white neighbours on either side.[34] Two years later Witten petitioned the government for land outside the city walls on which to build houses for himself and the other free blacks of the community. He also asked permission to cut timber so as to be self-employed and support his family. The new governor, Juan Nepomuceno de Quesada, agreed to the request but, as fate would have it, a French-inspired invasion from Charleston rocked the province that year and the panicked governor ordered all the northern settlements evacuated and burned to deny them to the enemy.[35] Three years later, Witten's son, Francisco, signed a petition, 'for my father who does not know how to write,' asking for land to cultivate south of the city, which the governor granted.[36]

In 1792 the free English-speaking mulatto, John Moore, petitioned for and received 350 acres near Trout Creek, for himself, his wife and four grown sons, however Governor Enrique White later required that land to pasture cattle herds belonging to Panton Leslie & Co. In place of those lands the governor reclaimed, Moore received an equal amount of acreage on the St. Johns River. He and his family began again and improved their claim by building a home on it, fencing the land, and cultivating fields. The family also raised cattle and seemed to be on an upward trajectory when Indian raids intervened (1800–3). Although Moore and his wife remained on the dangerous frontier to defend their homestead, their grown sons reported for militia service in St. Augustine. After the trouble settled, the sons returned to the farm and the Moore family held the land until after the end of the Spanish regime, when in 1823 Moore sold it for $1,200 to the American, Elihu Woodruff.[37]

In 1796 a new group of black refugees arrived in Spanish Florida, and they too began to work the system and claim rights as 'new homesteaders'. This time they came, not from the English-speaking north, but from the French-speaking Caribbean. After ceding Santo Domingo to France by the Treaty of Basle, Spain evacuated General Jorge Biassou and his 'family' of some 26 followers and their families to Saint Augustine. Although the presence of this band of seasoned black soldiers who had waged unrelenting war for the previous six years disturbed many of St. Augustine's citizens (and even more so the Anglo planters to the north) before long, the new immigrants were applying for and receiving homesteading lands. Although he lived in town, Biassou was soon clearing a plantation north of St. Augustine, lending the place its name of Bayou Mulatto. When he applied for land, the black Caudillo indicated that many of his countrymen would soon be establishing themselves nearby.[38]

Almost all free blacks who applied for land received it. Among them were the free mulatto, Stephen Cheves, who received 200 acres, the free negroes, Jerry Travers and Felipe Edimboro who each received 100 acres, Antonio Williams and Abraham Hannean, who received 50 acres, and Scipio, who received 25 acres. Free women of colour could petition under the same formula and among those who did were Flora Leslie, who received 500 acres and Isabella Wiggins, who received 300 acres.[39]

Another route to land ownership for free blacks was through membership in militias. As representatives of the Crown, governors could grant lands for meritorious service to the state, which included military service. By the early nineteenth century Spain was fighting invasions at home and revolutionary movements throughout the empire and could devote very few resources of any kind to Florida. Unfortunately, Florida was also under siege much of that time. In addition to the Genet-inspired invasion (1794–95), it suffered through repeated Indian attacks during the State of Muskogee's war against Spain (1800–3), another invasion during the so-called Patriot Rebellion (1812), in which the United States government supported Georgians attempting to take the province, and repeated violations of Spanish sovereignty by the United States, such as the US Navy's attack on the Negro Fort on the Apalachicola River (1816) and General Andrew Jackson's raids on the black and Seminole villages along the Suwannee River (1818). In its final years, Spanish Florida also suffered the seizure of Amelia Island by revolutionaries, pirates, and lastly, the US Navy. Given Spain's inability to protect Florida, desperate governors had to make do with the resources at hand, and their necessity created leverage for free blacks who saw service in all those crises.[40]

Free blacks had been organizing themselves into militia units under their own leaders in Florida since the seventeenth century, just as they had in other circum-Caribbean locales. Spanish governors paid the men for their service and the empire-wide military reforms of 1759 also entitled blacks to the military *fuero*, or exemption from civil prosecution and taxes. On orders from the governors and from white commanders of the frontier, black Floridians served as scouts, pilots, sailors, messengers, foot soldiers and cavalrymen. They manned the frontier and river posts outside the city as well as the batteries and lines of Florida's main fort, the Castillo de San Marcos. In the eighteenth and nineteenth century governors also posted black units among the Seminoles to encourage their continued loyalty to Spain. In their military correspondence Florida's governors commented frequently on the 'excellent' contributions of the black militia.[41]

The men had compelling reasons to serve. Most importantly, their interests lay with Spain, the nation that had freed them. They knew full well what would come of a United States take-over. Moreover, their service underscored their loyalty and citizenship and won them pay, titles, recognition and the gratitude of the beleaguered Spanish community. During the so-called Patriot Rebellion on 1812 Sergeant Prince Witten led a black and Indian unit in an attack on the United State Marines who were supporting the Patriot siege of St. Augustine and liberated vitally needed food supplies for the starving Spanish citizens.[42] Spain declared that it was 'well satisfied with the noble and loyal spirit which animates all the individuals of this company' and promised that 'each one's merit shall be magnanimously attended to and compensated with all the advantages the state can assign, and the national supreme government can support for their good services to the country'.[43] Despite the rhetoric, actual cash rewards were minimal, however such guerrilla operations provided free blacks the opportunity to enrich themselves at the expense of the enemy. Witten and the other black officers received orders which specified that they could appropriate any guns, powder, and provisions they might need from the rebels' sizeable plantations. In addition, horses, cattle, equipment, supplies, clothing and household goods went to the takers and these spoils of war no doubt were put to good use by the militiamen.[44] More importantly, as a result of their important service in 1812, a royal order of 1815 made black militiamen eligible for service-related land grants and many acquired land for the first time or added to their existing holdings.[45]

Florida's military dependence upon free blacks presented the militiamen with opportunities, but the ever-present danger also took its toll on black families and farmsteads. As we have seen, some black homesteaders lost their original homesteads during the invasion of 1794–5. During the Indian raids of 1800–3 others were forced to flee for their lives to the shelter of the city, and a decade later the Patriot Rebellion drove others from their land. On these occasions the black homesteaders reported their losses to Spanish authorities, who made an attempt to relocate them to new properties.

Some years after the fact, blacks also made claims against the United States government, which reviewed and paid for part of the damages for which it was liable as a result of its sponsorship of the Patriot Rebellion. At least 26 free blacks pressed claims against the United States. Their claims ranged from a high of $3,062 for well-connected free blacks such as Abraham McQueen, to a low of $320, for 'Segui, a free black' (without a surname, and presumably connections). The average claim was for approximately $2,000. The claims describe the black homesteads and the value of the losses sustained and also indicate how the free property holders worked their lands.[46]

The carpenter Lewis Sánchez and his wife, Diana, had a 'plantation' four miles from town on which they planted eight to ten acres of corn, as well as peas, potatoes, peanuts, pumpkins and melons in fenced fields. They owned a herd of 60 cattle, 26 hogs, 6 work horses, and a large number of poultry, housed in 4 chicken houses. Sánchez had built two log dwelling houses, corn cribs, poultry coops and a cookhouse on the land. He owned considerable farm equipment and carpentry tools, and the plantation was said to be 'in a flourishing state' when the family was forced to abandon it. Witnesses attested that Sánchez was an 'honest and hard-working man' and a 'good farmer' and supported his claims to losses worth $2,625.75.[47]

The Patriots also struck the homestead of Benjamin Wiggins, the mulatto son of Job Wiggins, and of the free Senegalese, Nancy Wiggins. Wiggins supported his family by raising cattle on a land grant west of St. Augustine. He was also a pilot for the black militia and served repeatedly in the many disturbances which shook Florida. Wiggins and his wife, Nicolasa, and their three children owned land adjacent to his father-in-law, Felipe Edimboro, and the families worked their holdings co-operatively. Wiggins owned a herd of 38 cattle, 2 yokes of oxen, 3 horses and poultry, and had planted crops of corn, potatoes, peas and pumpkins. Once again witnesses testified to support Wiggins' compensation claims for $1,196.50 stating that 'the circumstances of the claimant were very good for a person of colour before the rebellion', but that the family was 'entirely reduced' immediately afterward. They reported that Wiggins was a man 'who always had money…but kept it private' and that 'he must have expended it for the support of his family during the siege…for he was actually very poor directly afterwards'. Despite his losses, Wiggins's industry sustained the family in town. In addition to the pay he received as a pilot, he earned money fishing and oystering and Nicolasa added to their income by unspecified work. Witnesses also remarked that Wiggins had inherited some income from his (white) father's estate and 'is again getting up in the world'.[48]

Wiggins's claims point to another means by which free blacks acquired property. He and others in St. Augustine commonly inherited from their white fathers, who may not have married their mothers but who recognized their children at baptism and provided for the mothers and their children in their wills. José Sánchez, the natural son of the wealthy cattle rancher, Francisco Xavier Sánchez, married Lucía Ysnardy, the natural daughter of the royal accountant, Miguel Ysnardy. Both received inheritances from their fathers, including houses, land and slaves of considerable value. Sánchez also provided well for his natural daughters, leaving them houses and slaves.[49]

Finally, free blacks, like any other *vecino*, or citizen, could buy property, had they the resources. Juan Bautista Collins, a free mulatto from New Orleans had entered Florida in 1770 during the British occupation. In 1792 he petitioned for and received a new settlers' headright grant of 300 acres for himself, his mother and daughter, and two slaves. He may have entered Florida with some inherited money, but once there, he also engaged in a successful commercial career. He bought and traded items ranging from butter to cattle and horses to slaves in locations as diverse as Charleston, Havana, New Orleans, Pensacola and the Indian nations in the interior. He won the government meat contract and spent months among the Seminoles buying cattle to be taken to St. Augustine and Pensacola. By 1793 he had bought a town home in St. Augustine for himself, his mother, and daughter.[50]

After 1808 some free blacks moved from St. Augustine to the new and fast-growing town of Fernandina, on Amelia Island. Lying just south of the United States border and blessed with a good harbour, Fernandina boomed as a result of the US Embargo Act of 1807 and the Congressional cessation of the African slave trade in 1808. The same year Fernandina became a free port and soon was attracting smugglers and slave traders from every Atlantic port and many Caribbean ones. The haphazard growth of Fernandina disturbed Governor White who appointed a surveyor general, Don Jorge J.F. Clarke, to design an urban renewal plan which would bring Fernandina into line with the Spanish urban model. To encourage the beautification programme, all those who already held land and had built homes were guaranteed reimbursement for any moves or required changes to their homes, as well as title to their lots. By 1813 41 free blacks owned property in Fernandina and had constructed homes and businesses, some of considerable substance.[51] Don Jorge Clarke and his brother, Carlos, both had black consorts and many natural children whom they recognized, educated and named in their wills. The Clarkes moved their extended families to Fernandina in 1808 and seem to have functioned as patrons, sponsors, and supporters of many other free black Floridians. Some of the free blacks badly needed assistance after the brief Patriot Rebellion spread its destruction to Fernandina.[52]

The American and French revolutions had created havoc in Spanish Florida, but they had also made it possible for former slaves of the Southern colonies and of Spanish Santo Domingo to claim sanctuary and freedom in Florida.[53] Subsequent disturbances only hurt the free blacks of Florida, repeatedly undermining their hard-won prosperity, and the last years of Spanish tenure in Florida were especially hard.

Only five years after the Patriot Rebellion fizzled, and as black families were beginning to recuperate from the losses of that fiasco, Gregor MacGregor, a veteran of the Napoleonic wars and of the South American revolutions, seized Fernandina, with the stated intent of freeing all of Florida from monarchy. His 'Republic of the Floridas' failed to gain official United States support and within months he was gone. After MacGregor came a French corsair, Luis Aury, who also claimed to be advancing the causes of liberty and republicanism. With the aid of over 100 black Haitians, Aury claimed Fernandina for the 'Republic of Mexico' and also set up a government. Like the Spaniards, Aury planned to use land to reward loyalty, promising a private who would serve the republican cause for six months 320 acres of Florida land; those with longer service or higher rank would earn even more generous bounties. Since many of his own forces included freed blacks, this offer might have actually added to black property holdings, but Aury never had a chance to deliver on his promises. The fear of lost customs' profit and potential slave flight from the southern states inspired another US intervention. A naval squadron soon arrived to clear out the 'pirate's den', and take Fernandina.[54] Throughout the political turmoil black Floridians, many of whom were members of the Fernandina militia, fought bravely to defend their Fernandina homes.[55]

Although free blacks and Spaniards struggled to the best of their abilities to stave off the inevitable, in 1819 Spain conceded Florida to the United States. Once more Spain arranged a general exodus to Cuba and on 22 August 1821 a total of 145 free blacks, including 40 men, 27 women and 78 children, boarded ships leaving St. Augustine. Like their earlier counterparts they were resettled in Cuba at government expense and there began the arduous process of restructuring their lives.[56]

The few free blacks who trusted cession treaties and remained in the new territorial Florida found the white supremacist planters who immigrated into the area unable to tolerate such a challenge to the myth of black inadequacy. Over the next years these immigrants pressured many free blacks into selling what remained of their property at rock-bottom prices and in the years leading up to the United States Civil War, some free blacks joined later exiles going to Cuba and Mexico, where their histories have yet to be traced.[57]

In this brief review we have seen that several factors combined to facilitate the growth of a free black property-holding class in Florida, including law, custom and Spain's geopolitical necessity to hold a frontier under constant threat. Blacks who had once been counted as chattel themselves must have valued more than most the right to be free citizens, to own and dispose of property, and to take arms in defence of their families and homes. Given the opportunity, former slaves worked hard and made good lives for themselves and their families on Florida land and as some of the case studies above illustrate, many prospered until factors beyond their control ruined their efforts. As long as it could, and for its own purposes, the Spanish Crown continued to reward loyal black citizens with land grants and subsidies, and with that commitment in place black Floridians repeatedly rebuilt their lives, demonstrating not only great ambition but a fierce determination to succeed against the odds.

NOTES

1. William D. Phillips, Jr. *Slavery From Roman Times to the Early Transatlantic Trade* (Minneapolis, 1985), pp.28, 50.
2. José Luis Cortes López, *Los origines de la esclavitud negra en España* (Madrid, 1986), pp.141–2.
3. Alfonso Franco Silva, *Regesto documental sobre la esclavitud Sevillana (1453–1513)* (Seville, 1979). Early examples of propertied blacks include Ana Fernández, who rented a house to Catalina Gutiérrez, race unknown, in 1498, and the free black, Leonor Rodríguez, who rented a house to the free black, Juan García, in 1501. Two years later García rented a house on the corridor of the Lonja (the present-day Archive of the Indies) to the Genoese, Silvestre Vento. Ruth Pike contends that the surplus of unskilled labour and discriminatory guild regulations, combined with depressed economic conditions in Seville, drove many freed persons to the Americas. *Aristocrats and Traders: Sevillian Society in the Sixteenth Century* (Ithaca, 1972), p.189.
4. Lyle N. McAlister, *Spain and Portugal in the New World, 1492–1700* (Minneapolis, 1984), pp.3–8, 32, 133–52. Even conquered people might be acceptable settlers, provided that they swear allegiance to the Crown and pay tribute.
5. During the Reconquest of Spain from the Muslims (700–1492) the Crown resettled Spaniards into the newly-won areas. In the Americas, the Crown often relocated loyal Indian allies, like the Tlaxcalans, to threatened areas it wished to hold, and after the Indian population was diminished, the Crown also transported Galician and Canary Island populations across the Atlantic to fill critical voids. Numerous examples of homesteading and repopulation plans can be found documented in Ministerio de Cultura, *Documentación Indiana en Simancas* (Valladolid, 1990), pp.250–7.
6. Eugene Lyon, *The Enterprise of Spanish Florida: Pedro Menéndez de Avilés and the Spanish Conquest of 1565-1568* (Gainesville, 1974); The mulatto Francisco Galindo, former overseer of the Asile ranch, was freed in old age by Governor Horruitiner. 'Documentation Pertaining to the Asile Farm', extracted from Governor Diego de Rebolledo's residencia of his

predecessors and transcribed by John Hann, on file at the Bureau of Archaeological Research, Tallahassee, FL, p.67. For more on the Spanish development of the region see John. H. Hann, *Apalachee: The Land Between the Rivers* (Gainesville, 1988); Amy Bushnell, 'The Menéndez Marquez Barony at La Chua and the Determinants of Economic Expansion in Seventeenth-Century Florida', *Florida Historical Quarterly*, Vol.56 (1978), pp.407–31.

7. Governor Zúñiga described Espinosa's San Diego homestead as a small ranch or *hato* in recounting South Carolina Governor James Moore's invasion of 1702. Charles W. Arnade, *The Siege of St. Augustine in 1702* (Gainesville, 1959), p.60. Over the years the establishment grew in size and importance, was fortified, and became known as Fort San Diego. John J. TePaske, *The Governorship of Spanish Florida, 1700-1763* (Durham, 1964), pp.135–54.

8. John H. Hann, 'Apalachee Counterfeiters in St. Augustine', *Florida Historical Quarterly*, Vol.62 (1988), pp.54–5.

9. On the burning of St. Augustine by Francis Drake in 1586 and Indian wars and uprisings of the sixteenth and seventeenth century see Amy Bushnell, *The King's Coffer: Proprietors of the Spanish Florida Treasury, 1565-1702* (Gainesville, 1981), pp.4, 12–14. Drakes' raid is described in Contratación 4802, Archivo General de Indias, Seville (hereafter cited as AGI), in the John B. Stetson Collection, P.K. Yonge Library of Florida History, University of Florida, Gainesville (hereafter cited as PKY). The later raid of pirate Robert Searles is described in Francisco de la Guerra y de la Vega to King Charles II, 8 August 1668, 54-5-18, AGI, Connor Collection, Library of Congress, Washington, DC.

10. John E. Worth, *The Struggle for the Georgia Coast: An Eighteenth-Century Spanish Retrospective on Guale and Mocama* (Athens, 1995); Verner W. Crane, *The Southern Frontier, 1670–1732* (New York, 1981); TePaske, *Governorship* (Durham, 1964), pp.108–32.

11. Royal decree, 7 November 1693, AGI 58-1-2/74, John B. Stetson Collection, PKY.

12. Jane Landers, 'Gracia Real de Santa Teresa de Mose: A Free Black Town in Spanish Colonial Florida', *American Historical Review*, Vol.95 (1990), pp.9–30.

13. Fugitive Negroes of the English plantations to the King, 10 June 1738, AGI 58-1-31/62, cited in Irene A. Wright, 'Dispatches of Spanish Officials Bearing on the Free Negro Settlement of Gracia Real de Santa Teresa de Mose, Florida', *Journal of Negro History*, Vol.9 (1924), pp.144–93.

14. Landers, 'Gracia Real', p.16. Refugee Apalachee and Yamassee Indians had once populated Mose, but an epidemic in 1727 killed all but six of them. John H. Hann, 'St. Augustine's Fallout from the Yamassee War', *Florida Historical Quarterly*, Vol.68 (1989), p.193. The strategic location of the site, north of St. Augustine and blocking both land and water access to the city, made it imperative to hold. It is not surprising Governor Montiano assigned those lands to the newly-freed blacks.

15. Landers, 'Gracia Real'. Material on Mose and the fugitives is found in Santo Domingo 844, AGI, fols, 521–46, on microfilm reel 15, PKY. On the Spanish ideal of the 'ciudad perfecta' see Richard Morse, 'A Framework for Latin American Urban History', in Jorge Hardoy (ed.), *Urbanization in Latin America: Approaches and Issues* (Garden City, NJ, 1975), pp.57–107

16. TePaske, *Governorship*, pp.139–46.

17. TePaske, *Governorship*, pp.133–58. One widow of a Mose militiaman described how the family had left behind a St. Augustine home and all meagre belongings except clothing and bedding when forced to evacuate to Havana. Petition of María Gertrudis Rozo, 25 Sept. 1792, Santo Domingo 2577, AGI.

18. Evacuation report of Juan Jorge Elixio de la Puente, 22 Jan. 1764, Santo Domingo 2595, AGI. For more on the evacuation see Robert L. Gold, *Borderland Empires in Transition: The Triple Nation Transfer of Florida* (Carbondale and Edwardsville, 1969) and Jane Landers, 'An Eighteenth-Century Community in Exile: The Floridanos in Cuba', *New West Indian Guide*, Vol.70 (1996).

19. Dan Schafer, '"Yellow Silk Ferret Tied Round Their Wrists": African Americans in British East Florida, 1763-1784', in David Colburn and Jane Landers (eds.), *Race and Society in Florida: The African American Experience from Early Contact to the Present* (Gainesville,

1995), pp.71–103.

20. J. Leitch Wright, Jr. 'Blacks in British East Florida', *Florida Historical Quarterly*, Vol.54 (1970), p.427.

21. J. Leitch Wright, Jr. *Florida in the American Revolution* (Gainesville, 1975), pp.108–9. In his declaration made before evacuating to New Providence, the free black Jacob Steward stated he owned a home in which 'Negro rites in the style of Guinea' were celebrated. Census Returns, 1784–1814, bundle 323A, on microfilm reel 148, East Florida Papers (hereafter cited as EFP), PKY.

22. Susan R. Parker, 'In My Mother's House: Female Property Ownership in Spanish St. Augustine', paper delivered at the Florida Historical Society, St. Augustine, 1992, on file at the St. Augustine Historical Preservation Board.

23. Carlos Howard to Luis de las Casas, 2 July 1791, Cuba 1439, AGI.

24. Decree of Vicente Manuel de Zéspedes, 14 July 1784, in Joseph Byrne Lockey (ed.), *East Florida, 1783–1785: A File of Documents Assembled and Many of Them Translated* (Berkeley, 1949), pp.233–5; James A. Lewis, 'Cracker–Spanish Florida Style', *Florida Historical Quarterly*, Vol.63 (1984), p.202.

25. Ramon Romero-Cabot, 'La defensa de Florida en el segundo período Español' (Thesis, University of Seville, 1982), pp.39–44.

26. Proclamation of Vicente Manuel de Zéspedes, 26 July 1784, in Lockey, *East Florida*, pp.240–1.

27. Census returns, 1784–1811, bundle 323A, EFP, on microfilm reel 148, PKY. Jane Landers, 'Spanish Sanctuary: Fugitives in Florida, 1687–1790', *Florida Historical Quarterly*, Vol.63 (1984), pp.296–313.

28. Jane Landers, 'Black Society in Spanish St. Augustine, 1784–1821' (Ph.D. dissertation, University of Florida, 1988).

29. To demonstrate improvements a settler had to build a house with a suitable chimney, erect fences and maintain a prescribed number of livestock on the land. When tenure and improvements were proved by the sworn testimony of witnesses, the homesteader would receive title. Works Project Administration, *Spanish Land Grants in Florida*, Vol.I (Tallahassee, 1940), pp.xviii–xxiii.

30. Carlos Howard to Luis de las Casas, 2 July 1791, Cuba 1439, AGI.

31. For multiple examples see US Board of Land Commissioners, Miscellaneous Spanish Florida Land Records 1808–1849 (hereafter cited as SFLR), Record Group 000599, Series 992, Florida State Archives, Tallahassee, FL.

32. Census Returns, 1784–1821, EFP, reel 148, PKY. The family may have been in St. Augustine for several years before being required to register.

33. Black Baptisms, Cathedral Parish Records, Diocese of St. Augustine Catholic Center, Jacksonville, Fl (hereafter cited as CPR), Vol.1, pp.41, 118, on microfilm reel 284 J, PKY.

34. Census of 1793, EFP, reel 148, PKY. Witten's neighbours were Don Juan Leslie, head of the Panton Leslie & Co. Indian trading house, and Don John McQueen, of American revolutionary fame, and a major landholder and later, judge, in Spanish Florida.

35. Richard K. Murdoch, *The Georgia–Florida Frontier, 1793–1796: Spanish Reactions to French Intrigue and American Designs* (Berkeley, 1951); Carlos Howard to Luis de las Casas, 4 May 1796, Santo Domingo 2590, AGI.

36. Petition of Juan Bautista Wiet [*sic*], SFLR, Record Group 000599, Series 992, Box 12, Folder 35.

37. *Spanish Land Grants In Florida*, Vol.V., pp.223–4. Governor Enrique White amended the original head rights system, reducing grants to fifty acres for the head of the family, twenty-five for every child or servant over the age of sixteen, and fifteen acres for every child or servant between the ages of eight and sixteen years. Ibid., p.xxii.

38. Petition of Juan [*sic*] Buissou [*sic*], 7 July, 1797, Record Group 599, Series 992, Box 1, FF 32, SFLR. After Biassou's death in 1806, his brother-in-law, and military heir, Juan Jorge Jacobo, laid claim to Biassou's lands. See Jane Landers, 'The French Revolution on Spain's Northern Frontier: Rebellion and Royalism in Spanish Florida', in David Barry Gaspar and David Geggus (eds.), *A Turbulent Time: The Greater Caribbean in the Age of the French and Haitian Revolutions* (Bloomington, forthcoming).

39. 'Land Claims in East Florida', *American State Papers, Public Lands*, Vol.VI, pp.59, 70–1, 88. The complete petitions for land grants and the governmental responses are found in SFLR. Flora Leslie was the consort of St. Augustine's white surveyor, Jorge J.F. Clarke, and Isabella Wiggins was the consort of his brother, Carlos Clarke, which may explain their large awards. Louise Biles Hill, 'George J.F. Clarke, 1774–1836', *Florida Historical Quarterly*, Vol.21 (1943), pp.208–13. Another female property holder of substance was the former Anta Majigeen Ndiaye, enslaved in Senegal, but freed by her owner, Zephaniah Kingsley, within five years. She bore him children and managed his vast Florida estates and later her own estates in Florida and Haiti as well. Anna received some of her property from Kingsley, but other pieces, like her five acre farm near Mandarin and town property in Fernandina, were grants of the Spanish government. Daniel L. Schafer, 'Shade of Freedom: Anna Kingsley in Senegal, Florida and Haiti', in this volume.
40. Landers, 'Black Society'. On the French invasion see Murdoch, *The Georgia–Florida Frontier*. On the Muskogee State's war against Spain, see J. Leitch Wright, *William Augustus Bowles, Director General of the Creek Nation* (Athens, 1967), and on the Patriot Rebellion, see Rembert W. Patrick, *Florida Fiasco:Rampant Rebels on the Georgia–Florida Frontier, 1810–1815* (Athens, 1954). See also James W. Covington, 'The Negro Fort', *Gulf Coast Historical Review*, No.5 (Spring 1980), pp.78–91 and Canter Brown, Jr., 'The "Sarrazota", or Runaway Negro Plantations: Tampa Bay's First Black Community, 1812–1821', *Tampa Bay History*, Vol.12 (1990), pp.5–19.
41. Landers, 'Black Society'.
42. J. H. Alexander, 'The Ambush of Captain John Williams, U.S.M.C.: Failure of the East Florida Invasion', *Florida Historical Quarterly*, Vol.56 (1977), p.286. Patrick, *Florida Fiasco*, pp.179–344.
43. Review Lists for the Free Black Militia of St. Augustine, 1812, Cuba 357, AGI.
44. Orders to Jorge Jacobo, Prince Witten, and Benjamin Segui, 19 July 1812, EFP, reel 68, PKY.
45. *Spanish Land Grants in Florida*, pp.xxiv–xxv. Among those receiving service grants were Antonio Proctor, 185 acres, Pedro Sively, 150 acres, Prince Patton, 300 acres, Aysick Travers, 115 acres, Jerry Travers, 125 acres.
46. Patriot War Papers, St. Augustine Historical Society, MC 31, Folder 96, p.3. At least 26 free black claimants are recorded in this collection.
47. Claim of Susannah Sánchez, 9 September 1834, Patriot War Claims, MC 31, folder 69, St. Augustine Historical Society. When driven from his land Lewis Sánchez joined the black militia and served against the invaders who ruined him.
48. Ibid., MC 31, Folder 75. Felipe Edimboro also claimed damages to his own farm in the amount of $1,624.00. Sánchez Papers, Vault, MS Box, 12, PKY. Edimboro's farm was burned and his cattle, horses, and hogs robbed by the insurgents. On 28 April 1815 he asked for and received new lands. Record Group 990, Box 11, Folder 4, SFLR.
49. Marriage of José Sánchez and Lucía Ysnardy, 2 Feb. 1805, Black Marriages, CPR, vol. 1 on microfilm reel 284 L, PKY; Notarized Instruments, Testament of Miguel Ysnardy, 2 March 1803, EFP, reel 157, PKY. Testamentary Proceedings of F. X. Sánchez, 31 Nov. 1807, EFP. reel 8, PKY. Also see Landers, 'Black Society' and Schafer, 'Shades of Freedom'.
50. Petition of Juan Bautista Collins, 6 Aug. 1791, SFLR, Record Group 599, Series 992, Box 3, Folder 18. Notarized Instruments, Suits and sales by Juan Bautista Collins, 4 Sept. 1787, 22 March 1798, 9 May 1799, 23 June 1800, 8 Jan. 1801, 16 Jan. 1810, EFP, on microfilm reels 166–8, PKY.
51. Census of Fernandina and Amelia Island, 1814, EFP, on microfilm reel 148, PKY.
52. Hill, 'George J.F. Clarke'; SFLR. Clarke surveyed many land grants for free blacks and helped them document and retain these grants when the United States finally took Florida in 1821.
53. In 1796 General Jorge Biassou led a group of former Black Auxiliaries of Carlos IV from Santo Domingo to Florida, where many became propertied. Landers, 'The French Revolution on Spain's Northern Frontier'.
54. David Bushnell (ed.), *La República de las Floridas:Texts and Documents* (Mexico, 1986); Rufus Kay Wyllys, 'The Filibusters of Amelia Island', *Georgia Historical Quarterly*, Vol.23 (1928), p.311.

55. Fernandina Militia List, 12 Aug. 1811, EFP, reel 51, PKY. The black unit of Fernandina was headed by Sergeant Jorge Jacobo, heir to Jorge Biassou's command, and a veteran of the slave revolt of Santo Domingo. Jacobo was also a son-in-law of Prince Witten, with whom he often served. Aury's forces also included over 100 black Haitians, so Jacobo and other Fernandina troops from Santo Domingo may have faced off against some of their erstwhile countrymen.
56. Relation of the Florida Exiles, 22 Aug. 1821, Cuba 357, AGI.
57. Landers, 'Black Society'. Ruth B. Barr and Modeste Hargis, 'The Voluntary Exile of Free Negroes of Pensacola', *Florida Historical Quarterly*, Vol.17 (1938), pp.3–14.

Free Blacks and Coloureds in Plantation Suriname

ROSEMARIJN HOEFTE

Suriname on the South American mainland was a classic Caribbean plantation society. In the 1650s English colonists and Sephardi Jewish refugees from Brazil (arriving in two groups in 1652 and 1666) introduced the cultivation of sugar. When the Dutch took over from the British in 1667 some fifty sugar plantations already operated. Following an initial decrease in the number of estates, Suriname soon developed into a rather prosperous colony producing sugar and later coffee, cacao, and cotton as well. By 1745 there were 154 sugar and 140 coffee plantations. In the second half of the century, Suriname experienced its halcyon years. By 1770, some 400 plantations exported coffee and sugar, while the export value of the tropical products was highest between 1770 and 1789. In the nineteenth century this value dropped sharply: coffee and cotton in particular did badly, while the value of sugar exports was more stable despite the decline in the number of plantations.[1]

Needless to say, slave labour was instrumental in the plantation economy. In 1700 the planters employed some 10,000 slaves on approximately 100 sugar estates. Some ninety years later, in 1788 to be exact, the slaves numbered 50,000 out of a total population of 55,000. In that year there were in Paramaribo, the capital and only town in Suriname, two whites for every seven slaves, but in the rest of the colony the ratio was much more skewed: one white to sixty-five slaves. Many contemporaries expressed deep fear about the vast numerical superiority of the slaves. Although the colony experienced very few outright revolts, one author described Suriname in the 1730s and 1740s as a 'theatre of perpetual war'. The escape hatch of the slaves was the tropical rain forest, covering approximately 90 per cent of Suriname. By 1770 there were already five to six thousand maroons living in the jungle. After almost a century of protracted guerrilla wars the runaways established independent societies in the interior.[2] It was not until 1863 that slavery was finally abolished in the colony.

Given this history of the plantation colony it is not surprising that most attention of historians and social scientists, particularly anthropologists, has been directed towards the plantations and their overwhelming number of slaves[3] and to the fascinating and unique history and culture of the maroons.[4] The number of whites and free coloureds and blacks was so small that their histories have been largely neglected.[5] To be sure, in *Frontier Society*, R.A.J. van Lier's classic social history of Suriname, the 'white masters' and the 'free mulattos and negroes and the position of the manumitted' both get their own chapter, but the chapter on slaves has double the number of pages of the other two combined.[6] There exists no monograph, in any language, on the free population in pre-emancipation Suriname; fortunately there are several fine English-language articles on 'sub themes'. In an important essay based on her dissertation Rosemary Brana-Shute discusses manumission.[7] H. Hoetink compares the conditions of free coloureds and blacks in Suriname and Curaçao; for Suriname Hoetink leans on Van Lier, however.[8] This essay will sketch the social and economic lives of free coloureds and blacks.[9] Slaves in Suriname became free in two important ways: through military service and the judiciary. However, the number of slaves obtaining freedom was small. In addition, the colonial administration established a number of extra regulations to control freed slaves. This suggests that manumitted individuals were regarded as potentially dangerous individuals rather than as a buffer against the slaves. Slaves had to work hard to earn their freedom, and once they had achieved it life did not get much easier. Yet, against all odds, a small group of free coloureds and blacks did economically well. The importance of family networks in obtaining freedom, protection and assistance is unmistakable. In the nineteenth century emancipation and education were closely intertwined and a middle class of free coloureds was formed. Although racial prejudices permeated the colony, making social acceptance of free coloureds difficult, kinship ties continued to be important and overrode virtually all racial and social prejudices.

This overview is certainly not complete. Few eighteenth-century records have survived either in Suriname or the Netherlands and in so far as documents are available they very often cannot be consulted without prior restauration. It seems, however, that the colonial authorities recorded very little about free-born or manumitted blacks and coloureds. This essay presents a general history and shows the changes free coloureds and blacks underwent in the eighteenth and nineteenth centuries by using nineteenth-century colonial records, contemporary secondary sources and recent studies.

COLONIAL SOCIETY IN THE EIGHTEENTH CENTURY

In the eighteenth century Paramaribo developed into a charming town. When the Dutch took over in the late seventeenth century less than thirty houses made up the settlement, but J.D. Herlein, who had visited the colony, reported in 1718, in the first Dutch account, that Paramaribo consisted of some 500 wooden houses.[10] This estimate may have been too high as in the second half of the eighteenth century Governor Jan Nepveu believed there were less than 800 houses, even though the town had expanded substantially.[11]

Population data are generally unreliable, but it seems safe to say that approximately 20 per cent of the colony's population lived in town. In 1787 Paramaribo held 2,650 inhabitants, excluding military men. Two thousand of the town dwellers were white (the majority Germans and Jews) and the other 650 were free blacks and coloureds.[12] Most contemporary authors remark upon the cosmopolitan character of Paramaribo's population, which included Germans, Ashkenazi and Sephardi Jews, Dutch, French and English.[13] The governors did not hold this population in high regard. Much quoted are the words by Governor Jan Jacob Mauricius who wrote that the majority were 'good-for-nothings' and the 'scum of the nations'. Moreover, many had no intention to settle permanently and where there only to get rich as fast as possible.[14] And the colony indeed offered opportunities for social climbing and making a quick fortune. Even so, a strict social hierarchy was enforced in both town and districts. In Paramaribo there were several clubs or societies based on rank or religion. Senior colonial officials, planters and administrators[15] belonged to the highest echelon. Jews had a separate society.

This strict hierarchy was undermined, however, by the very unbalanced sex-ratio. Suriname had large numbers of single men on the plantations and in the army. The scarcity of white women encouraged the development of that typical colonial phenomenon of concubinage or a 'Suriname marriage' with coloured and black women.[16]

Most relationships involved European men and free or slave women of African descent, but there are at least two cases known in Suriname involving free white women and black men, in all likelihood slaves. In 1711 Barend Roelofs petitioned the Court of Policy and Criminal Justice (*Hof van Politie en Crimineele Justitie*) for divorce.[17] He stated 'that his wife, Maria Keijser, having [had] carnal intimacy with a negro and having become pregnant by him, had been delivered of a mulatto girl a few months previous'. During court deliberations the case of Judith de Castre passed in review. She also had a child by a black man but had since married a certain Jean Milton. The Court notified Judith that neither she nor anyone else was 'ever to bring her mulatto child, or have it brought, to Paramaribo, on penalty of arbitrary punishment'.[18] The reality that children were born out of these relationships made it impossible to deny the existence of sexual contact between white women and blacks, or white men and black or coloured women for that matter. In addition, if the few white women in the colony gave birth to coloured children, it would diminish the chances for white reproduction. Not surprisingly, European officials felt it was essential to prevent such relationships forming. Following the deliberations on these two cases, Governor Johan de Goyer promulgated an edict stipulating that a single white woman who had intercourse with a black man was liable to flogging and expulsion from the colony. A married women would also be branded. The men would receive the death penalty.[19] The fact that the Governor made this legal effort suggests that there might have been more liaisons between white women and black men, undermining the existing (colour) hierarchy. In 1730 indeed a slave named Jantje, owned by Jacob Aron Polack, was hanged because he had had carnal relations with Ganna, the white Jewish daughter of Levy Hartogh. Ganna was flogged and banned.[20]

WAYS TO FREEDOM: MILITARY SERVICE

From its very beginning the plantation colony was confronted by the problem of runaway slaves. Over the years the maroon threat only continued to grow and soon these runaways endangered the plantations and the colony as a whole. From the 1670s a citizen's militia mounted organized pursuits to capture maroons and destroy their settlements. In the early eighteenth century larger military expeditions, also employing Amerindians and slaves, were organized. This participation of slaves could lead to their manumission as freedom occasionally was granted to slaves in recognition of meritorious behaviour toward whites. The most celebrated example of such a slave was African-born Quassie, also known as Kwassie, Graman Quacy, Kwasi or in Saramakan Kwasímukámba.[21] From the 1730s to the 1780s he was one of the key players in the prolonged confrontation between colonial administration and runaway slaves.

According to John Stedman, Quassie was 'one of the most Extraordinary Black men in Surinam or Perhaps in the World'.[22] Quassie no doubt was an extraordinary man, yet his role in Suriname history is not undisputed. Stedman notes that Quassie was born on the coast of Guinea around 1690. He must have arrived in Suriname in the first decade of the eighteenth century because in 1712 'he Acted as Drummer & Beat the Alarm on his Masters Estate when the French Commodore Jacques Cassard Put the Colony under Contribution'.[23] In about 1730 Quassie's first claim to fame was recorded: he discovered the medicinal use of a tree in curing tropical fevers. Linnaeus named this tree *Quassia amara* (Quassi-bitter). Quassie became the colony's leading *lukuman* (diviner) and *dresiman* (curare), exercising great influence among all population groups. Stedman observed that 'The corps of Rangers [on these so-called Black Rangers see below] & all fighting free negroes are next under his command, to whom by selling his *healer* [obeahs] or *Amulets* to make them invulnerable, / they under the Power of his Superstition fearing no danger & fighting like bull dogs / he not only has done a Deal of Good to the Colony but fill'd his pockets with no inconsiderable Profits Also, while his Person is Adored & Respected like a God.'[24]

These powers represented only one side of Quassie's authority. In the guerrilla wars against the maroons he served as a scout locating runaway villages, secret agent, negotiator, obeahman and in his final years as an adviser to the newly established Black Rangers. In 1730 the Court of Policy presented Quassie with a gold breastplate bearing the inscription 'Quassie, faithful to the whites'. In 1744 Governor Mauricius bought Quassie to assist in the exploration of minerals, to hunt Indian slaves, and to teach the Governor's youngest son Negro-English, Carib and Arawak. Eleven years later Quassie was manumitted in appreciation of his services to the colony. He continued to conduct peace negotiations as well as expeditions to capture runaways. In addition, he expanded his activities by becoming a planter on the Perica Creek. In 1772 maroons raided his estate and some months later he joined a large expedition for the last time. In 1776 the colonial government bestowed upon him official thanks and in The Hague even the Prince of Orange received Quassie, showing his gratitude by presenting him with a coat of gold lace and a white feathered hat, a gold medal, a gold-headed cane, a silver gilt hanger, and two chests of wine.[25]

Upon his return from Holland, Quassie lived in Paramaribo in a house, served by two slaves, all gifts of the administration. When he passed away in 1787 he was so famous that several contemporaries composed mourning poems.[26] The tone, however, was often satirical, ridiculing his powers. The white population accepted Quassie's services gratefully, but at the same time clearly considered his powers, fame, astuteness and wealth a threat to the existing societal order.

Quassie's activities in the fight against the runaways were obviously appreciated by the whites, but how do the descendants of the runaways view Quassie? Richard Price's research reveals that among the Saramakas 'he is the prototypical symbol of betrayal ... First, he is known as a guide who led the whites on various military expeditions beyond the plantation area ... Next, they believe that he led the whites far upriver in an attempt to make peace ... But most important, they know him as a self-appointed secret agent, a spy who almost brought about a terrible defeat which, thanks to the Saramakas' gods, was transformed into a famous victory.'[27]

Had the granting of freedom to Quassie been arbitrary, in the 1770s the administration regulated the manumission of slaves through military service. To tackle the problem of the maroons and their attacks on plantations Governor Jan Nepveu decided not to wait for the arrival of European troops and in 1772 he bought some 300 male slaves to form the *Korps Zwarte Jagers* (Corps of the Black Rangers) to battle the maroons.[28] In Suriname these soldiers were commonly known as the *Redi Musu* (Red Berets). In return for their services the slaves were promised their freedom and a plot of land to cultivate when off duty. These parcels were located on the edge of Paramaribo and are still known as *Frimangron* (Free Men's Ground). In addition, the Redi Musu were permitted to visit their female companions and children who had stayed behind on the plantations. However, government officials had to issue written notices summoning the owners to indeed allow the soldiers' visits. Creation of this army made the administration the most important manumitter in Suriname, a double irony since the administration attempted to restrict manumission and slaves gained their freedom by chasing other slaves.

WAYS TO FREEDOM: MANUMISSION THROUGH THE COURT

In 1733 Suriname's most powerful institution, the Court of Policy and Criminal Justice, outlawed the private freeing of slaves.[29] The colonial administration sought to regulate the manumission of slaves by requiring owners to petition the Court for its permission. In addition, the petitioner had to guarantee that the slave in question was able to earn his or her own livelihood and educate him or her in Christianity. The administration established a distinction between free-born and freed individuals. Besides the normal benefits and obligations bestowed on free people, the manumitted carried some additional responsibilities. A freed person, as well as his descendants, was to continue 'to honor and respect' his former owner and his family. Moreover, the manumitted had the obligation to support his former patron financially should the latter fall into poverty and to give him a quarter of his property. The freed population was expressly forbidden to marry or cohabit with slaves.[30] Ignoring the latter regulation could lead to the dissolution of freedom. In 1760 and 1761 the Court promulgated the original law anew and emphasized the clause on the economic viability and the code of conduct of freed people and particularly that they not cohabit with slaves or attend slave dances. A new stipulation was that manumitted persons had to respect not only their former owners but all whites.[31] These regulations suggest that the whites not only feared slaves but also feared freed persons might conspire with slaves against the administration and the planters.

The effect of the manumission laws was clearly not as intended: the stricter the law, the more manumissions. In the period 1760–99 the Court freed 655 slaves. However, it should be kept in mind that the relative number of freed slaves was exceedingly small. Even though reliable population data for the eighteenth, and early nineteenth, century are missing, Brana-Shute's samples show that not even one per cent of the slaves was manumitted during any year for which she had specific documentation.[32]

Manumission petitions from the period 1760–1828 provide information regarding the sex, colour, age, residence and kinship of the slave as well as a profile of the owners and their motivations for manumissions. As in other slave societies, the majority of the manumitted slaves (62.5 per cent) was female, even though men formed the majority of the slave population.[33] Most manumitted slaves (54 per cent) were mulattoes, the second largest group (40 per cent) was black. The others were coloured, but not mulattoes. In other words, about 60 per cent of the freed slaves were coloured, while more than 90 per cent of the slave population was black. That coloureds constituted the majority of the manumitted slaves is not surprising. They were born and raised in Suriname and spoke the lingua franca, Sranan Tongo or Negro-English, and maybe a European language as well. In other words, they were more likely to develop a closer relationship with the owner or other free people than African-born slaves who did not yet know the culture, social code and language of plantation society.[34] Yet, as Brana-Shute emphasizes, it was a cluster of factors – including age, skills, residence, attractiveness and kinship – that decided whether a slave would be manumitted.

Brana-Shute stresses the need to reconsider non-economic reasons for manumission. A look at age shows that the owners apparently did not mind the high fees for manumitting slaves in the prime of their lives. Rather surprisingly, scarcely any of the freed individuals were classified as old. Children were the majority of the freed coloured persons. Not even one-fifth of the manumitted slaves came from plantations. Obviously Paramaribo, where many slaves were employed as artisans, semi-skilled labourers, soldiers or domestics, offered the best chances to meet free people, and thus potential patrons, and learn the legal ropes of obtaining manumission. In town men held a distinct advantage over women because their skills were in higher demand. On the other hand, women's roles as domestics, nannies, nurses, mistresses and mothers (of bastard children) provided better chances to obtain the necessary social skills and become familiar with free people.[35]

The characteristics of the manumitters changed dramatically over time: white women and coloured and black individuals, of both sexes, replaced white men.[36] Approximately 60 per cent of the petitioners were male and 40 per cent female and a little less than a quarter of the owners were coloured or black. There were twice as many males (69 per cent) as females among white manumitters; among blacks and coloureds women (63 per cent) formed the clear majority. The petitions reveal little about the social and economic status of the manumitters, but Brana-Shute argues that the stereotype in Suriname historiography of the white plantation owner as the most important manumitter is wrong.[37] Most male manumitters were middle- or lower-class townspeople, such as shopkeepers or artisans. Another interesting development is the increasing role of free blacks and coloureds as guarantors of the financial solvency of the manumitted. Many of these guarantors were clerks, including the revered Comvalius family who often acted as bondsmen and witnesses, and apparently were financially secure enough to undertake this task. To quote Brana-Shute: 'just as owners who manumitted slaves were increasingly colored and black over time, so too were the agents and allies of slaves'.[38]

The reasons mentioned for manumission included loyalty and affection (37 per cent), self-purchase (29 per cent) and kinship (22 per cent).[39] In the latter case, more than 95 per cent of the slaves had consanguinal ties with the owner and in almost 90 per cent of all 'kinship manumissions' the manumitters were black or coloured. Thus uniting families rather than the acknowledgement of paternity formed a major reason for freeing slaves.

In short, most slaves had worked hard to gain their freedom by fighting in the military or serving their masters well and thus obtaining their loyalty or earning and saving enough money for self-purchase. Yet even the most enterprising and tenacious individuals, qualities most manumitted slaves must have possessed, might have found it difficult to make a living in Suriname.

FREE COLOUREDS AND BLACKS IN THE EIGHTEENTH-CENTURY ECONOMY

The overwhelming majority of blacks and coloureds worked as plantation slaves. In the early days of the colony most blacks and coloureds in Paramaribo were concubines or domestic slaves of plantation owners and administrators who took up residence in town.[40] However, the scarce extant papers tell about a few free coloured and black individuals who earned a living as soldiers, landholders, or skilled labourers.[41] J.M. van der Linde mentions that in 1685 Thomas Herman was one of the first free blacks. He held a land title of twenty acres and was counted among 'kleine suikerheren' (small sugar gentlemen).[42] In the eighteenth century more coloured or black planters held estates, for example Quassie, who, as we have seen, owned a plantation along the Perica Creek. Thus free coloureds and blacks were allowed to own land and some of them made use of the opportunities in the colony to improve their economic position and achieve a certain degree of upward mobility, even though they were never accepted by the whites.

The lives of the majority of free blacks in particular were often uncomfortable. If they did not have viable economic opportunities and were not upwardly mobile whites treated them like slaves, as is illustrated by the case of Isabella.[43] Isabella was a free Christian black, but as she told minister Kals – who preached in Suriname between 1731 and 1733 – she found life as a free person unbearable. The whites scorned and mocked her while attending church. They called her a 'black animal' and told her that heaven was not made for blacks as they were the devil's children, created to plant sugar and coffee. Isabella told Kals that the white men wanted her to live with them but not to marry her. She instead opted to 'marry' a black man with whom she had several children. Isabella accepted her reduction to slavery on the condition that she be permitted to attend church again. Isabella almost certainly was no exception; there must have been many more free men and women who preferred to live among and with slaves, often relatives, rather than in the 'free' world.

In contrast to this great mass and the small middle group of small landowners, there was a very tiny elite of prominent and well-to-do free mulattoes, including exceedingly few free blacks, who shared in the general wealth of the colony, lived a sumptuous life and owned several houses as well as several plantations plus slaves. Some of them could afford to sail to the Netherlands. In the period 1729–49 seven free blacks and coloureds travelled to Holland and three returned, while in the period 1749–81 sixty-seven left and twenty-nine returned.[44] Elisabeth Samson was a member of this elite and the most famous free black in eighteenth-century Suriname. She was (in)famous because she was so rich and because she wanted to marry a white person.[45]

Research by Cynthia Mc Leod-Ferrier shows that Elisabeth Samson was born free in 1715. Her mother, Mariana, had by that time been manumitted but was still a slave named Nanoe when she gave birth to Elisabeth's older siblings. Nanoe had two free mulatto children, Charloo and Maria, with a planter from St. Kitts[46] and four slave children of whom the father(s) was/were unknown. Nanoe and her slave children were probably bought free by the eldest (free) child, Charloo, a builder and carpenter who had inherited his mother from his planter father.[47] Elisabeth was born after her mother was manumitted and grew up in the household of her free, mulatto half-sister Maria Jansz, a sister of Charloo, who was married to the white German Frederik Coenraad Bossé, a local merchant. This Bossé guaranteed that his manumitted relatives would be able to support themselves. The Bossés owned plantation Salzhalen and a town house in the most attractive section of Paramaribo. By the time of his death in 1742 Bossé was a member of the Court of Policy.

Elisabeth Samson's youth seems to have been comfortable, but soon her fortune turned. Elisabeth is at age nineteen already listed as a slave owner. Her starting capital was in all likelihood a small legacy by Charloo.[48] When she was still a young woman, she became involved in an interesting legal dispute, even though this controversy has not received as much attention as her later fortune or her marriage.[49] Elisabeth was accused of spreading malicious rumours about Governor Joan Raye, and in April 1737 she was found guilty and banned from the colony.[50] During the trial, the public prosecutor Van Meel had slanderously stated that this free black woman was known 'in the whole world' as a whore.[51] Elisabeth left for Holland and upon arrival immediately asked the States General (Dutch 'Parliament') for a retrial. The case dragged on for another one and a half years but in October 1739 the States General ruled against public prosecutor Van Meel and for Elisabeth. Thereupon Elisabeth returned to Suriname. Obviously she had spirit and money to take her case to the States General, retain a lawyer and await its ruling in a cold, foreign country where she could hardly have known anybody.

Back in Suriname she became the concubine of Carl Otto Creutz.[52] Their cohabitation was notarized in 1751; judging from legal documents both partners were childless.[53] Carl Otto Creutz was born in 1715 in Emmerich, Germany. He arrived in Suriname in 1733 as an eighteen-year-old cadet and soon made a career for himself. On his death in November 1762 he was the senior member of the Court of Policy.

The official inventory made following Creutz's death revealed that he and Elisabeth jointly owned a large townhouse and two adjacent premises, a country house/cattle ranch named La Solitude, and plantation Clevia.[54] Elisabeth inherited Creutz's half of the house and buildings in town and she became the usufractuary of Clevia and La Solitude. Clevia was a gift of the Governor of Mauritius to Creutz. On the plantation some 130 slaves took care of 1,100 coffee trees. Interestingly, the slaves were the private property of Elisabeth and not part of the inventory. La Solitude included a two-storey house, 13 slaves, 52 cows, 13 bulls and 32 calves. The thirty-one-page inventory of the townhouse reveals how well-off Elisabeth and Creutz were. It includes 21 male slaves, 23 female slaves, a rich assortment of furniture, expensive cloth, linen, (Japanese) porcelain, pottery, silverware, 500 bottles of beer and more than 200 bottles of wine.

Elisabeth Samson was an astute business woman in economically prosperous times. Following the death of Creutz she managed to increase the value of her real estate from 250,000 to one million guilders in a mere eight years. Her yearly income was estimated to be between 30,000 and 100,000 guilders.[55] In comparison, Governor Wigbold Crommelin earned 10,600 guilders per year.

Elisabeth seems to have had everything, except a legal husband. Thus a spouse she coveted next, and a white man to boot. She was the first black woman who officially requested the Commissioners of Marital Affairs to marry a white man.[56] This caused quite some commotion in Suriname, because such a racially mixed marriage was thought to be illegal. Elisabeth had to request the Court of Policy for permission to marry Christoph Policarpus Braband(t), organist and sexton of the Reformed Church and owner of a lumber mill. The Court did not know how to handle this sensitive case and so referred the problem to the Directors of the Society of Suriname in Amsterdam.[57] In a letter to Amsterdam the Court expressed its opinion that a mixed marriage would be morally wrong, yet it advanced a major argument to support this union. In time the younger husband would inherit his wife's fortune; her money and other possessions would thus transfer to the white community. As the Court of Policy stated 'this would not be bad: because to have too influential free persons among the Negroes, one has to fear trouble, because it would give our slaves the idea, that they are able to climb as high as we'.[58] It took more than three years before a decision was reached. Finally, the Dutch authorities announced that there existed no legal obstacles to racially mixed marriages and advised the Court of Policy to give its permission. By the time Elisabeth received the good news her groom-to-be had passed away. But his death did not deter her: she married the white Hermanus Daniel Zobre, twenty-two years her junior, instead. Zobre was born in The Hague in 1737 and migrated to Suriname to become a planter. The ceremonies took place in December 1767. Governor Crommelin deemed the marriage so important that he noted in his diary: 'today notice of the intended marriage of Elisabeth Samson, former housekeeper of Carl Otto Creutz'. Crommelin did not think it necessary to mention the name of the groom.[59]

There is little information about the joint lives of Elisabeth Samson and Hermanus Daniel Zobre. Economically they did well: the coffee harvests in 1768 and 1769 were very good and brought good prices in the Amsterdam market. The tide turned in the 1770s but Elisabeth did not live to see the downturn: she died on 21 or 22 April 1771 at the age of fifty-five. She had been married for three years and four months. Her property included six townhouses and half of another six houses; the ranch La Solitude; the plantations Clevia, De Goede Vreede, Toevlugt and Welgemoed; half of the plantations Belwaarde, Vlaardingen, Catharina'sburg and Onverwacht; a quarter of plantation Salzhalen; and half of a country estate. Her total worth was more than one million guilders.[60]

Elisabeth Samson was certainly an exception. The figures show how exceptional: in 1731 a free black was for the first time registered as a slave holder. In 1733 there were two, in 1735 six (including three women), in 1736 three, in 1743 seven (four women), in 1744 five (two women), and in 1752 five (four women).[61] These women included Elisabeth and her freed sisters, Nanette and Catharina Opperman. The life story of Elisabeth Samson is of interest not because she was representative of free blacks but because of what her history discloses about eighteenth-century Suriname society.

The white administration's ideal was a society in which there were no relations between the different population groups and it therefore decreed a strict separation between whites, coloureds, blacks and slaves.[62] Yet many whites belonging to the administration broke these very rules. For example, Frederik Coenraad Bossé, the husband of the mulatta Maria Jansz, and Carl Otto Creutz, who had a notarized relationship with the black Elisabeth Samson, were members of the Court of Policy and thus were among the very highest officials in the colony. Apparently, marrying a mulatta was socially acceptable, but, as the case of Elisabeth shows, a marriage between a black and a white certainly was not. The white men in the family with whom the black or coloured women had a relationship were very much involved in their lives and acted as advisors, witnesses, or guardians.

The Samson family almost represented colonial society: some were born slaves, some were born free. The family members ranged in colour from black to white and on the social ladder they occupied almost every rung: from the lowest (as slaves) to the highest. The black mother and her black slave children were manumitted by her free mulatto children. It illustrates Brana-Shute's argument that 'uniting families was a major motivation for manumitting a slave, particularly among free coloureds and free blacks'.[63]

COLONIAL SOCIETY IN THE NINETEENTH CENTURY

In the nineteenth century, following the English interim administration (1804–16), Suriname experienced several social and cultural changes. According to contemporaries and subsequent historians, the standard of culture improved markedly. The plantation directors and overseers were no longer recruited solely from the ranks of (former) soldiers and sailors;[64] increasingly these positions were filled by young Dutchmen from 'respectable' families. The Dutch agronomist M.D. Teenstra stated that the overseers now belonged to the most decent classes in the colony.[65] In addition, The Hague sent a new breed of officials who supposedly were virtuous as well as rational. Moreover, more than one-third of the whites had left the colony, while other whites were reduced to poverty. As a consequence the elite observed the proper forms and became more bourgeois and less frivolous, since the nineteenth-century lifestyle of the Dutch bourgeoisie was rather austere. Now it was the senior officials and some plantation administrators rather than the planters who set the tone and style. Social life became less grandiose: instead of grand balls the elite now enjoyed itself at home or at social clubs. The 'second tier' was formed by middle-ranking bureaucrats (*ambtenaren 2e klas*), judges, lawyers, doctors and pharmacists.[66]

In the first decades of this century the number of (illegal) manumissions and consequently the number of free blacks and coloureds grew appreciably. During the 'British interregnum' the cost of manumission had risen considerably. Healthy male slaves above the age of fourteen could still work their way out of slavery by serving in the Free Corps (*'s Lands Vrijcorps*) for three years without pay. Officially that was the only arrangement to gain freedom through labour rather than money. As Brana-Shute states, the 'growing costs and regulations imposed by the court served to undermine the very intentions of the laws by encouraging an increase in illegal manumissions in the early nineteenth century'.[67] A slave often paid his owner to buy himself free, an advantageous deal for both parties: the owner did not have to pay any costs and even made a profit, while the slave gained his freedom. Such an illegally manumitted slave was called a *piki njan*. A *piki njan* slave was free as far as the owner was concerned and therefore was free to make his own living.[68] Most *piki njan* slaves gravitated to Paramaribo and their growing visibility led the Court in 1825 to attempt to curb illegal manumissions through private arrangements between masters and slaves. Within the next five years, the administration effectively outlawed the status of *piki njan* slaves.

Even though the accuracy of Suriname population data is questionable, and the colonial administration often differentiated only by 'free' and 'slave', it seems safe to say that the absolute and relative number of free coloureds and free blacks rose sharply, particularly after 1820. Around the turn of the century there were less than 2,000 free coloureds and blacks, approximately three per cent of the total population and some forty-six per cent of the free population. Between 1802 and 1828, 1,660 slaves were manumitted through the court. During these decades the number of free coloureds and blacks hovered between 2,500 and 3,000. In the 1830s their number shot up to more than 5,000: about nine per cent of the total population and 66 per cent of the free population. Approximately two-thirds of this group was female.[69] By the middle of the decade Paramaribo numbered some 15,000 inhabitants: 1,145 coloured slaves, 7,435 black slaves, 2,043 whites (including 386 Dutchmen), 3,612 free coloureds and

1,030 free blacks. On the plantations lived 595 whites, 335 free coloureds and 64 free blacks in addition to 40,204 slaves.[70] In other words, more than ninety per cent of the free coloureds and blacks lived in town.

In the decades thereafter the number of freed individuals increased noticeably, especially after many restrictions on manumission were relaxed or even abolished.[71] Between 1855 and 1862, 2,160 persons – 855 men (forty per cent) and 1,305 women (sixty per cent) – were manumitted. The number of manumissions per year fluctuated between a low of 215 in 1857 and a high of 293 in 1861. The year 1862, one year before abolition, was clearly exceptional with 392 manumissions, of a total of more than 36,000 remaining slaves. The percentage of manumitted women fluctuated between fifty-seven and sixty-six per cent of the total number of manumissions. For the period 1855–62 data on the age of the manumitted show that of the 855 men forty-one per cent was younger than 12, forty-three per cent was between 12 and 40, fourteen per cent was over 40 years of age and of 1.5 per cent the age was unknown. Of the 1,305 women thirty per cent was under 12, forty-two per cent between 12 and 40, twenty-seven per cent older than 40 and two per cent unknown. Thus boys were manumitted more frequently than girls. In the age groups 12 to 40 years there was virtually no difference between men and women. In the age group over 40 relatively, and absolutely, more women than men were freed.[72] As in the eighteenth century, most manumissions occurred before age 40.

Given the number of slaves the rate of manumission was still not spectacular, but it was surely higher than in previous decades and swelled the ranks of the free coloureds and blacks. Paramaribo grew to more than 18,000 inhabitants in the final years before emancipation, and now some thirty-five per cent of the colony's population lived in town. At this time seventy-two per cent of the town's population was free. The percentage of Suriname's free people living in town gradually dropped from more than ninety per cent to approximately eighty per cent, while the number of free people in the districts grew from 864 in 1848 to 2,969 in 1862.

FREE COLOUREDS AND BLACKS IN THE NINETEENTH-CENTURY ECONOMY

The great majority of these free coloureds and blacks lived in poor conditions due to their lack of education and the difficult access to jobs held either by whites or (skilled) slaves. Even though free coloureds in particular had a good reputation as carpenters and cabinet makers, it was impossible to 'take over' the trade as owners hired out skilled slaves. According to the administration, market-gardening and cattle-breeding became more popular for this group.[73] Women, the majority of the free coloureds and blacks, could find work in such low paying, typical 'female' jobs as domestic servant, cook, laundress, and nanny. An alternative was becoming a huckster, but this was a highly competitive business as the market was crowded with both free people and slaves, who had to sell their masters' products.[74] According to the law, the patron or police could report freed individuals who did not regularly practice their occupation or remained idle. They could be sentenced to two to twelve months (paid) forced labour. Those who still did not 'better' their lives would be put to labour in jail.[75] The government regularly reported that the 'moral and social civilisation of the free population improves, as well as the desire for education ... and the industriousness of the lower classes'.[76]

Against the odds, a small coloured 'elite' began to develop in the nineteenth century. This advancement was helped by the fact that many whites had departed the colony, leaving room for a new middle class formed by a tiny group of free coloureds who had enjoyed some education.[77] Most of them were children of white higher- or middle-class fathers. Education and emancipation of the free coloureds went hand in hand. A few children were even sent to school in the Netherlands. The return of one of them, Johannes Vrolijk, as a teacher had important social and educational consequences. In 1809 Vrolijk founded a school for students of all races which helped to lift educational standards considerably. Van Lier calls him the 'first coloured man we see occupying a post of some importance'.[78] Other prominent coloured professionals soon followed in his footsteps. On the initiative of the coloured physician M.M.A. Coupijn, a group of them in 1827 founded the Benevolent Society (*Maatschappij van Weldadigheid*) to improve the living conditions of the (free) lower classes. The whites at first were suspicious as they believed the founders to have secret objectives. When Commissioner-General Johannes van den Bosch was in Suriname the Society requested and received his support, thus rescuing this first coloured organization. In 1832 the Benevolent Society had 227 members and helped the sick, supported a few poor on a monthly basis, and paid tuition for some fifty students.[79]

Perhaps the most eminent coloured man in the first half of the nineteenth century was the lawyer Hendrik Charles Focke.[80] Focke was born in Suriname in 1802. His father, Hendrik Everhard Focke, was a Dutch planter who had migrated to Suriname in 1789. His (coloured?) mother, Willemina Charlotta Esser, was born in the colony. In 1820 Hendrik Charles enrolled at Utrecht University and seven years later he obtained his doctorate. A few years later he fought in the Dutch army against secessionist Belgium. In 1834 he returned to his native country. He ultimately became president of the Court of Petty Session (*College van Kleine Zaken*). Besides his professional activities, Focke was a musician, a botanist, one of the founders of the short-lived journal *West-Indië* and the author of a Negro–English dictionary (*Neger-Engelsch woordenboek*, 1855).

Despite his prominence, his private life was fairly typical for a free coloured man. In 1839 the slave Matte, who already had two children, gave birth to his daughter, Bettina. In 1840 Focke manumitted Matte and her three children. Matte now was known as Maria Tomeshuizen. Focke and Maria had two more children: Henrietta (1841) and Jan (1843). In 1855 he officially requested that his children be allowed to carry the name Focke rather than Tomeshuizen. On his deathbed Focke married Maria Tomeshuizen, thus legitimating his three children. The legal marriage was performed on 18 June 1856, the church wedding a day later and Focke passed away ten days later, on 29 June.

RACE RELATIONS

The rise of a small coloured elite and the accompanying socio-cultural changes did not make the differences between the population groups disappear, although relations between whites and the coloured elite improved. The decision by Commissioner-General Van den Bosch in 1828 to grant equal rights to all free individuals and to make mulattoes and Jews eligible for government functions without discrimination led to great improvements in the social standing of both groups. In the second half of the century these two population groups together with Dutch officials formed the new administrative elite. Prominent mulattoes were able to marry into the white elite and mixed marriages no longer caused a sensation.[81] The Dutch captain G. van Lennep Coster, who returned to Paramaribo after a sixteen-year absence, observed that now coloured 'women' were to be found in the company of European 'ladies'.[82] Yet these social climbers made only a small dent in the existing hierarchy and the accompanying racial prejudices.[83] Church membership was indicative of the existing socio-economic structure. Several coloured families joined the white, and thus prestigious, Dutch Reformed and Lutheran churches, while the Catholics and Moravians attracted slaves and the great majority of the free population.[84] Teenstra, a Dutch gentleman-farmer and abolitionist, argued that there might have been less social distance between whites, Jews, and some coloureds but that the social hierarchy had become more rigid. There existed a social gap between senior and junior officials and grand merchants and minor traders. And even rich coloureds were barred from joining white clubs. According to Teenstra, life in Paramaribo was less 'pleasant' than it used to be. At the estates, however, the same *joie de vivre* and hospitality in the planters' houses continued to exist unabated.[85] Needless to say, this planter hospitality depended on slave servitude.

Contemporary whites expressed the colony's and their own racial prejudices in varying degrees of vehemence. According to Teenstra, even the lowliest white utterly despised coloureds and blacks, while whites, coloureds and blacks alike disdained Jews. The coloureds, free or slave, were looked down on by blacks and whites. Teenstra agreed that most coloureds were 'arrogant, proud, conceited, lazy and impertinent'. He claimed free blacks and coloureds found their greatest bliss in serene rest, and their greatest delight was sleeping with a rounded belly. The girls only showed off and had a strong desire for fancy clothes and jewellery, according to Teenstra, and whites considered mulattas as 'dress-up dolls, as filthy-coloured foam. A literal nothing in a great show'. Teenstra did not find it surprising that Suriname concubines had few domestic inclinations and instead loved spending money and being ostentatious, yet he also felt that mulattoes possessed some positive qualities such as 'hospitality, compassion, mildness and helpfulness'. The great majority of free blacks, on the other hand, he felt were extremely lazy and dirty and very shabby, and he claimed nobody treated slaves more harshly than a manumitted black.[86]

The Dutch agricultural expert W.H. Lans basically held the same opinion as Teenstra by saying that in coloured people 'arrogance and poverty are intertwined in the most peculiar manner'. He believed free coloureds and blacks only wanted white collar jobs or a position as a tailor in order to dress up. He tells the anecdote that he once visited two young coloured men, relaxing in their hammocks in their overgrown garden. When Lans remarked upon the poor condition of the yard, the men replied that they could not help it as they did not have slaves. Lans used this story to illustrate his opinion on the free man's disdain for even the lightest form of agricultural labour.[87]

Adriaan François Lammens was a Dutch official who served as a judge, and later President of the Court, from 1816 to 1835. His judgments were more progressive and milder, probably because he was married to a coloured woman. In contrast to most contemporaries, he considered free coloureds to be close to the whites. He turned against the 'preposterous idea, child of unlimited imperiousness' that in the administration of justice there should be made a difference between free people in favour of the 'first or privileged class, the whites'.[88] Lammens clearly did not understand the disdain of the whites for the coloureds, whom they thought to combine the vices of blacks and whites,[89] since it implied the estrangement between parents and children. He was more appreciative of the black contempt of coloureds because the latter treated their slaves much harsher than the whites.[90] Despite this sympathy for blacks and coloureds, Lammens was critical of them as well. Blacks, whether slave, manumitted or free born, were sluggish and lazy. He also claimed that both free blacks and free coloureds, with a very few exceptions, always complained about not having work, but were rarely in the mood to do anything. According to Lammens, their motto was not 'after the work is done repose is sweet', but rather 'we begin to rest, and when we are rested, we'll see if we want to work'.[91]

In other words, racial prejudices poisoned the colony. Free coloureds and blacks had no sympathy for the plight of the slaves and treated them more severely than the whites did. European contemporaries criticized the existing relations and racial biases, yet remarks by expatriates such as Teenstra, Lans and Lammens only fueled such prejudices. But we have seen when free coloureds and blacks were related to slaves they often did care for them and bought them free.

ON THE PLANTATIONS

Outside Paramaribo, in the districts, the situation for free coloureds improved as well. The most likely career was on the plantations, and some coloureds indeed managed to become plantation directors or owners. The Dutch agricultural expert, Lans, expressed some ambivalence about Suriname-born planters. He believed they could not handle a slave labour force as they were 'too close to the slaves', yet, on the other hand they were industrious, proud of their land, and less conservative than the Europeans. He also noted that the Suriname-born planters were willing to introduce new agricultural techniques.[92]

In April 1836 a missionary, Treu, visited plantations along the Saramacca River. In his diary he noted the racial background of a number of directors:

> Sonetta is in the possession of Miss Ketty Smith. She is the mother of the mulatto Lamith, who has left for Zeist [the main base of the Dutch Moravian Brethren] to receive an education at the boarding school. The co-owner of De Vier Hendrikken is Reyeg, a bastard relative of Fr. Weissenbruch. The director at Tyrol is Schütte, a mestizo son of a German. Herstelling is owned by Miss Vervuurt. The two children of her son are almost white and work as housekeepers. Margaretha's Gift is Miss Pottendorf's. The director is a mulatto son from a clergyman from Geldern. At Catharina Sophia the director has a fifteen-year-old mulatto girl, and another one on plantation Acconaribo and who knows how many more![93]

One of those coloured planters published his memoirs, one of the few egodocuments by a free coloured that has survived.[94] E.J. Bartelink gives us a glimpse of plantation life and relations in the second half of the nineteenth century. He started as an overseer in 1855 in the employment of Eyken

Sluyters en Mollinger, one of the most prominent *administrator* houses in the colony and worked his way up to plantation director (1864) and eventually owner.[95] At twenty-one years of age Bartelink went to work at estate Zeezigt where he and seven other colleagues had the supervision over 800 slaves.[96] Bartelink earned 150 guilders per year and enjoyed free housing, light, laundry and domestic service, tobacco and pipes, and board at the director's table.

Eyken Sluyters en Mollinger moved Bartelink around and he worked at some fourteen plantations.[97] The hardest times were at sugar plantations, where the water mill was in constant use during the season. Bartelink complained that the slaves got compensation for lost sleep whereas the overseers did not. He concluded that overseers might have been worse off than the slaves.

The best times were had at plantations Wederzorg, Geyersvlijt, Belwaarde and Ornamibo. In all these cases the plantations were led or owned by individuals, white or coloured, whom Bartelink greatly admired. The director at Wederzorg was Arnold Maynard, who enjoyed a solid reputation in planter circles. Bartelink characterized him as a 'distinguished coloured' who reminded him of a Spanish *grande*. 'Papa' Maynard was a gourmet, always inviting people for dinner.[98] The owner of Geyersvlijt was the prominent Eyken Sluyters family. They possessed several estates and most of their directors were coloured. This family was not racially prejudiced at all. 'Whichever prominent person visited the plantation, I, an ordinary coloured, was always introduced and treated as an equal with the same distinction'. At this time, in the 1860s, Bartelink earned 2400 guilders a year.[99]

Belwaarde was owned by another prominent white, G. Bosch Reitz, like Eyken Sluyters a member of the Colonial States. According to Bartelink, Bosch Reitz had a 'noble' character, in spite of one twist that Bartelink frowned upon. Bosch Reitz employed a carpenter named boss Palm, who had bought himself free. The master liked his employee so much that they were inseparable. He was invited to eat with guests and used as a 'court jester'. It was the latter that Bartelink did not like: Palm's inarticulate Dutch doubled up the guests with laughter.[100] Bartelink's final job as an overseer was at Ornamibo. This was the estate of the coloured Marius del Prado who had worked his way up from an artisan to a rich plantation owner. Bartelink called him a 'real gentleman', 'honest', who had remained himself and treated him like a brother.[101]

Bartelink followed in the footsteps of Del Prado and bought his own (cacao) plantation, although he in all likelihood did not become as rich. In his memoirs Bartelink looked back contended. He had worked hard and made a decent living. His oldest son received his education in Europe.

Parenthetically, he observed that the abolition of slavery (in 1863) had not had any effect on his career or life.[102] Bartelink gives the impression that the life of a coloured might have been easier in the districts than in Paramaribo with its rigid hierarchy.

In the second half of the nineteenth century the socio-economic advance of the 'respectable' coloureds languished temporarily, to the benefit of the Jews, still the only white permanent settlers. Throughout the century coloureds and Jews had vied with each other for the same positions.[103] Apparently many coloureds (and whites for that matter) decided after finishing their education in the Netherlands not to return to their home country and instead opted for a career in Europe or the Netherlands East Indies, thus leaving room for the Jewish population. Jews and coloureds, however, were united in their occasional outbursts of antipathy against the highest Dutch officials, who in turn often openly disdained these two population groups. This awakening nationalism came to full bloom in the middle decades of the twentieth century.

CONCLUSION

In relation to the overwhelming number of slaves in Suriname, only very few – one to three per cent – of them were manumitted. Yet the free blacks and coloureds made up a large proportion of the free population: their share grew from a quarter in the late eighteenth century to two-thirds in the 1830s and even more in the last years before the abolition of slavery. In his comparison of Suriname and Curaçao, Hoetink concludes that the 'mild, paternalistic type of slavery and an early and frequent use of manumission' in Curaçao did not lead to the early development of a coloured social elite. He very tentatively advances the thesis that a 'cruel slave system [in Suriname] tends to interest the whites in the creation of alliances with the free people, which may lead to the improvement of the latter's social and economic position'.[104]

Indeed there may have been more social and economic room for free coloureds and blacks in Suriname, but the great majority lived in dire circumstances and were unable to find sufficient employment. And the almost negligible group of well-to-do free blacks or coloureds was treated with fear and contempt by the Europeans, certainly in the eighteenth century. The comments of the Suriname authorities on Elisabeth Samson, especially the sentence 'to have too influential free persons among the Negroes, one has to fear trouble, because it would give our slaves the idea, that they are able to climb as high as we' speaks volumes. The Samson family demonstrates several points. First, the importance of family networks in freeing slaves and protecting and (financially) assisting them once free. Second, family ties were stronger than racial differences. Third, there was money in the free coloured and black community, but that wealth did not lead to social recognition. Only in the nineteenth century did a tiny elite – most often the male offspring of upper-and middle-class European fathers – manage to climb the social ladder and gain white acceptance.

Therefore, the idea that the free coloured and black population were used as a buffer against the demographically overwhelming slave population is questionable, particularly in the eighteenth century. Very few slaves were manumitted and, moreover, the administration issued special regulations to control this small freed group. Racial and socio-economic divisions permeated colonial society and prevented the formation of a free 'bloc' against the slaves. On the other hand, an alliance between all blacks and coloureds – free, manumitted and slaves – against the colonial administration was highly improbable given the way in which free blacks and coloureds despised slaves except kin. Broadly speaking the whites felt so superior that the formation of 'alliances' between the whites and the other free population groups did not occur; only particular coloured individuals and families were accepted. The fact that the coloureds were a product of white society made them suspect in both white and black eyes. Yet education enabled them to become upwardly mobile. Coloureds, in turn, despised blacks in general and slaves in particular. Jews and coloureds were competitors. Successful coloureds looked down on the great mass of free coloureds and blacks who were still living a hand-to-mouth existence.

Much research remains to be done to learn more about the free coloured and black population. The few recent studies on this subject, by Rosemary Brana-Shute and Cynthia McLeod-Ferrier in particular, have corrected received ideas and added much to our understanding of Suriname history. The eighteenth century may be partially 'lost' because not much was recorded and due to the poor condition of the extant archival material. Yet, a closer examination of nineteenth-century documents should reveal more about what happened to manumitted individuals and their descendants.

ACKNOWLEDGEMENTS

I would like to thank Gert Oostindie and particularly Jane Landers for their helpful comments and critical suggestions.

NOTES

1.   For a fine overview of Suriname's plantation economy see Alex van Stipriaan, *Surinaams contrast: Roofbouw en overleven in een Caraibische plantagekolonie 1750–1863* (Leiden, 1993). On pp.28–32 he places the Suriname plantation economy in a Caribbean context.

Even though Suriname was one of the oldest and one of the largest plantation colonies in the Caribbean it was never among the most important. The population of Suriname was comparable to Barbados, rather than to Saint Domingue, Jamaica, and later Cuba. The production and export of sugar in those latter three colonies were also much higher.

2. The number of escaped slaves was much higher than the number of maroons settling in the interior. Many were caught and others returned to the plantations by their own volition. The refugees withdrew behind natural obstacles such as waterfalls and rapids. Marronage seems to have occurred even in the English period before 1667. During the Dutch administration the maroon threat continued to grow and soon these 'runaways' posed a military threat to the plantations and the colony as a whole. From the 1670s a citizen's militia was organised to hunt maroons and destroy their villages. In 1685 the administration established bounties for the capture of runaways and these premiums increased over the years. In the early eighteenth century larger military expeditions, including Amerindians and slaves, were organised. According to David Nassy, *Essai historique sur la Colonie de Surinam ... par les Régens et Représentans de ladite Nation Juive Portugaise* (Paramaribo, 1788), Vol. I, p.87, in the 1730s and 1740s Suriname had become a theatre of perpetual war'. During this period the expeditions reached their maximum size and frequency. Nevertheless, most of them were unsuccessful. This lack of success and the growing costs forced the colonial administration to change course. In the 1760s peace treaties were concluded with the three main groups of maroons: with the Ndjuka in 1760, the Saramaka in 1762, and the Matawai in 1767. The Ndjuka and Saramaka at that time numbered between 2,500 to 3,000 each; the Matawai were a much smaller group of some 300. The maroons received autonomy and in turn pledged to refrain from acts of aggression against the colony. The maroons indeed kept to the treaties but the marronage problem continued to exist. Groups of runaway slaves continued to pose military threats to the plantation colony. In 1772 the *Redi Musu* or Black Rangers were founded to battle the maroons in the so-called Boni Wars (1765–93).

3. To mention only the most recent monographs: Humphrey E. Lamur, *The Production of Sugar and the Reproduction of Slaves at Vossenburg, Suriname 1705–1863* (Amsterdam, 1987); Gert Oostindie, *Roosenburg en Mon Bijou: Twee Surinaamse plantages* (Dordrecht, 1989); Van Stipriaan, *Surinaams contrast*; Ruud Beeldsnijder, *'Om werk van jullie te hebben': Plantageslaven in Suriname, 1730–1750* (Utrecht, 1994). Unfortunately there is no English–language monograph covering the seventeenth century to the abolition of slavery. In three volumes C.Ch. Goslinga has covered the history of the Dutch Caribbean: *The Dutch in the Caribbean and on the Wild Coast, 1580–1680* (Assen, 1971); *The Dutch in the Caribbean and in the Guianas, 1680–1791* (Assen, 1985); *The Dutch in the Caribbean and in Surinam, 1791/5–1942* (Assen, 1990). Some recent articles on plantations and slavery in English are Oostindie, 'The Economics of Surinam Slavery', *Economic and Social History in the Netherlands*, 5 (1993), pp.1–24; Oostindie, 'Voltaire, Stedman and Suriname Slavery', *Slavery & Abolition*, 14, 2 (1993), pp.1–34; and Van Stipriaan 'Debunking Debts. Image and Reality of a Colonial Crisis: Suriname at the end of the 18th century', *Itinerario*, 19, 1 (1995), pp.69–84.

4. The maroons are divided into six groups, each under its own leadership: the Aluku, Kwinti, Matawai, Ndjuka, Paramaka and Saramaka. The literature on maroons is vast and generally of a high standard. I will limit myself to mentioning some of the most important monographs in English. The best introduction to the literature is Richard Price, *The Guiana Maroons: A Historical and Bibliographical Introduction* (Baltimore, 1976). Richard Price's rich *oeuvre* focuses on the Saramaka, see his *Saramaka Social Structure: Analysis of a Maroon Society in Surinam* (Río Piedras, 1975); *To Slay the Hydra: Dutch Colonial Perspectives on the Saramaka Wars* (Ann Arbor, 1983); *First-Time: The Historical Vision of an Afro-American People* (Baltimore, 1983) and *Alabi's World* (Baltimore, 1990). With Sally Price he has written *Two Evenings in Saramaka* (Chicago, 1990) and *Afro-American Arts of the Suriname Rain Forest* (Berkeley, 1980). Sally Price has published *Co-wives and Calabashes* (Ann Arbor, 1984; reprint 1994). For the Matawai see Chris de Beet and Mirjam Sterman, *People in Between: The Matawai Maroons of Suriname* (Utrecht, 1981). On the Ndjuka see Silvia de Groot, *Djuka Society and Social Change: History of an Attempt to Develop a Bush Negro Community in Surinam, 1917–1926* (Assen, 1969) and

From Isolation towards Integration: The Surinam Maroons and Their Colonial Rulers (The Hague, 1977); and H.U.E. Thoden van Velzen and W. van Wetering, *The Great Father and the Danger: Religious Cults, Material Forces, and Collective Fantasies in the World of the Surinamese Maroons* (Dordrecht, 1988). On the Aluku or Boni see Wim Hoogbergen, *The Boni Maroon Wars in Suriname* (Leiden, 1990).

5. In Suriname the general colour distinctions were white, black and mixed or coloured (*kleurling*). The coloureds were subdivided into smaller categories based on their (perceived) racial ancestry: *mulatten* (black x white), *mestiezen* (white x mulatto), *kastiezen* (white x mestizo), *poestiezen* (white x *kastiezen*) and *karboegers* or *kabougres* (black x mulatto). See A.F. Lammens, *Bijdragen tot de kennis van de kolonie Suriname, tijdvak 1816 tot 1822.* Edited by G.A. de Bruijne (Amsterdam, 1982), p.99.

6. R.A.J. van Lier, *Frontier Society: A Social Analysis of the History of Surinam* (The Hague, 1971).

7. Rosemary Brana–Shute, 'Approaching Freedom: The Manumission of Slaves in Suriname, 1760–1828', *Slavery & Abolition*, 10, 3 (1989), pp.40–63. This article is based on her Ph.D. dissertation *The Manumission of Slaves in Suriname, 1760–1828*, Gainesville: University of Florida, 1985.

8. H. Hoetink, 'Surinam and Curaçao', in David W. Cohen and Jack P. Greene (eds.), *Neither Slave nor Free: The Freedman of African Descent in the Slave Societies of the New World* (Baltimore, 1982), pp.59–83.

9. Maroons are excluded from this overview since the administration did not consider them free citizens under colonial jurisdiction.

10. J.D. Herlein, *Nauwkeurige Beschrijvinge van Zuriname* (Leeuwarden, 1718), p.46.

11. Van Lier, *Frontier Society*, p.29, in Nassy, *Essai historique sur la Colonie de Surinam*, Vol.II, p.20 the number of houses counted is 1,119 in 1787. J. Wolbers, *Geschiedenis van Suriname* (Amsterdam, 1861), p.425 mentions 1,776 houses in 1790.

12. Nassy, *Essai historique*, II, p.37. In 1791 there were 11,500 inhabitants according to Van Lier, *Frontier Society*, p.29. Van Lier, p.97, also reports that between 1738 and 1787 the number of free people only increased by 52 persons: from 598 to 650. Other authors have recycled Van Lier's figures, see, for example, Hoetink, 'Surinam and Curaçao', p.62. This small increase, however, is rather questionable, especially given Brana-Shute's work. Beeldsnijder, pp.8 and 25–6, suggests that Van Lier's source, Dirk van Hogendorp's *Stukken Raakende den tegenwoordigen toestand der Bataafse Bezittingen in Oost-Indië* (The Hague, 1801) may contain a printing error. The year 1738 should have been 1783; in that case the increase was 52 free black and coloured individuals in four years. Ruud Beeldsnijder, 'Op de onderste trede: Over vrije negers en arme blanken in Suriname 1730–1750', *Oso* 10 (1991), pp.7–30.

13. See, for example, Herlein, *Nauwkeurige Beschrijvinge*, p.48 and M.D. Teenstra, *De negerslaven in de kolonie Suriname en de uitbreiding van het Christendom onder de heidensche bevolking* (Dordrecht, 1842). Van Lier, *Frontier Society*, pp.85–95, devotes a special chapter to the Jewish community.

14. The English translation of Mauricius's letter may be found in Van Lier, *Frontier Society*, p.38. Particularly Mauricius's expression *animus revertendi* has often been quoted. Many colonists indeed had no intention of settling, yet this should not obscure the fact that many white families did stay in Suriname, for whatever reason.

15. Administrators or estate superintendents (in Dutch *administrateurs*) were agents representing absentee owners. They were to become the most important members of the colonial society. The most influential administrators held dozens of administrations. In both the eighteenth and nineteenth centuries Suriname-born administrators were exceedingly scarce, see W.H. Lans, *Bijdrage tot de kennis der kolonie Suriname* (The Hague, 1842), pp.36–37, 39.

16. A 'Suriname marriage' stood midway between a legal and religious marriage and a random sexual relationship. The simple ceremony that inaugurated a 'Suriname marriage' was a sign of the 'permanence' of the relationship. 'The mother of the girl, accompanied by a female neighbor, brought her into the bedroom of the groom. The next morning, after man and wife left, the room was visited again by the mother and the neighbor, who then

proceeded to announce to the neighborhood that the marriage had become a fact', Hoetink, 'Surinam and Curaçao', p.61, n1. Needless to say, concubinage did not eradicate irregular sexual relationships.

17. This Court was the most important colonial institution. The Governor was obliged to consult this council and to carry out any of its resolutions, see Van Lier, *Frontier Society*, p.47.
18. Ibid., p.77.
19. Algemeen Rijksarchief The Hague (ARA) Raad van Politie (RvP) 217 folio 171; ARA Societeit van Suriname (SvS) 401 deel 1 folio 140; *West Indisch Plakaatboek: Plakaten, ordonnantiën en andere wetten uitgevaardigd in Suriname*. Edited by J.A. Schiltkamp and J.Th. de Smidt (Amsterdam, 1973), p.277.
20. Maria Lenders, *Strijders voor het Lam: Herrnhutterbroeders en -zusters in Suriname, 1735–1900* (Leiden, 1996), Chapter III.
21. On Quassie see, for example, J.G. Stedman, *Narrative of a Five Years Expedition against the Revolted Negroes of Surinam*. Edited by Richard Price and Sally Price (Baltimore, 1992), pp.582–84; Nassy, *Essai historique*, Vol.II, pp.71–6; Wolbers, *Geschiedenis van Suriname*, p.436; Charles Douglas, *Een blik in het verleden van Suriname: Beknopt verhaal omtrent de gebeurtenissen met de slaven en toestanden in Suriname gedurende de jaren 1630–1863* (Paramaribo, 1930), p.76; Beeldsnijder, 'Over vrije negers en arme blanken in Suriname 1730–1750', pp.11–12; Richard Price, 'Kwasímukámba's Gambit', *Bijdragen tot de Taal-, Land- en Volkenkunde* 135 (1979), pp.151–69 and *First-Time*, pp.153–9.
22. Stedman, *Narrative*, pp.581–2.
23. Ibid., p.582.
24. Ibid.
25. Stedman made a well-known portrait of 'The Celebrated Graman Quacy' in his 'royal' outfit, which was later engraved by William Blake. See ibid., p.583, also reproduced in Price 'Kwasímukámba's Gambit' next to p.158, Price, *First-Time*, p.156 and Ursy M. Lichtveld and Jan Voorhoeve, *Suriname: Spiegel der vaderlandse kooplieden, een historisch leesboek* (Zwolle, 1958) next to p.168.
26. Lichtveld and Voorhoeve, *Spiegel der vaderlandse kooplieden* includes a brief biography and three of these mourning poems, pp.168–74.
27. Price, 'Kwasímukámba's Gambit', p.163. The Saramakas killed the white expeditionary force led to their village by Kwasí. According to their story, Kwasí's life was spared, only his ear was cut off, ibid., pp.163–4. See Blake's portrait of Kwasí with severed ear. For the fascinating Saramaka opinion on and history of Kwasímukámba see Price 'Kwasímukámba's Gambit' and *First-Time*, pp.153–9.
28. On the Black Rangers see Silvia W. de Groot, 'Het Korps Zwarte Jagers in Suriname: Collaboratie en opstand, I', *Oso* 7 (1988), pp.147–60. The owners received some 800 to 3,400 guilders per slave. The colonial government organized free blacks and free coloureds into separate military companies, Hoetink, 'Surinam and Curaçao', p.63.
29. For this law: ARA, SvS 401 deel 2 folio 132–133 or *Plakaatboek*, pp.411–12. The most recent and by far the most extensive study on manumission in Suriname is Brana-Shute's dissertation *The Manumission of Slaves in Suriname*. She systematically sampled 943 petitions requesting freedom for 1,346 slaves, covering about one third of all manumissions in Suriname in the period 1760–1826. A pioneering M.A. thesis by Paul Koulen resulted in his article 'Schets van de historische ontwikkeling van de Manumissie in Suriname (1733–1863)', *Mededelingen Stichting Surinaams Museum* 12 (1973), pp.8–36. Koulen and Brana–Shute disagree on the reasons behind the manumission legislation. Koulen (p.9) thinks that it was aimed at preventing excessive (*veelvuldig*) manumissions, while Brana-Shute (p.143) argues that the Court hoped to prevent *undesirable* manumissions and that fiscal concerns were paramount. Another financial factor might have been that the administration attempted to siphon off money and property inherited by blacks and coloureds.
30. Brana-Shute, 'Approaching Freedom', p.43; Koulen, 'Schets van de historische ontwikkeling', p.13.
31. ARA, SvS 405 no.6; RvP 664; 223 no.6 and Svs 405 no.35; RvP 223 no.35 or *Plakaatboek*,

pp.690 and 726–7. Brana-Shute, *The Manumission of Slaves in Suriname*, pp.120–22. In 1764 followed a minor change in the manumission regulations, see ARA RvP 759 and SvS 403, no.6, *Plakaatboek*, p.789. In 1788 the government levied its first tax on manumission to subsidise the fight against the runaway slaves, see ARA SvS 406 no.126 and RvP 220 no.1184, *Plakaatboek*, pp.1117–18.

32. Brana-Shute, *The Manumission of Slaves in Suriname*, pp.202, 216; 'Approaching Freedom', p.45.

33. For demographic profiles of the slaves see Brana-Shute, *The Manumission of Slaves in Suriname*, pp.220–89; Brana-Shute, 'Approaching Freedom', pp.46–50.

34. Only one slave, a woman called Patientie, was listed as African-born. Her owner was A.J. Koopman, a free-born black or coloured, who had bought Patientie for his fishing business. He manumitted her to acknowledge her service. He guaranteed her livelihood by keeping her in his employment, Brana-Shute, *The Manumission of Slaves in Suriname*, pp.265–6.

35. Only in a very few cases was the occupation of the manumitted listed in the petition. Ibid., p.253, lists the work of 21 females: one was a fisher, one a master carpenter and all the other worked as servants in households or as washerwomen, seamstress, or personal companion. Of the 16 males, 2 were apprentices, one a soldier, one a footboy, and the others were skilled labourers, including a master smith, a potter, carpenters, a cooper, a clothes maker and a tailor. Combining the sex and colour variables shows that coloured men had a better chance than coloured women to be freed, but that black females had a greater chance than black males. If one adds residence it turns out that black men on the plantations had virtually no chance at all to be freed: the lighter the skin the better the chance of freedom. In Paramaribo it was exactly the other way around: the darker the greater the opportunity for manumission.

36. For a profile of the manumitters see Brana-Shute, *The Manumission of Slaves in Suriname*, pp.290–342; 'Approaching Freedom', pp.50–3. In over a quarter of the samples sex was not listed.

37. See for example, Van Lier, *Frontier Society*, p.99, 'Manumitted persons were mostly concubines and their children who had been released by the white men with whom they had entered into a relationship'.

38. Brana-Shute, *The Manumission of Slaves in Suriname*, p.315.

39. For the motivations for manumissions see Brana-Shute ibid., pp.343–89 and Brana-Shute, 'Approaching Freedom', pp.53–7. She assumes that manumission through self-purchase was under-reported. Brana-Shute found out that only 7 of 67 slaves freed on account of kinship were freed by white owners acknowledging their paternity. The remaining 60 were manumitted by coloured and black kinsmen and women. The desire to unite families also partly explains why many owners bought slaves and then immediately freed them. Even if manumission was financially impossible kin owned by relatives did not have to fear separation by being sold to another owner.

40. Visitors regularly criticized the ostentatiousness and indolence of colonial life. Women – whites, mulatta and mestiza concubines – dressed in silk, lace, and linen and wearing richly decorated hats paraded through town followed by a cortège of slaves. The men loved to show their wealth through (imported) horses and magnificent carriages. See, for example, Philip Fermin, *Nieuwe Algemeene Beschryving van de colonie van Suriname, behelzende al het merkwaardige van dezelve, met betrekking tot de historie, aardryks- en natuurkunde* (Harlingen, 1770), pp.86–92 and J.R. Thompson, *Overzicht der geschiedenis van Suriname* (The Hague, 1901), p.70.

41. J.D. Kunitz, *Surinam und seine Bewohner oder Nachrichte ueber die geographischen, physischen, statistischen, moralischen, und politischen Verhaeltnisse dieses Landes waehrend eined zwanzigjaehrigen Aufenthalt daselbst* (Erfurt, 1805) states that there existed an easy way to tell the difference between manumitted and free-born persons. He mentions that only free-born coloureds and blacks were allowed to wear socks and shoes and that manumitted individuals could wear shoes but no socks, pp.73–4. (Slaves, of course, were prohibited to wear shoes.) However, I have not been able to find this in the *Plakaatboek*.

42. J.M. van der Linde, *Surinaamse suikerheren en hun kerk: Plantagekolonie en handelskerk ten*

tijde van Johannes Basseliers, predikant en planter in Suriname, 1667–1689 (Wageningen, 1966), p.97.

43. The history of Isabella is related by minister J.G. Kals in his tract *Neerlands Hooft-en Wortel-sonde, het verzuym van de bekeringe der Heydenen* (Leeuwarden, 1756) and reproduced and commented upon in Lichtveld and Voorhoeve, *Spiegel der vaderlandse kooplieden*, pp.122–40.

44. Gert Oostindie and Emy Maduro, *In het land van de overheerser: Antillianen en Surinamers in Nederland* (Dordrecht, 1986), p.7.

45. See for example Jan Jacob Hartsinck, *Beschryving van Guiana, of de Wilde Kust, in Zuid-Amerika ...* (Amsterdam, 1770), p 865, Charles Douglas, *Een blik in het verleden van Suriname*, pp.47–8, Hoetink, 'Surinam and Curaçao', p.78 and Stedman, *Narrative*, p.79. The latter wrote 'A great Hubbub was made here on account of a free Negro Woman call'd Eliz. *Sampson* going to be married to an European, she was worth above a hundred thousand pound Sterling inherited from her Master whose Slave she had formerly been and having addressed herself to their High and Mightinesses her Request was Granted, and accordingly being Christened she enthered in the Lawful Bond of Matrimony with one Mr Zubli'. Van Lier, *Frontier Society*, p.67 assumes that, given her name, she had inherited her fortune from a 'Jewish owner who gave her her freedom and left her his fortune'. As the following account will show, both Van Lier and Stedman got some major facts wrong.

46. The family settled in Suriname in 1705. After the planter's death, Nanoe gave birth to four slave children: Jakje or Isaak Hanibal, Quackoe, Cato or Catherina Opperman, and Nanoe or Nanette Samson. On the genealogy of Elisabeth Samson's family see Cynthia Mc Leod-Ferrier, *Elisabeth Samson: Een vrije zwarte vrouw in het achttiende–eeuwse Suriname* (Utrecht, 1993), pp.25–38.

47. In 1730 Charloo requested the Court of Policy to manumit the four children of his mother Mariana as he now had the means to buy them free. Given her name, the mother by that time was free already.

48. Charloo left her 200 guilders. Mc Leod-Ferrier, *Elisabeth Samson*, pp.25, 27, 40.

49. See ibid., pp.40–6; Beeldsnijder, 'Een vrije negerin en een arme blanke: Twee portretten uit Suriname in de jaren dertig van de achttiende eeuw', *De Gids* 153 (1990), pp.839–41.

50. A certain Pelser told Elisabeth that the Governor when in the military had been forced to hand in his sword. Elisabeth told the Governor about this accusation. When questioned Pelser denied ever having said anything and in turn Elisabeth was accused of slander.

51. Beeldsnijder, 'Een vrije negerin', p.840.

52. On Creutz see Mc Leod, *Elisabeth Samson*, pp.47–51.

53. Notarization of cohabitation was common when property was involved.

54. On this inheritance see ibid., pp.53–9, 102–4. Noteworthy is that neither this inventory nor any later inventories mention any mortgages on the properties.

55. Hartsinck, *Beschryving van Guiana*, p.865 and Douglas, *Een blik in het verleden van Suriname*, p.47 mention 30 to 40,000 guilders. Van Lier, *Frontier Society*, p.67 quotes Nepveu who estimated her income at 80 to 100,000 guilders.

56. The Suriname authorities clearly stated that they thought a mixed mariage was morally repugnant. Their worst fear was that 'lascivious' white women might want to manumit black men to marry them. They referred to the edict of Johan de Rayer forbidding relations between white women and black men. Mc Leod-Ferrier, *Elisabeth Samson*, pp.67–74.

57. After an brief period of administration by the Dutch province of Zeeland and after that the West India Company, Suriname fell under the control of de *Geoctroyeerde Societeit van Suriname* (Chartered Society of Suriname). The West India Company, the city of Amsterdam, and the Van Aerssen van Sommelsdijck family each owned one-third of the Society's shares.

58. McLeod-Ferrier, *Elisabeth Samson*, pp.68–9.

59. Ibid., p.74. Housekeeper (*huisvrouw* or *huishoudster*) is a common term in the Dutch colonies in the East and West to describe a common-law wife.

60. Ibid., pp.81–7. To give but one indication of the worth of Elisabeth Samson's possessions: a new slave at that time cost 250 to 300 guilders.

61. Beeldsnijder, 'Over vrije negers en arme blanken in Suriname 1730–1750', p.11.

62. On this European institutional ideal see Sidney W. Mintz and Richard Price, *The Birth of African-American Culture: An Anthropological Perspective* (Boston, 1992), esp. pp.5–6.
63. Brana-Shute, 'Approaching Freedom', p.56.
64. Called 'ill-mannered lummoxes' by Teenstra, *De negerslaven*, p.18; See also Lans, *Bijdrage tot de kennis der kolonie Suriname*, p.37; Van Lier, *Frontier Society*, p.46.
65. Teenstra, *De negerslaven*, p.18.
66. G. Van Lennep Coster, *Aanteekeningen, gehouden gedurende mijn verblijf in de West–Indiën in de jaren 1837–1840* (Amsterdam, 1842), p.40; Teenstra, *De negerslaven*, pp.11, 41, 68–9; Van Lier, *Frontier Society*, pp.81–2.
67. Brana-Shute, 'Approaching Freedom', pp.43–4.
68. The term *piki njan* derives from the Sranan (the lingua franca in Suriname) expression *waka piki njan*: walking around gathering food. There is very little information about *piki njan* slaves. See Brana-Shute, *Manumission of Slaves in Suriname*, pp.151–60.
69. Ibid., pp.99, 303.
70. Teenstra, *De negerslaven*, pp.5, 10, 34. Lans, *Bijdrage tot de kennis der kolonie Suriname*, p.197 provides similar data for the population of Paramaribo. Van Lennep Coster, *Aanteekeningen*, p.33, mentions that the majority of Paramaribo's population is coloured.
71. The manumission laws were relaxed for the first time in 1843. Now a request for manumission had to include a financial guarantee (200 to 400 guilders) or a deposit in the colonial coffers (75 to 100 guilders); proof of church membership; and proof of registration in the slave register. The manumitted slave would only receive full civil rights after ten years and during that period he/she was not allowed to leave the colony, *Koloniaal Verslag* 1849, p.349.
72. Calculated from *Koloniale Verslagen* 1855–1862.
73. *Koloniaal Verslag* 1847–48, p.37.
74. Teenstra, *De negerslaven*, p.43; Brana-Shute, *Manumission of Slaves in Suriname*, pp.302–4.
75. *Koloniaal Verslag* 1849, p.350.
76. Ibid., 1850, p.135; see also *Koloniale Verslagen* 1851, p.3; 1852, p.8; 1853, p.3.
77. More than one third of the whites had left the colony within a twelve-year period. Governor Wichers actively fostered this emancipation by appointing free coloureds in lower- and middle-level administrative positions. Instead of continuing the policy of importing more slaves and recruiting white colonists, he wanted to form a middle class of coloured individuals who would stay in the colony. According to Van Lier, *Frontier Society*, p.108, the increasing number of manumissions during Wichers's term of office is to be explained by the personal influence of this Governor.
78. Van Lier, *Frontier Society*, p.111. On Vrolijk see also Wolbers, *Geschiedenis van Suriname*, pp.559–60 and Oostindie, *In het land van de overheerser*, p.31.
79. On the Benevolent Society see Wolbers, *Geschiedenis van Suriname*, p.645 and J. Marten W. Schalkwijk, *Plantation Societies: Structural Analysis and Changing Elite Networks in Suriname, 1650–1920* (Ph.D. Dissertation, Cornell University, Ithaca, 1994), pp.233–4.
80. On H. Ch. Focke see John Focke, 'Mr. Hendrik Charles Focke 1802–1856 (een vergeten Surinamer?)', *Mededelingen van het Surinaams Museum* 40 (1983), pp.26–34.
81. The administration reported that, albeit slowly, the number of marriages among the free coloureds and blacks increased, particularly because of the moral pressure in the Moravian Church, *Koloniale Verslagen*, 1854, p.3 and 1855, p.7. On the Moravians and their obsession with marriage and sexual relationships see Lenders, *Strijders voor het Lam*, Chapters III en IV.
82. Van Lennep Coster, *Aanteekeningen*, p.40.
83. Van Lier, *Frontier Society*, pp.111–13.
84. The eminence of the Reformed Church did not preclude the fact that the great majority (often close to 80 per cent) of the children receiving baptism were bastards. In contrast to the Reformed Church, the Lutheran Church had some coloured elders (Wolbers, *Geschiedenis van Suriname*, p.769). On the popularity and influence of the Moravian Brethren see Lenders, *Strijders voor het Lam*.
85. Teenstra, *De negerslaven*, pp.47, 68–9.

86. Ibid., pp.45–67. As an abolitionist Teenstra protested against the excesses of slavery, but that obviously did not diminish his belief in white supremacy. Wolbers, *Geschiedenis van Suriname*, p.638, agreed that around 1830 the prejudices against coloureds and Jews had not abated.
87. Lans, *Bijdrage tot de kennis der kolonie Suriname*, pp.40–1.
88. Lammens, *Bijdragen tot de Kennis van de Kolonie Suriname*, p.xv.
89. According to Van Lier, *Frontier Society*, p.106, the prejudice against the inferior half-caste was a nineteenth-century phenomenon. In the eighteenth century discrimination had been based on the slave origins of the free coloureds.
90. Ibid., pp.57–8.
91. Ibid., pp.105–6.
92. Lans, *Bijdrage tot de kennis der kolonie Suriname*, p.40.
93. Dagboek Treu quoted in Lenders, *Strijders voor het Lam*, Chapter III.
94. E.J. Bartelink, *Hoe de tijden veranderen: herinneringen van een ouden planter* (Paramaribo, 1916).
95. Almost all directors in the service of Eyken Sluyters en Mollinger were mulattos. According to Bartelink, ibid., p.43, 'the directors were held in high esteem by the administrators, when they performed well, and were given much freedom in their job, there were certain rules which had to be strictly adhered to. The administrators believed that a director had to be present on the plantation and discouraged him from coming to town. Overseers and directors needed permission for trips to town'. Lans, *Bijdrage tot de kennis der kolonie Suriname*, p.36 mentions that one needed at least three years experience as an overseer to become a director. Teenstra, *De negerslaven*, p.24 calls the director the most useful person in the colony. Several times Bartelink switched employers, including the administrators Paul Planteau and Bouguenon.
96. In these first years he had the benefit of the advice of a washerwoman, who had a child by the previous director. This child was bought by the father and sent to Holland for further studies, Bartelink, *Herinneringen*, p.17.
97. Zeezigt, Voorburg, Wederzorg, Barbados, Ornamibo a/d Para, Potribo, Wederzorg, Geyersvlijt, Reynsdorp, Concordia, Caledonia, Leliendaal, Belwaarde, Ornamibo.
98. Bartelink, *Herinneringen*, p.24.
99. Ibid., pp.54–6.
100. Ibid., pp.76–8.
101. Ibid., p.82.
102. Ibid., p.59. This seems to indicate the possibility that the majority of free coloureds, even those in the plantation business, did not pay much attention to the social consequences of the emancipation of the slaves.
103. During the first half of the century it was the coloured population who occupied most administrative positions, in the latter part the Jews were in the majority. A very small buffer was formed by a group of coloured Jews. Robert Cohen, 'Patterns of Marriage and Remarriage among the Sephardi Jews of Surinam, 1788–1818', in *The Jewish Nation in Suriname: Historical Essays*, edited by Robert Cohen, pp.89–100 (Amsterdam, 1982), p.94 mentions that by 1830 there were only 50 coloured Jews. Hoetink, 'Surinam and Curaçao', p.64 mentions a few hundred in the later nineteenth century. See also Robert Cohen, *Jews in Another Environment: Surinam in the Second Half of the Eighteenth Century* (Leiden, 1991), pp.156–74.
104. Hoetink, 'Surinam and Curaçao', p.81.

Shades of Freedom:
Anna Kingsley in Senegal, Florida and Haiti

DANIEL L. SCHAFER

For hours the horsemen rode through the countryside of Kajoor into the dry and barren landscape of Jolof. It was April 1806, temperatures were moderate and the roads still passable as the heavy seasonal rains had not yet disrupted travel in Senegal. The fierce-looking men with long braided hair and warrior apparel stopped occasionally to rest the horses and fire their passion for battle with deep swigs of alcohol. The raiders hit Anta Majigeen Ndiaye's village just before dawn.[1]

Had the local villagers detected the horsemen, panic would have spread quickly, for these were the Tyeddo warriors feared throughout the region, the royal slaves of Amari Ngoone Ndella, the Damel (king) of Kajoor, a Wolof state located south and west of the Jolof nation. Owing allegiance only to Ndella, they were a standing army of professional soldiers trained to protect Kajoor and its ruler and to raid and plunder enemy villages and march the survivors to the coast to sell to European slave traders. In exchange, Ndella received cloth, alcohol and luxury goods, and more importantly, the guns and powder necessary to resupply his war machine.[2]

The mounted warriors approached Anta's home that day in the same manner they had converged on dozens of Jolof villages in preceding months. Conditions had been unsettled in Senegal since 1790 when religious wars broke out in the kingdom of Kajoor, one of four Wolof kingdoms to survive the legendary Jolof empire that ruled in Senegal for centuries. Most Wolof people had converted to the religion of Islam long before 1790. The leaders of many villages were Muslim clerics. Pious farmers, fond of quiet family life in rural villages, forbidden to imbibe alcohol or engage in other sinful acts, the Wolof Muslims had grown resentful of the immorality of their ruling families.[3] Especially troublesome were the flamboyant Tyeddo, whose attacks were supposed to be directed only at non-Wolof peoples. But when supplies of luxury goods or weapons ran low, rulers winked at raids on distant and unsuspecting Wolof villages.

In Kajoor, resentment led to nearly two decades of rebellion. As Ndella's repression worsened, thousands of Muslims fled south and west to form their own state at the Cape Vert peninsula, enclosing themselves in walled villages for protection against the Tyeddo cavalrymen. But Ndella's warriors pursued, spreading destruction beyond the borders of Kajoor to pit one Wolof state against another. Even non-Wolof people like the Fulbe of Futa Toro were engulfed in the fighting. Warfare was suspended in 1806 but the Tyeddo raids continued in to Jolof to punish that state for past support of Futa Toro.[4] The Tyeddo tortured and killed some of the male captives as lessons to the rebellious. The others were taken to the coastal town of Rufisque and sold into the Atlantic slave trade from the Island of Goree.

Had Anta been awake in the pre-dawn darkness she might have heard the horses stomping restlessly in the sand and scrub beyond the millet fields surrounding the housing compounds. But she slept until the sounds of charging horses and the terrifying shouts of the Tyeddo burst into the dwelling houses in her family's compound. Her father was cut down as he resisted the intruders. Anta and the surviving members of her family were herded into the centre of the village with the other victims. Over the walls came sounds of resistance from neighbouring compounds. The soldiers searched the family compounds, pillaging objects of value and destroying anything impeding their progress. It was late morning before the looting ended and the captives were marched away. Behind them the signs of violence were everywhere beneath the smoke rising from fires set by the looters. Bodies of men lay where they were shot by the intruders. This would be Anta's last memory of her home.

The captives were forced to march south and west toward Rufisque in a column that grew longer as it progressed as captives from nearby slave villages were forced into its ranks. Most slaves lived in such detached agricultural villages and worked the millet fields of their owners. Purchased at markets or captured in warfare, slaves of the Wolof were generally Sereer people captured in raids on villages located to the south toward the Gambia River, or were captives from the Bambara states or from other nations to the east of Senegal. Anta's family had owned numerous slaves, many of them women who worked as 'pileuses' pounding millet kernels and preparing meals in the family compounds, or fetching water from the well and performing other menial tasks. Anta had grown up in a highly stratified society of inherited classes of nobles, free farmers and slaves.

Although it may not have been apparent to her captors as they traversed the sandy roads that day, Anta was a member of a proud and noble family. Anta inherited from her father the Ndiaye name which descended from the legendary Njaajaan Njaay, the founder of the Jolof Empire. For generations the Ndiaye men had been free farmers who prized their independence and social standing, the owners of slaves and land and cattle. Each Jolof king had come from one of the hundreds of heads of family in the Ndiaye patrilineage. Anta's sudden loss of freedom was both a painful and humiliating experience.[5]

It was rare to see Wolof of either gender enslaved and brought to the coast. Located near the European trading posts, the Wolof had expanded their production of grain and other foodstuffs to sell to the ship captains whose profits depended on keeping their human cargoes alive during the passage to the Americas. For decades Wolof had raided and traded to acquire labourers from other African nations for the prospering Wolof enterprises.[6] But these were unusual times. Ndella's warriors had crushed Muslim rebels in Kajoor and exported large numbers of them. When the wars widened beyond the boundaries of Kajoor, Ndella's soldiers brought captives from Jolof, even Fulbe from Futa Toro, to the markets at Rufisque and St. Louis. The wars were temporarily halted in 1806, yet Anta and other women captured by the Tyeddo were enslaved and sold at Goree.

At Rufisque, Anta's coffle was taken to the central market where buyers walked among them judging their strength and health. The buyers were the metis traders, offspring of French officials and Wolof women known as 'signares'. After the French left Senegal, the 'signares' headed the family-based companies headquartered at Goree and St. Louis that dominated mercantile activities along the rivers and coastal areas.[7]

Late that afternoon Anta's group was placed in long, narrow canoes used by the traders from Goree. The oarsmen pushed quickly into the harbour waters and paddled west toward the tip of Cape Vert, skirting the coastline *en route* to Goree, a rocky island two-miles offshore. Goree is a narrow island only a few hundred yards wide and less than a mile long with steep cliffs on the side facing toward the mainland. Frequented by Portuguese and Dutch traders from the middle of the fifteenth century, Goree was seized by the French in 1677 and fought over and alternately possessed by the French and British until Senegal became independent in 1960. When Anta reached its shores, the British controlled Goree.[8]

Before dark the canoes rounded the arm of land that reaches into the sea and protects Goree's snug harbour and were pulled on to the soft sand of the shore. Anta was led up a slight incline toward two-storey buildings flanked by long and narrow one-storey structures and stone fences enclosing inner courtyards. The guards stopped Anta before a large double door and led her into a courtyard surrounded by low-ceiling rooms with chains and manacles lining the dank walls.

Days later the thirteen-year-old Muslim girl from Jolof finally emerged from her cell shielding her eyes from the sunlight and descended the hillside toward the canoes in the harbour. Riding at anchor offshore was a European ship waiting to load its human cargo. Barrels of water, food and other items were packed in the crowded hold beneath the deck. Already aboard were huge iron cooking pots and assorted utensils necessary to prepare food during the voyage ahead. Waves pitched the canoe against the sides of the ship as Anta cautiously made her way up the boarding plank to the deck and down into the hold. She walked through wooden half-bunks protruding from the sides, three feet below the decks; on these and on the planks below, Anta and her shipmates were packed. She recognized some of the captives and was able to speak to them in her language, a source of comfort in the terror-filled days ahead. No one recorded Anta Majigeen Ndiaye's thoughts when she was forced below deck. Only a few weeks before she had been a teenage girl safe in the loving arms of family. When the anchor was hauled in and the sails raised to catch the easterly winds, Anta was carried away from everything that had given her comfort and identity, away from homeland and family, toward a new land and a new life.

HAVANA: ZEPHANIAH KINGSLEY, JR.

In Cuba the demand for Africans was high in 1806. Planters had developed huge sugar plantations in the rural provinces following Haiti's rebellion of 1789–1803 and the collapse of its sugar economy. Other nations were moving toward abolition of the Atlantic slave trade – Denmark in 1802, England in 1807, and the United States in 1808 – but in Cuba the demand for Africans remained insatiable. Ship captains knew the truth of the old Cuban saying, 'sugar is made with blood'. As long as sugar and slavery were inseparable in Cuba, high death rates were certain and African traders were assured of a profitable market.[9]

It was the promise of profit that brought Captain Francis Ghisolfi and the *Sally* to Havana in July 1806 under the flag of Denmark. Ghisolfi had been in Havana several times before, but never with a cargo of more females than males. Normally, the ratio had been two males to every female. On this voyage the *Sally* carried 120 Africans; 99 were women – better than an 80 per cent ratio – of whom 22 were young teenagers. The *Sally* arrived from the Island of St. Thomas in the Danish West Indies, where Charlotte-Amalie was an important trans-shipment centre in the Atlantic trade.[10]

Prodded by the rough men who had been her guards for five weeks, Anta Majigeen Ndiaye joined her shipmates moving slowly down the gangplank of the *Sally* and along the Havana dock. Merchants from France, Norway, the Caribbean islands and South America supplied the bustling Havana market where crowds of buyers haggled for lumber and salt fish from New England, meats and grain from other American states, cloth and manufactured goods from England, and slaves from Africa. Ships departed daily for other Spanish colonies loaded with sugar, rum, pork and African slaves.

Merchants at the waterfront had been watching the *Sally* for days, aware that it was filled with new Africans the Cubans called 'bozales'. Africans often arrived at American ports suffering from a variety of ailments. Those who had died during the crossing had been dumped into the ocean without ceremony.[11] Cuban doctors would have given Anta and her shipmates a perfunctory medical inspection soon after the ship anchored and ordered a brief quarantine if they detected epidemic diseases. During these immobile days crew members prepared the Africans for sale, adding fresh vegetables and fruits to their diets and bathing and oiling their skin to make them look shiny and healthy for buyer inspections.

On the September day that Anta was exhibited for sale, a merchant from Spanish East Florida mingled amidst the crowd of buyers. A slaver himself and the owner of a Florida plantation, Zephaniah Kingsley, Jr. noticed the tall Wolof girl with shiny black skin among the hundreds of Africans for sale. Kingsley was the high bidder that day, purchasing Anta Majigeen Ndiaye and two other African females.[12]

Kingsley was in Havana as the owner and business manager of the *Esther*, an American schooner that carried 45 Africans, all males, into port. He later testified that he purchased Anta 'as a bozal in the port of Havana from a slave cargo'.[13] Thus, Anta could have been one of the 22 young females who arrived in Havana aboard the *Sally*. Many years later, however, Kingsley said in an interview that he first saw Anta on the coast of Africa, and in his will stated they married 'in a foreign land' where the ceremony was 'celebrated and solemnized by her native African custom, altho' never celebrated according to the forms of Christian usage'.[14]

Kingsley remained in Havana while his cargo of male slaves was sold and the *Esther* was loaded with four hogsheads of molasses, 28 half pipes and 12 whole pipes of rum. At departure, the shipping manifest also recorded additional cargo: 'tres negras bozales' (three black females). Cuban customs officers had counted 45 male 'bozales' aboard the *Esther* when it entered Havana, with no mention of females. The 'tres negras bozales' counted when the ship departed were purchased in Havana and Anta was one of the three.

The *Esther* left Havana on 10 October 1806 and fourteen days later it lay at anchor off St. Augustine, Florida. Kingsley rowed ashore to register three new female residents of the province and the following day the *Esther* sailed north to the St. John's River and turned inland. From the deck Anta could see miles of sandy beaches and huge expanses of marsh grasses, occasional fields of corn and cotton and widely-scattered settlements. The most common sight was pine forest, with occasional oak hammocks and stretches of cypress and bay trees. There were no rocky outcroppings like those on the Senegal coast, and only rarely were there hills.

The schooner came to anchor at Doctor's Lake, an inlet to the west of the St. John's River forty miles from its mouth. At the wharf black men waited to secure it to the pilings. Adjacent to the dock other black men were building a ship, and beyond lay agricultural fields and large citrus groves. Once again, Anta walked down a ship's gangplank, this time to step ashore at Laurel Grove, her new home. Familiar with the Wolof language from his travels in Africa, Kingsley was able to communicate with Anta during their days together in Havana and aboard the *Esther*. When they reached the sandy soil beyond the wharf, Kingsley directed her beyond the wooden houses of the slave quarters toward the dwelling house where they would live together. Already, Anta was carrying Kingsley's child.

For the remaining thirty-seven years of his life, Kingsley would refer to Anta as his wife. She would be known as Anna Magigine Jai Kingsley, reflecting the way her African names were transposed into Spanish and English by officials in Florida and her decision to keep the memory of her mother and father alive in the Americas. Anna Magigine Jai's retentions of her parental names reflected the pride and adaptability for which Wolof women were noted.

LAUREL GROVE: ANNA MAGIGINE JAI

At an age when Wolof girls were only beginning to put aside childhood games to learn the first lessons of womanhood from their mothers, Anna had been torn from parents and homeland and sold across the ocean as a slave. Still in her thirteenth year, she had become the wife of a white plantation owner in Florida and in the months before the birth of her first child, Anna became the household manager at Laurel Grove, in charge of all activities related to life in the owner's housing complex. She later expanded that role to assume supervisory responsibilities for the health of the labour force and to manage the estate when her husband was absent. This meant overseeing agricultural activities, the shipyard and cotton gins on the estate, and a store stocked with tools and other items for trade with families and planters in the surrounding area. Kingsley's enterprise was far more elaborate than any of the slave villages Anna had seen in Jolof.

But Anna's orientation to life at Laurel Grove was made easier by the ways in which it reminded her of Jolof. Although the soil types, vegetation and levels of precipitation at Laurel Grove differed greatly from conditions in Jolof, Anna would have noticed similarities between the reserve lands Kingsley owned and the shifting cultivation patterns of West Africans, who moved crops and even villages on to idle brush-covered land when soil fertility in the millet fields diminished. And with the exception of her husband and occasional craftsmen hired to work at the shipyards, nearly everyone was from Africa. Ibo and Susu and Sereer men performed the skilled labour tasks at the carpentry and blacksmith shops just as Bambara and Fula and Sereer men had woven cloth in Wolof villages.

Kingsley's slave families were housed in rows of wooden cabins at Laurel Grove and at a nearby subdivision called Springfield. Each location had dwelling houses, slave quarters, poultry coops, cart houses, carpentry shops, mill houses, corn and pea cribs, and barns for cotton gins, bales of cotton, horses and mules. The estate's citrus grove had 760 Mandarin orange trees, surrounded by a picket fence and a 2,000 foot hedge of bearing orange trees. Kingsley also maintained several large fields of potatoes, corn and beans to feed his workers throughout the year. Each slave family also planted their own corn and vegetable gardens on land Kingsley assigned to them.

Kingsley's slave force of more than 100 workers came from several West and East African nations. Their languages and cultures were remarkably diverse, yet they worked and lived together amicably and were creating a medium of communication and a creole culture.[15] The field hand, Jacob, was from the Ibo nation of Nigeria. His wife, Camilla, was a SuSu from Rio Pongo on the Guinea Coast, and their son, Jim, was born at Laurel Grove. Another couple, Jack and Tamassa, were from an East African nation Kingsley called 'Zinguibara' (Zanzibar). In 1812 they were the parents of four children: Ben, M'toto, Molly and Rose, all born at Laurel Grove.

Abraham Hannahan, Laurel Grove's general manager, was a mulatto slave born and reared in the Charleston household of Kingsley's father. Kingsley brought Abraham to East Florida in 1804 and placed him in charge of Laurel Grove, where in consultation with trusted slave 'drivers', Abraham assigned daily work tasks and watched to see that they were completed.[16]

Kingsley chose an African named Peter to supervise Springfield, and Peter was second in command under Abraham. Kingsley called Peter a 'mechanic and valuable manager' worth at least $1,000 in 1812. Under Peter's direction the slaves left the quarters at sunrise to work at assigned tasks in the fields or forests until two o'clock each afternoon. Peter's slave crew produced 800 bushels of corn and 400 bushels of field peas in a year, in addition to caring for poultry, hogs and cattle. Peter was also in charge of the mill house where slaves processed the Sea Island cotton grown on 200 acres of the estate.

At Laurel Grove Anna had the companionship of another Jolof woman transported with her from Goree to Havana, and later to East Florida, and the women were able to talk about their homeland in the Wolof language they shared. As 'shipmates' in such a traumatic experience as the passage from Africa to Florida, Anna and Sophie Chigigine formed bonds that functioned as kinship ties in later years. Sophie became the wife of Laurel Grove's manager, Abraham Hannahan. Zephaniah later freed Abraham and Sophie and their children and the lives of the two families would remain intertwined for decades.[17]

In the months after her arrival at Laurel Grove, Anna met other plantation owners who had African wives and workers. John Fraser owned two cotton and rice plantations on which 370 Africans laboured. Fraser's African wife, Phenda, remained behind at their home on Rio Pongo on the Guinea Coast. There, Fraser owned a 'factory' or a fortified holding pen for slaves whom he transported to slave markets in the Americas aboard his own ships.[18]

Other African wives and mistresses of white men also lived nearby. Molly Erwin was the wife of James Erwin, who worked fifty slaves on his rice plantation on the St. Marys River. The two African wives of George Clarke, an important official with the Spanish government of East Florida, were well known in the area. Francis Richard, Francisco Xavier Sánchez and several other prominent men in Florida also had black wives and raised their interracial children in familial bonds. Only the interracial nature of these unions would have been outside Anna's experiences in Jolof. A familiar route to freedom for slave women in Wolof villages was marriage to their owners or other freeborn men in the compounds and giving birth to their children.[19]

Planters like Kingsley, Clarke, and Richard saw in Florida's climate, soil, and waterways the opportunity to become rich and they believed that only through slavery could they obtain the workers necessary for prosperity. Yet they felt race did not automatically and permanently consign persons of colour to either slavery or freedom. According to Kingsley, 'color ought not be the badge of degradation. The only distinction should be between slave and free, not between white and colored.'[20] Kingsley justified enslaving Africans by claiming they were more suited to work in the heat of the Florida sun than their pale European counterparts. 'Nature,' he wrote, 'has not fitted a white complexion for hard work in the sun, as it is evident that the darkness of complexion here is a measure of capacity for endurance of labor.'[21] In Kingsley's opinion, whites had two alternatives in Florida: either abandon the land or employ large numbers of black slaves.

Kingsley chose to employ black slaves, but he advocated humane treatment and encouraged slaves to live in family units and perpetuate their African customs. But more was needed to ensure the personal safety of the white patriarchs. Kingsley called for liberal manumission laws and policies which could convince 'the free colored population to be attached to good order and have a friendly feeling towards the white population'.[22] He believed men like Abraham Hannahan who had talent and leadership ability should be freed and given personal property rights and encouraged to join with white slaveowners. Once united, they could control the much larger group of black laborers who created the riches that justified the overall system. Acting on these principles, Kingsley freed Hannahan in 1811.[23] Kingsley permitted his slaves to purchase their freedom for one-half their evaluated price.[24]

The relationship between Anna and Zephaniah was open and familial and would continue so for nearly forty years. Kingsley always acknowledged Anna as his wife and praised her 'truth, honor, integrity, moral conduct and good sense', but he continued to keep other slave mistresses who also gave birth to his children. Anna was the senior figure, carrying the authority of the recognized first wife in a polygamous household, a familiar circumstance in her African homeland but controversial in Florida. Reared in Africa in a polygamous family, Anna would have been familiar with co-wife relationships, tolerant of them, and cooperative with the other women. Those who met Anna when she first arrived in Florida recognized her special relationship with Zephaniah and concluded from it that she was a free woman. John M. Bowden testified in the 1830s that he had known Anna 'from the time she first came into the country and she was always called and considered a free person of color'.[25]

And yet, Anna was legally a slave. Kingsley was thirty years her senior and engaged in a dangerous life as ship captain and slave plantation owner. Were his ship to go down during one of his Caribbean voyages, Anna would have appeared on a subsequent property inventory and she and her children would have been sold at auction. Kingsley once said he was unsure how his marriage to Anna would be considered under the law. They were married 'in a foreign land' where the ceremony was 'celebrated and solemnized by her native African custom, altho' never celebrated according to the forms of Christian usage'.[26] But there was never any doubt about her status: 'She has always been respected as my wife and as such I acknowledge her, nor do I think that her truth, honor, integrity, moral conduct or good sense will lose in comparison with anyone.'

Kingsley formally emancipated the eighteen-year-old Anna on 4 March 1811. On the manumission document Kingsley wrote:

> Let it be known that I...possessed as a slave a black woman called Anna, around eighteen years of age, bought as a bozal in the port of Havana from a slave cargo, who with the permission of the government was introduced here; the said black woman has given birth to three mulatto children: George, about 3 years 9 months, Martha, 20 months old, and Mary, one month old. And regarding the

> good qualities shown by the said black woman, the nicety and fidelity
> which she has shown me, and for other reasons, I have resolved to set
> her free...and the same to her three children.[27]

After almost five years of enslavement, Anna Kingsley became a free
woman again and her three children shared her freedom. Events in her life
had moved with amazing rapidity. After gaining her freedom Anna
remained at Laurel Grove as the wife of Zephaniah Kingsley and manager
of his household.

Abraham Hannahan, whom Kingsley emancipated in the same year,
continued on as plantation manager. Given land at Laurel Grove, Hannahan
built a house and barn and expanded his responsibilities by assuming some
of the duties for Kingsley's store. But when Abraham travelled on the St.
John's River selling goods to farmers and to Seminole Indians, Anna
assumed more responsibilities at Laurel Grove and Kingsley later said her
managerial abilities rivalled his own.[28]

Having responsible management at Laurel Grove was of major
significance because Kingsley was seldom in residence. For years he had
relied on slaves to manage while he sailed in the West Indies trade with an
all black crew. His diversified enterprises made Kingsley a rich man. In
1811 he owned several plantations and other properties and his merchant
operations were prospering. Given her husband's affluence, it is unlikely
that lack of material comforts would have led Anna to make significant
changes in her life. And yet, in 1812, she moved away from Laurel Grove.

Mandarin

Throughout her adult years Anna proved to be an independent and capable
woman, concerned about business investments and actively involved in
management of her family's financial affairs. Perhaps it was that
independence that prompted her to strike out on her own. She would
continue her relationship with Kingsley in the years ahead, but in 1812 she
moved across the St. John's River and established a home of her own in
Mandarin on a homestead granted by the Spanish government.

It was not unusual for the Spanish colonial government to recognize
Anna Kingsley's freedom, nor to grant her land and permit her to own
slaves. Racial prejudice existed in Spanish East Florida, but it lacked the
rigidity of racist exclusion found in nearby Georgia and South Carolina.
Manumission was encouraged, and once freed, black women and men were
able to work the Spanish system through baptism, marriage, land grants,
litigation and kinship networks – real or fictive. Faced with invasions and
internal rebellions occurring with a disturbing frequency, and plagued by an
army which was inadequate to meet these challenges, governor after

governor was forced to depend on free black militia units and Indian allies to retain control of the province. The geopolitical situation thus worked to keep a relaxed racial system in place while it was vanishing in nearby Spanish Cuba.[29]

As a free black woman in the frontier society of Spanish East Florida, Anna Jai was entitled to specific rights and privileges enjoyed under medieval Spanish law. She could hold and manage property, testify and litigate in the courts, and engage in business activities. She utilized the Catholic Church to protect her rights and bound her family to powerful patrons through extended kinship networks under godparent ties. Fictive kinship networks linked by mutual obligations were significant in Hispanic communities, as they had been in her Jolof village and Anna would continue to use these kinship ties, even after Florida became an American territory.[30]

At Mandarin Anna built a two-storey home; stone on the first floor and hewn logs on the second. The lower floor served as a store house for 600 bushels of corn in 1813, as well as for nails, spikes, chains, axes and other farming tools. Anna, George, Martha and Mary lived in the comfortably furnished second storey of the building. Outside were farm animals and cleared fields and a poultry yard praised by her neighbours as 'the greatest in the country'.[31]

Although a former slave herself, Anna became the owner of twelve slaves after her own emancipation. Her roots and conceptions of social relationships had been shaped in an African society where slavery had been integral to the social fabric for centuries. Nor would Anna's neighbours have thought it unusual that she owned slaves; other examples of free black owners of slaves abounded in the province. The unfree status of Spanish slaves was neither preordained nor indelibly permanent.[32]

In the same year that Anna established her own estate, the 'Patriot Rebellion' began. Instigated and financed covertly by the President of the United States, James Madison, and his Secretary of State, James Monroe, and supported by American soldiers and sailors who crossed East Florida's northern border as advisers to the insurgents, the Patriots took Fernandina and moved south to control the St. Johns River and begin a siege outside St. Augustine.[33]

By July 1812 Governor Sebastian Kindelan knew he would have to surrender if food supplies could not be found for the St. Augustine population. He ordered his Seminole allies to attack the outlying settlements, assuming that many of the rebels would be forced to leave the siege lines to defend their homes and families. The strategy worked, although it devastated Florida's previously thriving plantations. For Kingsley it meant the destruction of most of Laurel Grove and the loss of forty-one of his valuable Africans to the Seminole raiders.

The rebellion shortly failed, but widespread looting and burning followed as the Patriot affair turned into guerrilla warfare and border marauding. Anna had more to fear than the destruction of her property. She knew that if she and her family were captured by the marauders they would be driven to Georgia and sold as slaves. Hundreds of slaves and free blacks had been captured and driven north in the previous months of fighting. To be captured and driven in a slave coffle again, this time with her children marching beside her, must have been an unthinkable horror to Anna.

In the event of an attack by the rebels, she and her family could either escape to the woods and swamps, a perilous venture given the ages of her children, or seek shelter on the Spanish gunboats patrolling the St. John's River.[34] In November 1813 Colonel Samuel Alexander, a notorious plunderer and slave catcher from Georgia, led the feared attack on Anna's farm. Crewmen on the Spanish gunboats on the river saw the rebels as they approached but were unable to stop their march. Instead, the gunboat commander met briefly with Anna in her poultry yard, surrounded by her children and twelve slaves. Anna had already chosen a course of action: she emptied the houses quickly and carried the furnishings to a hiding spot in the woods nearby, then placed her children in the care of her slaves and hid them in the woods by the shoreline.

Before joining her children, Anna lit a torch and burned her home and the cabins of her slaves. She then ran through the woods to her family and led them to the gunboat. The gunboat returned to its command post at San Nicolas, just downriver from the ferry crossing at Cowford. When Thomas Llorente, commander at San Nicolas, learned of Anna's heroic actions he wrote to the governor: 'Anna M. Kingsley deserves any favor the governor can grant her. Rather than afford shelter and provisions to the enemies of His Majesty...[she] burned it all up and remained unsheltered from the weather; the royal order provides rewards for such services.'[35] The governor later awarded Anna a 350-acre land grant as compensation for her losses and for her heroic contribution to the defence of the province.

Kingsley joined Anna at San Nicolas in December, after his remaining buildings at Laurel Grove were destroyed by the rebels. The couple stayed there until the outlying plantations were again secure from marauders and in January 1814 they rafted their remaining property and slaves to safety in Fernandina.

Fort George Island

Early in March 1814, Anna and Zephaniah Kingsley sailed from Fernandina to their new home at Fort George Island. Accompanied by their three children, George, Martha, and Mary, and followed by a flotilla of rafts carrying slaves and plantation equipment, the Kingsleys travelled south via the inland waterway. From the deep water channels west of Amelia Island, Anna saw the ruins of plantations left by the Patriots as they withdrew. Continuing down the inland waterway along the western shore of Big Talbot Island Anna could see only two homesteads along the shore.

As the ship approached the southern point of the island, the anxious children ran to the forward deck rail to look across the inlet that separated Talbot from Fort George Island. Looking ahead from the rail the children could see a large two-storey white house with a long brick walkway leading to a wharf on Fort George Inlet. The observation deck on the rooftop faced east with an unimpeded view of the Atlantic Ocean.

Signs of the recent violence were everywhere. With the exception of the owner's quarters, not a single building had been spared. Damage to the main house was extensive – the rebels had even stolen the locks from the doors. But hard scrubbing and repair by the carpenters brought that dwelling into a livable state before nightfall. Only charred ruins remained where more than 200 slaves had once been housed. The magnitude of the work ahead was sobering.[36] Using building materials brought by the flotilla from Fernandina, the slaves immediately began building new shelters, although the project was made more difficult by the loss of the African carpenters, Jack and M'Sooma, abducted from Laurel Grove by Indian raiders in 1812. The women fashioned palm fronds into African-style thatch roofs for the temporary quarters.[37]

Once the slaves were sheltered, Kingsley sent them to prepare weed-filled fields for planting. The delay at Fernandina, and the loss of more than forty hands during the 1812 attacks on Laurel Grove retarded the planting schedule for 1814, but in the following months Kingsley's slaves restored Fort George Island's cotton and provisions fields to profitability.[38] That done, the slaves planted citrus groves and cane fields like those at Laurel Grove.

Kingsley followed a 'task' system of planting. Drivers assigned each labourer a task sufficient to occupy his time from dawn until mid-afternoon Monday through Friday, and until noon on Saturday. Anna Kingsley checked the health of the workers daily and filled in as manager during her husband's absences. She also directed the labours of her own slaves, who were quartered with the other workers. After completing their tasks, each slave was at liberty to work his or her own garden or to go fishing or hunting to supplement the weekly provisions Kingsley supplied. In the spring Kingsley gave his workers time off to plant corn and fresh vegetables in personal garden plots and in early October another holiday permitted them to harvest their crops.[39]

Anna's children enjoyed an idyllic childhood on Fort George island. They enjoyed pony rides, explored the huge oyster shell mounds deposited

centuries before by the Timucuan Indians, and met the ships which stopped
at the wharf to leave mail and packages and occasional visitors, and to load
plantation produce. George fished and hunted with playmates from the slave
quarters while Martha and Mary delighted in trips to Mount Cornelia, the
highest point on the island, or helped their mother with her daily work.[40]
Many years later, Mary would fondly remember helping her mother and
several slaves plant the long rows of palm trees on each side of the road
leading up to the big house.[41] George, who was nearly seven years old when
the family arrived, lived on Fort George Island for more than two decades.
He learned from his father and the drivers how to manage plantations for
himself, and in 1831 became the owner of Kingsley Plantation. That same
year he married Anatoile Françoise Vantravers and began his own family on
the island.[42]

Over time Kingsley's slaves built many new structures at the estate.
Gathering oyster shells from the abundant mounds on the island, the
carpenters mixed them with equal parts of lime, sand and water to make a
concrete-like material called tabby. A semi-circle of these durable tabby
cabins replaced the temporary slave quarters with larger quarters at each end
for the drivers.[43] Farther north and close to the main house, the slaves
constructed a two-storey tabby building to stable work animals and the
high-quality riding horses of which Kingsley was notably fond.[44]

Anna lived in a separate dwelling connected to Zephaniah's home by a
walkway. Built of tabby bricks on the first floor and wood frame above, the
'Ma'am Anna House' as it would be called for decades provided the spatial
separation for husband and wife that Anna expected based on her African
experiences with polygamous families.[45] Slave cooks prepared meals in a
large kitchen in the first floor of the Anna House and carried it to the
basement warming kitchen of the main house, where dinners were served in
the 'great room' on the first floor. The long rectangular room with fireplaces
at each end and windows looking across an open porch to Talbot Island was
a grand setting for family gatherings.

Ten years after beginning life anew at Fort George Island, the surprise
arrival of a second son brought joy to the Kingsley family. When Anna was
thirty-one and Zephaniah nearly sixty, their fourth and last child, John
Maxwell Kingsley was born 22 November 1824.[46] Five years later Anna
arranged a large Catholic baptism for John Maxwell and some of the other
children born at Fort George Island. Undoubtedly a Muslim in her youth,
Anna had become a Catholic during her stay on the St. John's River,
probably converted by a Spanish priest during one of his annual visits to the
rural settlements. Zephaniah had converted to Catholicism from his parents'
Quaker faith at some time prior to taking the oath of loyalty at St. Augustine
in 1803. John Maxwell was baptized alongside three other children. Two

were sons of African slaves, and the third was Mary Martha Mattier Kingsley, the free colored child of Fatimah Kingsley, Zephaniah's daughter by co-wife Munsilna McGundo. Luis Mattier, a white planter and Mary Martha's father, was in attendance. The wealthy planter, José María Ugarte was Mary Martha's godfather, and Zephaniah and Anna's daughter, Martha, served as godmother. John Maxwell's godparents were his uncle, Zephaniah C. Gibbs, and his sister, Mary. The Irish priest who travelled from St. Augustine to perform the ceremony, Father Edward Mayne, must have wondered about the mix of colours, cultures, and continents represented at the gathering.[47]

East Florida had been a Spanish colony when Anna and Zephaniah commenced planting at Fort George; it was a territory of the United States when John Maxwell was born. The change of flags brought the stability and security lacking under Spanish rule, prompting Kingsley to purchase additional plantations. Like others, he was optimistic about Florida's economic future, but he was alarmed by the new system of race relations imported by the Americans. In 1823 President James Monroe appointed Kingsley to the Territorial Council, an experience which increased his alarm.

Kingsley had supported the relatively liberal race laws of Spain that encouraged owners to manumit their slaves and incorporate them into a three-caste society of whites, free people of colour, and slaves. But the Americans arriving in the new US territory in record numbers viewed all black people, slave and free alike, as members of an inferior race and unworthy of freedom. The new society would be composed of two-castes only; there would be free whites and enslaved blacks, with no place for free blacks.[48]

Kingsley was a proud father. He believed 'the intermediate grades of color are not only healthy, but when condition is favorable, they are improved in shape, strength and beauty, and susceptible of every amelioration'.[49] His children were intelligent and well educated, yet the new laws categorized them as uncivilized and strictly regulated their activities in fear they might inspire slave rebellions. Kingsley urged the Territorial Council to pass laws encouraging emancipation. But the assembly barred free blacks from entering Florida, limited their right to assemble, carry firearms, serve on juries, or testify against whites in court proceedings. Town councils taxed free blacks unfairly and empowered sheriffs to impress them for manual labour projects. They could be whipped for misdemeanours, subjected to curfews, even forced back into slavery to satisfy debts or fines.

Two laws affected the Kingsley family directly. The first prohibited interracial marriages and made children of mixed-race couples ineligible to inherit their parents' estates. The second imposed severe penalties on white men found guilty of sexual liaisons with black women. In 1829 the assembly moved to curtail manumission by requiring owners to forfeit $200 for each person emancipated, and to post a security bond as well. Within thirty days the freedman was required to permanently emigrate or be sold back into slavery. Had this law been in effect when Kingsley freed Anna in 1811, he would have been forced to send her and the children away. The Kingsley family had immunity from some of the new laws, since they had been residents of Spanish Florida and were given special protections under the treaty of cession. But Kingsley could never be sure how the territorial courts would interpret the new laws, and John Maxwell was born after Florida was ceded to the United States.

Wealth and influence could shield the family for a few years, but the future was ominous. Kingsley added a codicil to his will warning his loved ones of the 'illiberal and inequitable laws of this territory [which] will not afford to them and to their children that protection and justice [due] in every civilized society to every human being'. Keep a legally executed will at hand, he urged, until they could emigrate 'to some land of liberty and equal rights, where the conditions of society are governed by some law less absurd than that of color'.

Alarmed by the rising tide of racism in Florida, Kingsley acted to ensure the economic security of his family. He deeded title to Fort George Island and estates in Putnam and St. Johns County to George Kingsley and his wife, Anatoile, in 1831 and 1832. The deed to Fort George provided that Anna 'shall possess the use of her house and whatever ground she may desire to plant during her life'. It also stated that co-wife 'Munsilna McGundo, with her daughter Fatimah shall possess the use of her house and four acres of land also rations during life.'[50] Kingsley deeded Anna title to an 1000-acre estate in St. John's County at Deep Creek on the St. John's River, in exchange for 'wages and faithful services during twenty five years together'. She still owned the 350-acre plot at Dunn's Creek granted by the Spanish government to compensate for her losses at Mandarin in 1813.[51] To his daughters, Martha and Mary, Kingsley deeded two plantations at San Jose on the St. John's River in Duval County. He gave his co-wife Flora Hannahan, a 300 acre farm at Goodby's Creek adjacent to San Jose. Flora was the daughter of Abraham Hannahan and Sophie Chigigine and a slave whom Zephaniah freed when she became the mother of his son, Charles.[52]

After making provisions for his family, the ageing Kingsley moved to White Oak Plantation on the St. Mary's River in Nassau County, and resumed his maritime travels.[53] He sailed to New York and Washington to meet with prominent abolitionists, and then rejoined his family with news of a programme initiated by the President of Haiti, Jean Pierre Boyer, to recruit free blacks from North America to restore Haiti's former prosperity.

Kingsley knew Haiti's potential from a three-year residence there in the 1790s. As the only free black republic in the Western Hemisphere, Haiti beckoned as a sanctuary from the racial turmoil in Florida and the Kingsley family decided to emigrate to the 'Island of Liberty'. Zephaniah would retain a residence in Florida from which to supervise his economic empire.

Leaving Fort George Island in 1837 was painful for Anna. She had lived there for nearly a quarter-century, longer than she had lived at any single location. She had watched her children grow up there and it was there her son had married and young men had courted her daughters. Anna approved of the stable and prosperous Scotsmen from the north whom her daughters chose. Martha married Oran Baxter, a ship builder and planter, and Mary wed John S. Sammis, a planter, sawmill owner, and merchant. Martha and Mary would remain in Florida when Anna and her sons moved to Haiti.

It was an emotional farewell for Anna. She carried with her fond memories of family happiness, safety and peace. Isolated and secure, Fort George Island had been a place of refuge from the dangers of the Patriot era. But once again the outside world had intruded with threats to the freedom of her family.

HAITI: RETURN TO THE ST. JOHN'S RIVER

Zephaniah Kingsley first sailed from the St. John's River to Haiti's north shore in 1835. The seventy-year-old anchored at Cabaret Harbor and explored the island by horseback, crossing the mountains to meet with President Boyer at the national palace.[54] The revolution that ended three decades earlier had left people of African descent in control of the island but years of warfare and turmoil had destroyed a thriving export economy, and few citizens remained who were experienced with plantation management and tropical agriculture. Eventually, 6,000 free blacks from North America accepted Boyer's challenge to help bring prosperity back to the island.

Zephaniah learned on his horseback journey that the soils were still rich, and he knew that his son George and many of the Africans who worked his Florida plantations had the agricultural skills Boyer was seeking. He purchased several tracts in what had been the Spanish part of the island, with the principal site, Mayorasgo de Koka, located twenty-seven miles east of Puerto Plata.

In 1836 Zephaniah brought George and eight of his most experienced workers to begin the colony. The following year Anna and John Maxwell arrived. By 1840 nearly sixty persons had immigrated from Kingsley's estates in Florida, including Anna's-co-wives, Flora Hannahan and Sarah Murphy, and their families. The others were slaves whom Kingsley had promised freedom and land after nine years of labour, as well as an annual division of the estate's profits.

Mayorasgo de Koka proved to be a profitable venture. Inland from the beach and harbour, a coastal plain of rich soils supported sugar and cotton production, citrus groves, and corn and vegetable gardens. Two creeks wound through the tract. Its mountain hillsides were rich with mahogany and cedar forests and provided the setting for a sawmill. Cabaret Creek fed a deep freshwater lake where George Kingsley located his settlement, and meandered beyond through orange groves, gardens, a Royal Palm and plantain walk, and meadows and cane fields before merging with the Yasica River and entering the ocean. In July 1842 Zephaniah described Mayorasgo de Koka as '... in a fine, rich valley, heavily timbered with mahogany all around, well watered, flowers so beautiful, fruits in abundance, so delicious that you could not refrain from stopping to eat, till you could eat no more. My son has laid out good roads, and built bridges and mills; the people are improving, and everything is prosperous.'[55]

Anna lived at George's settlement on Cabaret Creek. She also had a place at Cabaret Village that descendants many generations later would remember in legend as 'spreading into the sea, a place where Anna could relax', wearing long cotton gowns and gold jewellery in the styles she remembered from her days in Jolof.[56] For the next decade Anna lived in comfort from shares of the proceeds of Mayorasgo de Koka, supplemented with income from rentals of her slaves and lands in Florida.

After selling Fort George Island to his nephew, Kingsley Beatty Gibbs, Kingsley moved his Florida residence and approximately eighty of his slaves to San Jose Plantation, which another nephew, Charles McNeill, supervised. Kingsley sold his White Oak Plantation in Nassau County and either rented his other estates or placed them under overseers. Meanwhile, Kingsley made frequent trips to Cabaret. [57]

Kingsley last visited Mayorasgo de Koka in May 1842. After spending time with Anna and John Maxwell, and George and Anatoile and their children, he visited at Puerto Plata with Flora. Before he departed in early December, Flora gave birth to their fifth child, Roxanne Marguerite Kingsley.[58]

The ageing mariner died the following September aged seventy-eight. He was then in New York preparing to sail again to Haiti. Anna had lost her husband of thirty-seven years. Fifty-years old at the time, living a prosperous and tranquil life in Haiti, she would soon make major changes.[59]

Zephaniah Kingsley willed land and personal property to his nephews, Kingsley B. Gibbs, George C. Gibbs, and Charles J. McNeill, and recommended that his property and investments be divided into twelve equal shares. He assigned Anna one share, George, four and John Maxwell, two. He also assigned two shares to co-wife, Flora Hannahan and her sons, and one to his son, Micanopy, whose mother was his co-wife, Sarah Murphy. The remaining shares went to nephews, Kingsley B. Gibbs and Charles J. McNeill. In contemporary monetary values, Kingsley left an inheritance worth millions, enough to encourage the baser instincts of relatives not named as legatees.[60]

Soon after Kingsley's will was read, several white relatives sued to break the will, charging that the legatees in Haiti were of African descent and thus ineligible to inherit from their white father under Florida law. Zephaniah had predicted this would happen only months before his death. Kingsley's legatees appealed the case to the Florida Supreme Court where their rights were upheld. The court ruled the Adams-Onís Treaty that ceded Spanish East Florida to the United States guaranteed full citizenship rights to all free persons of color then in the colony and the executors distributed the proceeds as Kingsley had directed. Thousands of dollars were paid to Anna and the other legatees, whose signed receipts still remain in the court file.

But disputes continued over assignments of assets left by Zephaniah. In 1846 George Kingsley sailed for Jacksonville to challenge the executor's plans for distribution of lands in the estate. Some properties scheduled for sale at public auction had been deeded to George in the early 1830s. Between Puerto Plata and Jacksonville, however, his ship was caught in a severe storm and George was drowned aged thirty-nine. His younger brother, John Maxwell Kingsley, age twenty-two, took control of Mayorasgo de Koka. Shortly afterwards, Anna returned to Florida to monitor distribution of Kingsley's assets. She took an active interest, bringing suit to remove Charles McNeill as overseer of San Jose plantation, accusing him of mismanagement and asking the judge to rent out the land and slaves to enhance profits. After an extensive investigation, and depositions from many local planters, the judge ruled against Anna's motion, citing testimony about the inevitable overwork, harsh treatment and decline in the health and well-being of the slave families that would result if the labourers were rented out. Anna's actions in this matter leave little doubt that she was a tough-minded businesswoman, zealous in pursuit of family interests.[61]

Anna's reasons for re-establishing permanent residency in Duval County are not entirely clear, especially since racial tensions in Florida increased in step with the national sectional disputes of the 1850s. But the 'Island of Liberty' experienced tensions during Anna's residence: Haiti's black rulers were driven from the former Spanish part of the island, followed by an independence movement against Spain. Violence shook the north shore region near Cabaret during these episodes, and the citizenship rights of free persons of colour were once again threatened. Profits at Mayorasgo de Koka also suffered, as timber resources declined and laborers left the estate.[62]

Between 1847 and 1854 Anna resided at Chesterfield, a twenty-two acre estate on the St. John's River, conveniently located between the residences of her two daughters. Anna became matriarch of the Kingsley clan, consulting with and working through her white guardian as required by Florida law and the Jacksonville municipal codes. Anna still owned other properties in Florida, along with a continuing interest in her late husband's estate. She also took an active role in the lives of her children. In 1848 she arranged the baptisms of three children of Martha Baxter's daughters: her great-grandchildren, Emma Jane and Julia Catherine, and Osmond Edward.[63]

Anna could expect help and security from her daughters. Martha Baxter, a widow by then, was one of the five wealthiest persons living in Duval County in 1860. Mary and John Sammis were even more affluent.[64] Anna's home was at Point St. Isabel on the east side of the St. John's River where it bends sharply to the east and drains toward the Atlantic Ocean. Point St. Isabel was owned by Anna's daughter, Martha, whom Anna appointed as attorney to act in trust for her. Martha shared her house with her daughter, Anna B. Carroll, and her son-in-law, Charles B. Carroll, a white man from New York. Also living with Martha was daughter, Isabella Baxter. Anna Kingsley lived in a separate dwelling located adjacent to Martha's residence and with her lived Bella (Isabella), the eleven-year-old daughter of John Maxwell Kingsley, who still managed Mayorasgo de Koka in the Dominican Republic. Also living at Point St. Isabel were Emma Baxter, Martha's twenty-two-year-old daughter, Emma's husband, Joseph Moes, a music teacher born in Hungary, and their children, Osmond and Julia.[65]

Approximately three miles south of Point St. Isabel was the home of Anna's other daughter, Mary Sammis and her family. The Sammis estate once encompassed 8,000 acres filled with live oak, cedar and pine, a saw mill, cotton gin and sugar mill, all water-powered, and a brickyard and grits mill. Sea Island cotton grew on 700 cleared acres, and in the nearby wetlands, dams and dikes had been erected to raise rice. Herds of cattle and sheep grazed on pasture lands and the estate also boasted large vegetable and fruit gardens, a mineral spring and a large boathouse.[66]

The three mile stretch along the St. John's River between the Baxter and Sammis plantations was unique in north-east Florida. In addition to the extended Kingsley family, eight households of free coloured persons, comprising nearly forty men, women and children lived there. Most of them were former slaves of Anna and Zephaniah who had formed patron–client bonds with the Kingsley kin after they were emancipated. These were reminiscent of patron–client ties formed between Wolof slave-owners and their liberated bondsmen in Jolof villages in Senegal.

This unique community, and all free African Americans in north-east

Florida was thrown in to turmoil in January 1861, when the state's leaders met in Tallahassee to secede from the Union. In April, Florida joined the Confederate States of America. In the next year, north-east Florida would experience Confederate occupation, vigilante violence, burning and looting, and invasion and occupation by Union troops.[67] In April 1862, following a brief occupation of Jacksonville by Union forces, Anna boarded a naval transport with the Sammis family and was transported to safety at Hilton Head, South Carolina. From there they travelled to Philadelphia and New York. As strong Union supporters, Anna's family would have been in dire danger when Confederate forces re-occupied north Florida.

When peace was restored, Anna returned to Duval County to pass the remaining years of her life in tranquillity at her daughter's estates on the St. John's River. The death of her daughter, Martha, in February 1870 would mar her final months – but she was surrounded and comforted by numerous grandchildren and great-grandchildren – one grandson, Egbert Sammis, was elected to the Florida State Senate in 1884.

Anta Majigeen Ndiaye, the Wolof teenager who became Anna Magigine Jai Kingsley in Florida, found security and contentment at the close of her life. She died in July 1870. It is believed that she spent her final months with her daughter, Mary, and was buried in an unmarked grave in the Sammis family cemetery behind the residence. Her presence is most acutely felt at Kingsley Plantation on Fort George Island, a National Park Service site. Her house still stands, beside the residence of Zephaniah, the stables, and portions of the tabby slave cabins.

NOTES

1. An earlier version of this essay was published by the St. Augustine Historical Society (SAHS). Because the evidence is missing for some specific circumstances, narrative historical reconstruction is used to bridge gaps with speculation based on recent scholarship and documented comparable events. Many people helped with this manuscript. Joan Peters in a 1989 seminar paper; Bruce S.Chappell with the East Florida Papers; James Donlan with translations; Jane Landers with Parish Records data; Page Edwards and Kathy Tilford with editing. Bryan Peters arranged grants from Eastern National Park and Monument Association for research in Africa, Denmark, England and the Dominican Republic. The University of North Florida provided sabbatical and travel support. Andre Zaaiman and Katy Diop of the Goree Institute arranged housing, meetings and transportation in Senegal; Tony and Sandra Lebrón arranged interviews with Kingsley descendants in the Dominican Republic and transportation; Manuel Labron, a descendant of John Maxwell Kingsley, translated. I have an unpayable debt to Joan E. Moore, my wife, who helped in the archives, contributed ideas, and helped edit. Her companionship makes most things possible for me.

2. I chose Jolof as Anta's homeland. James Searing considers Kajoor more likely and any of the four Wolof states a possibility. Mbaye Gaye, Penda Mbow, and Mamadou Diouf at Cheikh Anta Diop University chose Jolof. I thank them and Boubakar Barry for reading my essay and for interviews in November 1994 in Dakar, Senegal. English sources on slavery among the Wolof are Philip Curtin, *Economic Change in Precolonial Africa: Senegal in the Era of*

the Slave Trade (Madison, 1975); Martin A. Klein, 'Servitude among the Wolof and Sereer of Senegambia', in Igor Kopytoff and Suzanne Miers (eds.), *Slavery in Africa* (Madison, 1977); 'Women and Slavery in the Western Sudan', in C.C. Robertson and Martin A. Klein (eds.), *Women and Slavery in Africa* (Madison, 1983); 'The Impact of the Atlantic Slave Trade on the Societies of the Western Sudan', in Joseph E. Inikori and Stanley L. Engerman (eds.), *The Atlantic Slave Trade: Effects on Economies, Societies, and Peoples in Africa, the Americas, and Europe* (Durham, 1992); James Searing, *West African Slavery and Atlantic Commerce: The Senegal River Valley, 1700–1860* (New York, 1993). Also helpful was Eunice A. Charles, 'A History of the Kingdom of Jolof (Senegal), 1800–1890', (Ph.D. thesis, unpublished, Boston University, 1973). Victoria Bomba Coifman contributed information on Wolof names and constant encouragement. Throughout, debts to M.A. Klein and Searing are apparent. In French, Boubacar Barry, *La Sénégambie du dix-cinquième au dix-neuvième siècle: Traite négrière, Islam et conquête coloniale* (Paris, 1988); Charles Becker, 'Conditions écologiques, crises de subsistance et histoire de la population à l'époque de la traite des esclaves en Sénégambie (dix septième-dix-huitième siècle)', *Canadian Journal of African Studies*, Vol.20 (1986), pp.357–76; and with Victor Martin, 'Kayor et Baol: Royaumes sénégalais et traite des esclaves au dix-huitième siècle', *Revue française d'histoire d'outre-mer*, 62 (1975), pp.270–300.

3. Searing, *West African Slavery*, explores the religious wars.

4. Mamadou Diouf, oral interview, Dakar, Senegal, Nov. 1994.

5. Searing corrected my identification of Majigeen as a lineage name: Anta was her first or given name, Majigeen her mother's given name, and Ndiaye (or Njaay) her father's family name. Personal correspondence, 30 Aug. 1994. Polygamous households with children of multiple wives identified which wife was the mother of each child. I kept Ndiaye as a lineage name after Mbaye Gaye, Penda Mbow, and Mamadou Diouf found the adaptability and character of Anta in the Americas a likely sign of descent from noble origins.

6. Searing, *African Slavery*, discusses increased food production and commerce as a result of European trade contacts.

7. George E. Brooks, 'The Signares of Saint-Louis and Goree: Women Entrepreneurs in Eighteenth-Century Senegal', in N.J. Hafkin and E.G. Bay (eds.), *Women in Africa: Studies in Social and Economic Change* (Stanford, 1976), and Searing, *African Slavery* are excellent on 'signares' and metis traders.

8. *Goree: The Island and the Historical Museum* (IFAN – Cheikh Anta Diop: Publication of the Historical Museum, 1993).

9. Hugh Thomas, *Cuba: The Pursuit of Freedom* (New York, 1971); David R. Murray, *Odious Commerce: Britain, Spain and the Abolition of the Cuban Slave Trade* (Cambridge, 1980); Kenneth F. Kiple, *Blacks in Colonial Cuba, 1774–1899* (Gainesville, 1976); Allan J. Kuethe, 'Havana in the Eighteenth Century', in Franklin W. Knight and Peggy K. Liss (eds.), *Atlantic Port Cities: Economy, Culture, and Society in the Atlantic World, 1650–1850* (Knoxville, 1991); and James Lewis, 'Anglo Merchants in Cuba in the Eighteenth Century', in Jacques A. Barbier and Allan J. Kuethe (eds.), *The North American Role in the Spanish Imperial Economy, 1760–1819* (Dover, 1984). For slavery in Cuba, see Franklin Knight, *Slave Society in Cuba during the Nineteenth Century* (Madison, 1970), and Robert L. Paquette, *Sugar is Made with Blood: The Conspiracy of La Escalera and the Conflict between Empires over Slavery in Cuba* (Middletown, 1988). On the Atlantic Slave Trade, see Philip D. Curtin, *The Atlantic Slave Trade: A Census* (Madison, 1969); Paul E. Lovejoy, 'The Volume of the Atlantic Slave Trade: A Synthesis', *Journal of African History*, 23, 4 (1982), pp.473–501; David Richardson, 'Slave Exports from West and West-Central Africa, 1700–1810', *Journal of African History*, 30 (1989), pp.1–22; David Eltis, *Economic Growth and the Ending of the Transatlantic Slave Trade* (New York, 1987); Roger Anstey and P.E.H. Hair (eds.), *Liverpool, the African Slave Trade, and Abolition* (Chippenham, 1989); James Rawley, *The Transatlantic Slave Trade* (New York, 1981); Herbert Klein, 'The Cuban Slave Trade', *The Middle Passage: Comparative Studies in the Atlantic Slave Trade* (Princeton, 1978).

10. Herbert S. Klein (comp.), 'Computerized data on slave ships arriving at Havana, 1790–1821', AGI, Audiencia de Santo Domingo, 'legajo' 1835 (copy available on magnetic tape, University of Florida Libraries). Voyages to and from St. Thomas are in the Danish

National Archives (Rigsarkiv), Copenhagen. For Kingsley and St. Thomas, see RA: Notarial Protocol (St. Thomas), 1804–1806; GTK Afskrift af St. Jan & St. Thomas Søpasprotokoller, 1788–1807; VL, West Indian passport and citizenry registers, St. Thomas Police Station, registers of persons arriving 1805–9; VRR, Toldregnskaber, 7 Nov. 1802, Liquidations Beregning; and VL, Harbormaster Reports. See also, Svend E. Green-Pedersen, 'The Scope and Structure of the Danish Negro Slave Trade', *The Scandinavian Economic History Review*, 19 (1971), pp.149–97; and 'Colonial Trade under the Danish Flag. A Cast Study of the Danish slave Trade to Cuba 1790–1807', *Scandinavian Journal of History*, 5 (1980), pp.93–120. I am indebted to Svend E. Holsoe for help in Copenhagen in Nov. 1994 and for copies and translations of important documents. Peter Sørensen, Per Nielsen, and Poul Olsen also assisted. The inclusion of Anta in this shipment is speculative, but is based upon the unusual preponderance of females on this ship and the correct time frame for Anta's established presence in Havana.

11. Kenneth F. Kiple and Brian T. Higgins, 'Mortality Caused by Dehydration during the Middle Passage', in Inikori and Engerman, *Atlantic Slave Trade*.

12. The East Florida Papers (EFP), Spanish records, 1784–1821, were invaluable. Microfilms at P.K. Yonge Library of Florida History (PKY), University of Florida. For Kingsley at Havana in 1806, Reel 97 Bundle 231J18 and R172 B231N21; arrival at Florida R163 B350U4.

13. EFP, R172 B376.

14. Lydia Maria Childs, *Letters from New York* (New York, 1843), pp.111–19. A copy of Kingsley's Last Will and Testament is in Duval County Probates, 1203. Kingsley's shipping activities for 1804–12 are in EFP, R57 B140J11; R58 B142J11; R59 B144A12; R59 B145B12; R60 B146C12; R97 B230I18; R97 B231J18; R98 B233L18; R133 B299P7; and R133 B300. Also see Stephen D. Behrendt, 'The British slave trade, 1785–1807: Volume, profitability, and mortality' (Ph.D. thesis, unpublished, University of Wisconsin, 1993).

15. All commentary on Laurel Grove comes from EFP R62 B144F12 and Superior and Circuit Court Records, Box 131, Folder 16, SAHS.

16. The senior Kingsley was a Quaker merchant and Loyalist supporter of King George III who took the family into exile in Nova Scotia during the American Revolution. At that time he deeded Abraham to his son. In 1793 Zephaniah, Jr., returned to Charleston, but later lived in Haiti, St. Thomas, and East Florida. *Royal Gazette and New Brunswick Advertiser*, 18 Dec. 1787; 16 Jan. 1789; 'Ward Chipman Papers', H.T. Hazen Collection; Andrew S. Beyea, 'A History of French Village...' unpublished ms., p.66, all at The New Brunswick Museum, St. John. Kingsley Sr., Loyalist Claim, in Alexander Fraser, 'Second Report of the Bureau of Archives for the Province of Ontario' (Toronto, 1904). For South Carolina, see Brent H. Holcomb, *Probate Records of South Carolina*, 2 (Easley, S.C., 1978), pp.177, 213, 216, 262; and *South Carolina Naturalizations, 1783–1850* (Baltimore, 1985), p.93; James W. Hagy, *People and Professions of Charleston, South Carolina, 1782–1802* (Baltimore, 1992).

17. Deed Book H, 17 March 1828, St. Johns County.'Sophy Chidgegane is a woman of Jalof, thirty-six years of age, about five feet high, black complexion'. The 20 March 1828 emancipation entry for Flora Hanahan Kingsley describes her as: 'a mulatto-colored woman of 20 years of age, a native of Florida and daughter to Sophy Chidgigaine [*sic*]...five feet high'.

18. Although Fraser brought his son to South Carolina, Phenda and their daughters remained in Africa. John Fraser material is in EFP R165, Testamentary Proceedings; R145, Inventarios, no. 16; R168 B364 and R173 B385, Bruce L. Mouser, 'Trade, Coasters, and Conflict in the Rio Pongo From 1790 to 1808', *Journal of African History*, 14 (Jan. 1973), pp.45–64, and 'Women Slavers of Guinea-Conakry', in Klein and Robertson, *Women and Slavery in Africa*.

19. For James Irwin, Patriot War Claims (PWC) MC 31, File 52, SAHS; For Richard, Clarke and Sánchez see Daniel L. Schafer, '"A Class of People neither Freemen nor Slaves": From Spanish to American Race Relations in Florida, 1821–1861', *Journal of Social History*, 26 (Spring 1993), pp.587–609.

20. Philip S. May, 'Zephaniah Kingsley, Nonconformist', *Florida Historical Quarterly*, 23 (Jan. 1945), pp.145–59; Charles Bennett, 'Zephaniah Kingsley, Jr.', *Twelve on the St. Johns* (Jacksonville, 1989), pp.89–113; Jean B. Stephens, 'Zephaniah Kingsley and the Recaptured Africans', *El Escribano; The St. Augustine Journal of History*, 15 (1978), pp.71–6; Karen Jo

Walker, 'Kingsley and His Slaves: Anthropological Interpretation and Evaluation', *Volumes in Historical Archaeology*, 5 (Columbia, 1989). Kingsley wrote *A Treatise on the Patriarchal or Cooperative System of Society as it Exists in Some Governments and Colonies in America, and in the United States, under the Name of Slavery, with its Necessity and Advantages* (Freeport, 1971 reprint of an 1829 publication); 'Address to the Legislative Council of Florida on the Subject of its Colored Population' (typescript, circa 1829, Tallahassee); *The Rural Code of Haiti; Literally Translated from a Publication by the Government Press; Together with Letters from that Country concerning its Present Condition, by a Southern Planter* (Middletown, 1837). Quote is from Kingsley, *Treatise*, p.7.

21. Kingsley, *Treatise*, p.1.
22. Kingsley, 'Address to the Territorial Legislature', p.4.
23. EFP R172 B376.
24. Kingsley Will, Probate 1203.
25. Kingsley, PWC.
26. Kingsley's will, probate 1203.
27. EFP R172 B376.
28. EFP: R62 B144F12, and PWC: Box 131, Folder 16; PWC, Abraham Hannahan Claim, Box 124, Folder 24.
29. Ibid. and Schafer, 'A class of people neither freemen nor slaves'.
30. Jane Landers, 'African and African American Women and Their Pursuit of Rights through Eighteenth-Century Texts', in Anne Goodwyn Jones and Susan V. Donaldson (eds.), *Haunted Bodies: Gender and Southern Texts* (Charlottesville, forthcoming).
31. Anna Kingsley, Patriot War Claim, MC 31, File 58, SAHS.
32. See Jane Landers, 'Black Society in Spanish St. Augustine, 1784–1821' (Ph.D. thesis, unpublished, University of Florida, 1988).
33. Rembert W. Patrick, *Florida Fiasco: Rampant Rebels on the Georgia–Florida Frontier, 1810–1815* (Athens, 1954), is the most complete source, but Francis P.Ferreira vs. U.S. Appellants, *Land Claims* (U.S. Congress: Senate Report, 1856–86), has crucial eyewitness testimony.
34. The reports of Thomas Llorente, commander at San Nicolas recount activities along the river in late 1813, including Anna's actions. See EFP R62 B149f12 (25 Oct.; 24, 26, 27 Nov.; 13, 17 Dec.).
35. EFP R62 B149f12 26, 26 Nov. 1813.
36. Patriot War Claims of John H. McIntosh, typescript, PKY.
37. Temporary housing is speculation based on records of African slaves owned by James Grant, first governor of British East Florida. See Daniel L. Schafer, ' "Yellow Silk Ferret Tied Round Their Wrists": African Americans in British East Florida, 1763–1784', David R. Colburn and Jane L. Landers (eds.), *The African American Heritage of Florida* (Gainesville, 1995).
38. Jacqueline K. Fretwell (ed.), *Kingsley Beatty Gibbs and His Journal of 1840–1843* (St. Augustine, 1984).
39. Ibid. Philip D. Morgan, 'Work and Culture: The Task System and the World of Low Country Blacks, 1700–1880', *William and Mary Quarterly*, 39 (1982), pp.563–99.
40. Gertrude Rollins Wilson, 'Notes Concerning the Old Plantation on Fort George Island', typescript, Kingsley Plantation Office, describes the island and buildings in the late-nineteenth century. Gertrude's father, John Rollins, bought Fort George Island in 1868. See also Julia B. Dodge, 'An Island by the Sea', *Scribner's Magazine* (Sept. 1877), and Samuel G.W. Benjamen, 'The Sea Islands', *Harpers New Monthly Magazine* (Nov. 1878).
41. William F. Hawley interview, Works Progress Administration, Florida Room, Main Library, Jacksonville. See also, *The Arlingtonian*, Vol.8, 1 May 1842, Special Collections, Jacksonville University Library.
42. *Duval County Marriages* (1823–64), 1, 1940. The inter-racial marriage was performed by Kingsley's nephew, Sam Kingsley, Justice of the Peace, on 5 May 1831.
43. Gertrude R. Wilson, 'Notes'.
44. Inference from Kingsley, PWC, and the enduring oral legend of his love for horses.
45. Gertrude R. Wilson, 'Notes'.
46. St. Augustine Parish Records for the baptism of John Maxwell Kingsley (microfilm roll 3,

entry 650, 30 Jan. 1829) give the date of birth as 22 Nov. 1824.

47. St. Augustine Parish Records, microfilm roll 3, no. 650, 30 Jan. 1829. Michael Gannon, *The Cross in the Sand; The Early Catholic Church in Florida, 1513–1870* (Gainesville, 1965), pp.139–49, explores Father Mayne's difficult times in St. Augustine.

48. See Schafer, 'A class of people neither slave nor free'.

49. Kingsley, *Treatise*, p.10.

50. Kingsley land holdings can be traced in the Archibald Abstracts of Historical Property Records in the Duval County Courthouse; in Works Progress Administration, *Spanish Land Grants in Florida* (Tallahassee, 1942), 4, Confirmed Claims, 6–37; in the Department of Natural Resources, Tallahassee, and in Deed Records: St. Johns, Putnam, Nassau and Volusia Counties. Archibald listings are mostly chronological. The Fort George Island sale to George Kingsley was 20 July 1831, in Book B, p.20. Buena Vista and Drayton Island also went to George Kingsley; see St. Johns County, Deed Book I-J, p.488 (20 Dec. 1832).

51. St. John's County Deed Book I-J, p.389 (21 Dec. 1832).

52. Mary's 300 acres are recorded in Archibald, Book B, p.10 (20 July 1831); Martha's 350 acres, p.12 (15 Aug.); Flora's on p.10 (26 June 1829) in trust for her and her son, Charles, under the care of Kingsley's son, George, and brother-in-law, George Gibbs.

53. St. Augustine *Florida Herald*, 9 Aug. 1832.

54. For the Kingsley colony in Haiti (now Dominican Republic), see Kingsley, *The Rural Code of Haiti*, and José Augusto Puig Ortiz, *Emigración de Libertos Norte Americanos a Puerto Plata en la Primera Mitad del Siglo XIX* (Dominican Republic: La Iglesia Metodista Wesleyana, 1978). Neit Finke and Pablo Juan Brugal, Puerto Plata, shared genealogical resources, land records and legends in Dec. 1993 and 1994 interviews.

55. Childs, *Letters from New York*, p.114.

56. Oral interviews, Dec. 1993 and 1994, with Kingsley descendants, translated by Manuel Lebrón.

57. Probate 1203.

58. K.B. Gibbs noted Kingsley's departures and arrivals in his diary. See Fretwell, *Kingsley Beatty Gibbs*. The Childs interview in N.Y. was 7 July 1842. Very few records of the Kingsleys in the Dominican Republic survive, making Pablo Juan Brugal's gift of a copy of the Certificate of Naturalization, Children of Zephaniah Kingsley and Flora Hannahan Kingsley, Nov. 1842, Haitian Archives at Puerto Plata, all the more welcome.

59. Obituary, the St. Augustine *News*, 30 Sept. 1843. Date of death given was 13 Sept.

60. Estate proceedings are in Probate 1203; Broward vs. Kingsley (19 Florida 722), Supreme Court of Florida, Tallahassee; and Superior Court Files 131/12 and 131/16, SAHS. See May, 'Zephaniah Kingsley, Nonconformist', for an attorney's account of legal challenges.

61. Probate 1203; George Kingsley's will and estate proceedings are Probate 1205. James Johnson, 'History of Zephaniah Kingsley and Family', typescript, 4 Jan. 1937, Federal Writers Project American Guide (Negro Writers Unit), copy at Special Collections, Jacksonville University, has details now missing from Probate 1205.

62. Telephone conversation, Oct. 1995, Alphonso Lockward, Santo Domingo. Frank Moya Pons, *The Dominican Republic: A National History* (New Rochelle, 1994), chapters 7–10, surveys the racial tensions and guerrilla campaigns, 1843–1865.

63. St. Augustine Parish Records, microfilm roll 3, 'Colored Baptisms' 23 Nov. 1848.

64. Archibald Transcripts, Bk G, p.16 (Jan. 1847) and p.285 (5 July 1854). Jacksonville University campus encloses this property today.

65. U.S. Census of 1850, Duval County, Free Schedules, the listing under Martha Baxter's household.

66. Photographs and an essay on the Sammis house are in Wayne W. Wood, *Jacksonville's Architectural Heritage: Landmarks for the Future* (Jacksonville, 1989).

67. See my compilation of Kingsleys and related families based on the U.S. Censuses 1830–1870, Kingsley Plantation Office. Until the 1880s, a distinct African American community known as Chaseville existed in the area. For the years 1861–1865, see Richard A. Martin and Daniel L. Schafer, *Jacksonville's Ordeal by Fire: A Civil War History* (Jacksonville, 1984).

Notes on Contributors

John Garrigus is Associate Professor of History at Jacksonville University. Educated at the Johns Hopkins University, he is completing a book on Saint-Domingue's free people of colour entitled *Sons of the Same Father: Free People of Colour and Whites in French Saint-Domingue*. His article 'Blue and Brown: Contraband Indigo and the Rise of a Free Colored Planter Class in French Saint-Domingue' was awarded the 1994 Tibesar Prize by the Conference of Latin American Historians.

Kimberly Hanger is Assistant Professor of Latin American History at the University of Tulsa. Educated at the University of Florida, she is the author of several articles on free people of African descent in Spanish New Orleans. She is completing a book on free blacks in Spanish New Orleans which will be published by Duke University Press.

Rosemarijn Hoefte is deputy head of the Department of Caribbean Studies of the KILTV/Royal Institute of Linguistics and Anthropology in Leiden, the Netherlands. Educated at the University of Florida, she publishes regularly on the Dutch Caribbean. She is completing a social history of Asian indentured labourers in Suriname.

Paul Lachance is Associate Professor of History at the University of Ottawa. Educated at the University of Wisconsin, he is the author of articles on Saint-Domingue refugees and on demographic and economic factors affecting French cultural persistence in New Orleans after the Louisiana Purchase.

Jane G. Landers is Assistant Professor of History and a member of the Center for Latin American and Iberian Studies at Vanderbilt University. Educated at the University of Florida, she has published a number of articles on Africans in the Spanish circum-Caribbean and is co-editor of *The African American Heritage of Florida*. She is completing a book entitled *Black Society in Spanish Florida* which will be published by the University of Illinois Press.

Robert Olwell is Assistant Professor of History at the University of Texas at Austin. Educated at the Johns Hopkins University, he is writing a book entitled *Slaves and Kings: The Culture of Power in a Colonial Slave Society, the South Carolina Lowcountry, 1740–1782*.

Daniel L. Schafer is Professor of History at the University of North Florida. Educated at the University of Minnesota, he has published a number of articles on Africans in the American South-east. He is currently writing a biography of Zephaniah Kingsley.

Index

Printed in the United States
83785LV00005B/391-417/A

9 780714 642543